GENERALLY SPEAKING

GENERALLY
SPEAKING

Lieutenant General
Claudia J. Kennedy (Ret.)
with Malcolm McConnell

WARNER BOOKS

An AOL Time Warner Company

Warner Books, Inc., 1271 Avenue of the Americas, New York, NY 10020

Visit our Web site at www.twbookmark.com.

For information on Time Warner Trade Publishing's online publishing program,
visit www.ipublish.com.

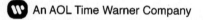 An AOL Time Warner Company

Printed in the United States of America

First Printing: September 2001
10 9 8 7 6 5 4 3 2 1

Library of Congress Cataloging-in-Publication Data

Kennedy, Claudia J.
    Generally speaking / Claudia J. Kennedy with Malcolm McConnell.
       p.   cm.
    ISBN 0-446-52793-9
       1. Kennedy, Claudia J. 2. Women generals—United States—Biography. 3.
Generals—United States—Biography. 4. United States, Army—Biography. I.
McConnell, Malcolm. II. Title.

U53.K455 A3 2001
355'.0092—dc21
[B]
                                                             2001026876

Book design by H. Roberts

To Lillian Strong Haygood and Virgie Crain Kennedy, my wonderful grandmothers, who were strong, independent, resourceful women. They would like who women today have become—indeed, they were of the generation who made this possible.

Acknowledgments

I would like to thank many friends and colleagues who helped make this book possible.

Those who encouraged me to write it: Dr. Jenny Lincoln, Betty Friedan, Dr. Kathleen Reardon, and many fellow soldiers.

Those who introduced me to the world of writing and publishing: Jill Bronson, Norman Brokaw, Mel Berger, Malcolm and Carol McConnell, Larry Kirshbaum, Maureen Egen, Emi Battaglia, Tina Andreadis, Michele Bidelspach, Maja Thomas, Fred Chase, Jackie Joiner, Mari Okuda, and Jackie Meyer.

Those who have placed confidence in me: Jean and Cary Kennedy, Walter and Selma Kaye, Valerie and Larry Thompson.

Those who read and commented on the earliest drafts: Sally Murphy, Kay and Ginger Snider, Doris Caldwell, General Jack Merritt (Ret.), General Gordon Sullivan (Ret.), Susan Ohle, Mugs Flott, Richard Swann, Terry Marsh, Kathy Bonk, and Nicole Harburger.

Of course a number of animal friends must be acknowledged: Sterling; Ashley; Molly; Sophie; Khaki; Kitty Hawk; and the grizzled veteran, Lina.

Contents

Introduction

The Pentagon, June 2, 2000

The ceremony marking my retirement from the United States Army took place in the Pentagon central courtyard on the stifling Friday morning of June 2, 2000, exactly thirty-one years after my father administered the oath commissioning me a second lieutenant in the Women's Army Corps.

When I enlisted in the 1960s, women were not allowed to command men or advance higher than the rank of colonel. But I was the daughter of a career soldier, and I had a feeling then that, if women were ever going to achieve equality in the military, the changes were going to have to evolve from within. In 1969, America was at war in Vietnam, and although some of my sorority sisters at Southwestern at Memphis were bemused when I told them I was joining the Army, young men were being drafted, and I didn't think it was fair for them to shoulder the entire burden when women were exempted. I also didn't believe women could claim equal privileges of citizenship without understanding and accepting the equal responsibilities of a citizen.

As I stepped onto the stage with Secretary of the Army Louis Caldera and surveyed the hundreds of guests, I saw small groups of senior military women, the bright sun glinting on the stars and gold braid of their rank. I was proud to see many who had risen beyond the rank of colonel and were now generals or admirals. I was the Army's highest-ranking woman, the first to attain three-star rank, and one of four in the military to have earned that grade. I shared this honor with Navy Vice Admiral Patricia A. Tracey, Deputy Assistant Secretary of Defense for Personnel, Lieutenant General Leslie F. Kenne, commander of the Air Force's Electronic System Center, and retired Marine Lieutenant General Carol A. Mutter.

As Deputy Chief of Staff for Intelligence, I was responsible for the Army's Intelligence Corps, which comprised almost 45,000 officers and enlisted soldiers and civilians around the world, 80 percent men, 20 percent women.

In fact, the entire U.S. military had changed in the thirty-one years since I raised my hand and took the simple soldier's oath to "defend the Constitution of the United States against all enemies, foreign and domestic." Hundreds of specialties previously reserved for men had opened to women, who now made up approximately 15 percent of the total force. Women officers and noncommissioned officers were rising steadily through the ranks. Although only eleven of the Army's 300 generals were women, there were scores of well-qualified women colonels eligible for selection to brigadier general.

As always at these Pentagon ceremonies, the U.S. Army Band, Pershing's Own, had played appropriately stirring music. Now an African-American sergeant with a clear, powerful contralto voice sang the National Anthem. Looking down at the massed ranks of my friends and colleagues—Army green with a scattering of Navy white and Air Force blue—I could sense the common patriotism and pride these women and men shared. They had come here today to celebrate my career, to honor the Army and the American military.

Lieutenant General Larry R. Ellis and his wife, Jean, were seated near the front. He was the Deputy Chief of Staff for Operations and Plans, a key Army leadership position. Larry controlled all the decisions about priorities and resources. He was a Vietnam veteran with solid credentials as an Infantry soldier who had always supported me. Jean had her own profession in the government, which she had to "pack up" each time the family moved during Larry's career, the situation of so many military wives over the decades, and a definite cause of concern among today's two-career households that the Pentagon is going to have to address if it expects to retain its most promising young officers.

Taking my seat on the platform as Secretary Caldera prepared to speak, I felt intensely proud to have played a part in the Army's measured and steady march toward fairness and equality. All I'd ever wanted was the chance to serve my country. The Army had given me the chance to earn the respect of my fellow soldiers, a fundamental requisite of leadership.

Most of the people in uniform attending the ceremony were men, many generals with whom I had served at the Pentagon or at other commands. I was heartened to see them. Their presence was both an act of personal friendship and also a sign of respect to the Army as an institution.

The final year of my long service had been marred by unfortunate and inaccurate publicity concerning a serious incident. In 1996, when I was a major general and alone in my Pentagon office, Brigadier General Larry G. Smith made sudden, inappropriate sexual contact. I remained quiet at the time because I handled the situation privately, and also because the Army was still reeling from multiple incidents of similar, though more serious, misconduct.

But in September 1999, after General Smith was nominated to be the Deputy Inspector General of the Army—a position that involves, among other duties, investigating misconduct and sexual harassment by senior officers—I could no longer remain silent. I took my information to the Inspector General, who opened a formal investigation, which continued through the next spring. By June 2, the media reported that the investigation of General Smith's contact had substantiated my report and that he would be officially reprimanded and would retire immediately. The Army's process had moved slowly, but with appropriate deliberation. In the end, justice had been served.

Would I have preferred these unpleasant matters to have been quietly resolved? Of course. Was I sorry I raised the issue with the IG in September 1999? Certainly not. An officer like General Smith, no matter how excellent his prior record, had no place serving as the Army's Deputy Inspector General where one of his main responsibilities would be to oversee complaints about general officer conduct and sexual harassment. But I also knew that the Smith case had raised the hackles of many traditional generals, active-duty and retired.

That was one reason why I was so pleased to see such a fine representation of senior officers whose uniforms displayed multiple combat decorations from Vietnam and the Persian Gulf. They were my friends and colleagues. They understood I had acted honorably in the Smith case, with the Army's best interest in mind.

But there was another dynamic at play. Many of these men had daughters in the Army. The fathers might have been helicopter platoon leaders in Vietnam, while their daughters could have flown big CH-47 Chinook helicopters to the banks of the Euphrates during Operation Desert Storm. As I had told the staff and faculty at West Point some years before, "It's not your father's Army." And no father would want his daughter assaulted by a fellow soldier.

In Secretary Caldera's remarks, he described me as "not only a role model for service women of our armed forces, but to girls and women across our nation, no matter what their professions and aspirations." I looked out from the shaded stage at the sunny courtyard. Among the glittering uniforms sat white-haired women in lovely flowered dresses and wide-brimmed hats. They were *my* role models. All three were World War II veterans and had made the Army their career. Colonel Mary A. Hallaren had been director of the Women's Army Corps during the Korean War, Colonel Bettie J. Morden, a WAC deputy director in the 1970s, when I was a young officer. And Brigadier General Elizabeth P. Hoisington, WAC Director during the Vietnam War, was the first Women's Army Corps officer to earn the rank of general. Any one of them could have been a three-star general in today's Army.

I had thought hard about my own remarks, wanting my comments to reflect my deep love for the Army, and also my conviction that the American military, which has led the country in breaking down the racial walls that divided us, had also been a pioneer in attacking the barrier of gender that once denied opportunity to more than half of all Americans. But I wanted to make it clear that there is still ample room for women soldiers to advance beyond my achievements.

Citing the Army recruiting ad, "Be all you can be," I told the audience, "I've been all that I could have been. I've risen farther than I ever dared to hope. All I wanted was to be a leader and to serve my country. When I joined the Army I never dreamed there'd be stars on my shoulders."

I noted that people sometimes view the Army as an impenetrable, tradition-bound institution, but that "it is actually one of the most effective organizations in our government: responsive, changing, and highly accountable."

I knew the true story of the Army was not found in newspaper headlines or television sound bites, but rather in the small details of soldiers' daily lives of duty, discipline, and selfless service. Periodically, the country called on them to fight battles, large and small, to keep the peace in lonely, troubled corners of the world, to combat terrorism in all its forms, and to draw on the soldier's traditional values of honor and courage. This was the Army in which I had matured as a leader, and of which I now spoke.

"Best of all, the Army is a cohesive collection of soldiers who share bonds across many dimensions.

"These bonds are: with leaders, peers, and juniors in current units and previous units."

Looking into the audience, I saw retired Colonel Edwin Tivol, who had been my brigade commander when I com-

xvi ★ ★ ★ LIEUTENANT GENERAL CLAUDIA J. KENNEDY (RET.)

manded a Military Intelligence battalion in Germany in the 1980s. Ed Tivol, an old school soldier, who demanded excellence from himself and all who served in his command, always treated me as a soldier first. I considered him an important mentor.

Squinting into the glare, I spotted Master Sergeant Wayne Smith standing at ease at the edge of the crowd. He had been my enlisted aide for the past three years. My life could be divided into Before Master Sergeant Smith (BMS) and After Master Sergeant Smith (AMS). BMS, my daily logistics teetered on the brink of complex chaos, requiring three outfits: morning Physical Training (PT), duty uniform, and dress uniform or comparable civilian clothing for constant official social events in the evening. My day was always long, from early morning to late at night, with little time for trips to the dry cleaner. AMS I actually had meals ready for me—no more gulping down a can of tomatoes over the sink. AMS I had shined military shoes and perfectly pressed uniforms. When I entertained, the parties were fun. I did my job; Master Sergeant Smith did his. For a senior officer, an aide is a necessity not a luxury. And most of my general colleagues had enlisted aides *and* wives to assist them through the day.

Sergeant Major of the Army (SMA) Robert E. Hall, the senior enlisted soldier in the Army, was in the front row. I was gratified to see him there because I considered him a personal friend and professional representative of the noncommissioned officer corps with whom I had always worked closely. The SMA is one of the Army's key soldiers, serving as a bridge between the enlisted ranks and the Chief of Staff of the Army. SMA Robert Hall had restored the Army's trust and confidence to his position following the very disappointing tenure of his immediate predecessor, SMA Gene C. McKinney, who had been court-martialed on nineteen criminal charges, mainly concerning sexual misconduct, and found guilty on one count of obstructing justice, reprimanded, and reduced in grade to master sergeant before retiring.

I noted that "I believe in reform, not revolution. But just as we would not have a democratic society today had it not been for the Revolutionary War, I would not be retiring as a three-star general had it not been for those women and men who, for decades, worked from within for change and for improvements. This is often the greatest act of loyalty to a large institution—to help it improve and modernize."

Acknowledging that the progress of military women had been "measured and steady," I noted it had also occurred within the context of societal change since the 1960s, decades during which the position of women in politics, sports, religion, academia, and corporate America had dramatically expanded.

Although I was the first of the Army's women to reach three-star rank, I predicted I certainly would not be the last. "These days the sound you hear overhead, in the Army and at the Pentagon, isn't an airplane breaking the sound barrier. It's the sound of a glass ceiling being shattered. And the Army and the Pentagon are the better because of it."

I was leaving the Army that had fought and won the seemingly endless Cold War. But as a senior professional intelligence officer, I took this opportunity to note the dangers our country faced in this uncertain world. A new generation of soldiers had to be trained and ready to confront and defeat a wide variety of threats: "terrorists, nonstate actors, weapons of mass destruction, cyber-bandits, transnational crime, near-peer competitors [Beltway code for China, other emerging military powers, and possible coalitions], ethnic and religious strife, narcotraffickers, and illegal technology transfers, which threaten our economic future. These are in addition to our need to be prepared for major regional conflicts."

Given the challenging nature of these new threats, many of which involve complex and evolving information technology, I knew military women would play a vital role in defending our country in the coming years and decades. Thinking of the next generation of women military leaders, I spoke of the "first woman to break the four-star barrier, the first woman to be the

Sergeant Major of the Army, and the first woman to be Secretary of the Department of Defense."

There were probably some in the audience who did not accept the idea of a woman four-star general or Defense Secretary, and certainly not the Sergeant Major of the Army. But I knew my prediction would be borne out. And I prefaced my comments by noting:

"One of my favorite quotes is by the French author Emile Zola, who said: 'If you asked me what I came into this world to do, I will tell you—I came to live out loud.'"

As I spoke, I glanced down at my family members. My cousin Valerie Haygood Thompson's husband, Larry, beamed back at me. Larry joined the Army the same year I did, even though he could have avoided service through a deferment. He served as a young enlisted engineer in Vietnam, then, in the tradition of Cincinnatus, returned to his civilian business and raised a family. Valerie and Larry and their four daughters had attended all of my promotions since I received my first star.

Tommie Jean Kennedy, my mother, also sat proudly in the front row, a position that reflected her place in my life. Although no longer married to my father, for thirty-one years she had been an Army wife in the most traditional sense. My mother made a home for her husband and four children under the most trying conditions, which Army wives of her day all faced (some of which persist today): frequent moves, very little money, resettling children in school, scouts, and church every year or two, finding homes for a surprise litter of kittens, the hours working as volunteers in the post thrift shop (which supported Army scholarships), and leadership of wives clubs, obligations expected of an officer's wife. Then there were the months when my father was away on unaccompanied assignments in Korea and Vietnam, during which she had to shepherd the family through crises ranging from a child's asthma attacks to hurricanes to packing household goods for ocean crossings. But to her, this was the life she had chosen. She loved her children, her husband, and the Army adventure.

Looking at my mother from the speaker's Pentagon rostrum, the three decades separating my commissioning as a second lieutenant in 1969 and my retirement as a lieutenant general in 2000 seemed to dissolve. For a moment I was a young woman on a sunny June day back in Memphis again.

But how had I changed in those years? What had I learned about myself as a leader and about the nature of leadership? What attributes had I acquired during thirty years as a soldier as I advanced to become the Army's first woman three-star general? What specific human lessons had I learned in my career that I could pass on to other women working in professions traditionally led by men, to other women and men in uniform, and to parents of talented daughters considering their future? And what of value had I also learned in my years as a military leader that could benefit everyone both in uniform and the private sector who wishes to understand our promising and dynamic human environment?

At a dinner in the fall of 1999 for women prominent in their career fields, I first met Betty Friedan, the founder of modern feminism. Supreme Court Justice Sandra Day O'Connor, Senator Kay Bailey Hutchison, and journalist Eleanor Clift were in attendance. I was in uniform. Ms. Friedan discovered I was the highest-ranking woman ever in the U.S. Army. "You must write a book," she said. "But don't write about abstract ideas. Write about the concrete events in your life that brought you to this point." Later, retired General Jack Merritt, president emeritus of the Association of the U.S. Army, suggested I tell my readers why I wrote this book. I want to explain how important the Army has been in forming me as a person and as a leader. Despite times of personal sacrifice, the experience has been overwhelmingly positive. The Army is more than a job; it's a life, a community of soldiers who become permanent friends. But perhaps most significantly, the Army is a team in which the leadership values of honor and selfless service have endured.

GENERALLY SPEAKING

1

A Soldier's Daughter

I was born into the Army.

My father, Cary A. Kennedy, was a Reserve Officer Training Corps (ROTC) cadet in his senior year at the University of Tennessee at Nashville when the Japanese bombed Pearl Harbor on December 7, 1941. He was commissioned a second lieutenant in the Infantry and spent World War II in the European Theater of Operations. In 1946 he came home to Memphis, married my mother, Tommie Jean Haygood, and the young couple soon embarked—literally—on an Army career, taking a troopship to Germany.

As Daddy would later wryly tell us, he decided to stay in the Army because he was energetic enough to walk up stairs to a processing station on the second floor. When the war was over, officers were given the choice of applying for a regular commission or mustering out. The line for immediate discharge, he said, formed on the first floor of an administration building, while there was another line of officers who wanted to stay in the service on the second floor. Daddy was a major. He liked the Army, but, given the option of remaining in the Infantry or selecting another branch, he chose the Transportation Corps.

I was born in Frankfurt, Germany, in 1947. A year later, my father sent Mother and me home to Memphis because the Cold War seemed about to flare into open conflict. The Soviets had cut off Allied ground access to Berlin. The West responded with the Berlin Airlift. Although tensions remained high for eleven months, the Soviets eventually relented and opened the land corridor to the Allied sectors of Berlin. But the Iron Curtain now divided Europe.

My father was reassigned to Fort Eustis, Virginia, on the James River near Williamsburg, headquarters of the Transportation Corps. Over the coming years, we would repeatedly return to this post. That's where my brother, Andy, and my sisters, Nancy and Elizabeth, were born, between assignments that took the family back to Germany, to Japan, and later even to Israel, where my father served as an assistant Army attaché.

Both my parents were strong influences on my character. Obviously, my father, a career soldier, formed my model of a professional officer. But my mother, Jean, has also always been a strong individual. She taught me that a woman could have independent political and social opinions at a time when *Father Knows Best* was as much a national ethos as popular entertainment. Almost fifty years later, I clearly remember an afternoon when she first made me aware that women could hold independent views on important issues.

It was early fall 1952, and the presidential election race between Democratic candidate Adlai Stevenson and Republican candidate Dwight Eisenhower was heating up. I was skipping rope in the yard and came inside to find Mama ironing and watching the grainy black-and-white image on the large screen of our light oak television set. It was Mr. Stevenson giving a speech.

"Who are we for, Mama?" I asked.

"Well, *we're* for Stevenson," my mother said, nodding toward the man on the TV. "But don't tell your father."

This was exciting stuff for a kid of five. Mama was talking to me like a grown-up. Daddy was a politically conservative Army officer who would naturally vote for General Eisenhower. But

Mama had independent political views, which were more liberal than my father's.

Both my parents, however, taught their children that their personal lives had to be disciplined, whatever individual social views they held. They also taught us to examine our own motives and not accept the opinions of others whole cloth. I can't think of a better preparation in childhood for the character of a future leader.

Like most Army children, I learned to make friends fast, not be surprised when we had to move after a year or two, and to endure the isolation of being the new kid when I was put into the middle of a strange class at a new school. And I also experienced some wonderful educational opportunities that civilians rarely had. As a second-grader at the Yoyogi School for military dependents in Tokyo in the mid-1950s, for example, I practiced the dances that all young Japanese girls were taught and even took a class in making traditional silk dolls. At the post school in Boeblingen, Germany, a few years later, I began to practice the polysyllabic mysteries of German.

When we went to Israel in 1962, Daddy was assigned to the embassy. I started tenth grade at Tabeetha School, run by the Church of Scotland. The curriculum was demanding, particularly the English and Latin courses, but I enjoyed the challenge because I had decided three years earlier that I wanted to be a doctor. I had reached that decision in an unusual way. When I was in seventh grade, there simply were not many professions open to women other than teaching and nursing. So I had decided I would be a nurse.

But one evening in Williamsburg, I had told Daddy of my ambition.

"Why not be a doctor?" he responded. I saw he was serious.

I chose my eighth- and ninth-grade courses, including algebra and Latin, based on that ambition. In Israel, I learned mammalian anatomy quite well by dissecting a dead rabbit. But, in the process, I also discovered that I had no further interest in becoming either a doctor or a nurse.

In 1964, we got news that my father, who had been promoted to full colonel, had been assigned to command the Brooklyn Army Terminal. We would live at nearby Fort Hamilton. I had become attached to my friends in Israel. I did *not* want to go to a third high school.

"I'll stay in Israel and finish my senior year," I told my father. I was eager to be independent, to be an adult.

We were at dinner. That evening Father was tired but patient. "You can't support yourself. You're sixteen."

"I'll get a job and pay board. There won't be any problem."

"You need a work permit, and you're not Jewish. It's not going to work, Claudia."

Naturally, I went home with the family. And I was unhappy that year. Fort Hamilton High was a civilian school near the post. The seismic shock waves of the 1960s counterculture hadn't hit yet, and the social scene was still frozen in a 1950s teenage time warp. Belonging to the right clique, whether it was centered on student government, sports, or neighborhoods, seemed a matter of dire importance.

With four children and an Army salary, my parents were saving every dime they had for our college education. The trendy pleated skirts from Neiman Marcus were out of the question. Nobody asked me to the prom. In fact, I didn't have a single date that last year of high school. For some girls, that would have been a tragedy. I decided to concentrate on my classes. And I read a lot for fun, mostly biography, which I'd enjoyed since grade school, then branched into Ayn Rand and Dostoyevsky.

We had already decided that I would attend my mother's alma mater, Southwestern at Memphis, a small co-ed liberal arts college founded by the Presbyterian Church in 1843. My mother's family had a long association with the school. Both aunts and one uncle had attended, and my grandfather had taught math and coached football there. Another advantage of attending Southwestern was I could live with one of my grandmothers. Daddy had promised all the children four years of college, but after that, as he always reminded us, "You graduate from college in four years, get a job, pack your bags, and live on your own. You'll always be welcome home for brief, pleasant visits." His emphasis was on brief. That was the Army colonel speaking.

The start of my freshman year in August 1965 coincided with the true beginning of the "sixties," the social cataclysm that shook the Western world for the next decade. Even though Southwestern was a Southern campus where weekly chapel attendance was mandatory, it was viewed as liberal in comparison with the local state college. Anti–Vietnam War demonstrations and protests over dorm rules and fraternity and sorority culture became commonplace during my college years. But in Memphis, retaining its Old South civility, these events lacked the strident tone or violence found on larger, more radical campuses. And many of the students simply remained aloof, preferring traditional college pursuits and confining their probing of deeper issues such as the civil rights movement or the war in Vietnam to intellectual expression, rather than taking the debate to the streets.

Although I joined the Kappa Delta sorority, I was hardly a leader: My most memorable responsibility was keeping the Coke machine filled; somebody else even emptied the dimes and delivered them to the vendor. I eventually opted for a philosophy major because it was interesting and permitted the most electives. And my father was dubious: "Just exactly what kind of job do you plan to *do* with that degree, Claudia?" That was hard to answer, but I had come to enjoy acquiring and synthesizing diverse knowledge for its own sake, valuable traits for a future Army intelligence officer. My big treat each month was taking myself to McDonald's, where I could afford two out of three items: a small burger, small fries, or a small Coke.

I was not interested in marching in campus demonstrations or in going to rock concerts. But I was starting to consider what kind of job I would get to fill the years between graduation and the apparent inevitability of marriage and motherhood. Real estate came naturally to mind because my grandmother Kennedy had run her own office for years, and I would always remember coveting her shiny Burroughs adding machine when I was a little girl of five. And my godmother, Meredith Moorehead, had worked her whole life in an office. She had her own lovely apartment in Memphis that I can remember as one of the most sophisticated and appealing places I visited as a child. As I read Socrates and struggled through economics and French literature, I considered the possibility of my own independence after college, not the mounting tensions on campus.

My father's next assignment brought the war home to me, however. He went off to command the port of Saigon at the height of the American military buildup in Vietnam. And now the steadily mounting draft calls for the war meant that many of the boys who were my friends were forced to consider how to navigate among the competing demands of college, graduate school, and the draft. The antiwar protests became more vocal.

Although I was personally troubled by our government's disregard of the public's legitimate concerns about Vietnam and South Vietnamese suppression of opposition groups, including Buddhist monks burning themselves alive on Saigon sidewalks, I did not believe national policy should be set by people's individual acts of civil disobedience during wartime. It was all well and good for college students enjoying their deferments to loudly debate the war. But the Iowa farm boy or inner-city black kid didn't have that option. They were over there in Vietnam. Just like my father. I felt they deserved our support, no matter what we thought of the war itself.

In the spring of my junior year, Southwestern hosted a seminar as part of the annual week-long Dilemma series on ethical issues in which a civilian speaker defended American policy in Vietnam. The lecture hall was packed with opponents to the war, students, faculty, and people from town. But the speaker handled himself well, even when the questions and audience responses to his answers got heated.

At the end of the program, as we stood outside the auditorium in an informal continuation of the discussion, I addressed him. "Despite all this controversy about the war, sir," I said, my voice a little uncertain, "there are Americans dying every day in Vietnam. What can we do about *them*?"

He looked around the lobby, then at me. "You can live every day of your life in honor of their sacrifice."

The people around me were silent. There were none of the groans or boos that had greeted his earlier statements. His words have stayed with me over three decades as a professional soldier, and have sustained me through the losses of a growing number of fellow soldiers.

* * *

A few weeks later, the postman found a copy of *Cosmopolitan* with a missing mailing label in his bag. He knew a college girl lived at my grandmother's house, so he put the magazine in the box. I read about the hot fashions and rather innocent dating advice, then happened to spot a full-page advertisement showing a photo of a dancing couple. They wore Army green uniforms. "Be an Intelligence Analyst," the caption read. The ad sought enlisted applicants for the Women's Army Corps. Intrigued, I sent in a postcard and received information about the WAC summer program for college juniors considering becoming officers after graduation. Suddenly I remembered the WACs I had seen near the gate of Fort Hamilton when I was on the way to high school. They had looked sharp and purposeful in their summer cord uniforms.

The WAC College Junior Program, I learned, was a four-week orientation held each summer at Fort McClellan, Alabama, for 150 college women between their junior and senior years. From this group, the WACs hoped to select about ninety potential officers who would be paid $200 a month as Army corporals during their senior college year, then be commissioned second lieutenants and return to Fort McClellan to begin the four-month Officer Basic Course the next summer. Once commissioned, they would have a minimum two-year service obligation.

Looking at the brochures, I saw photos of women officers leading formations of WACs and doing staff work in offices. To a
young person raised near Army posts, it seemed natural that
women officers were the counterparts of their male colleagues:
leaders. For the first time in my life, I recognized the possibility
that I might enjoy being a leader.

But I was still just twenty years old, and I didn't want to take
the plunge alone. So I approached one of my friends and a
sorority sister in Kappa Delta, Marilyn Gates.

"What are you going to do this summer, Marilyn?"

"I guess I'll work at TG&Y," she said unenthusiastically, naming a local drugstore, "just like always."

I showed her the WAC College Junior Program brochure. "If
you'll do it, I'll do it."

"I think that would be neat," she said.

Now I was committed.

I had to obtain faculty references to complete my application. When I approached one of my science professors, he wasn't
very receptive. "I don't approve of the military," he honestly admitted. "But I do believe it's important for women to work. Have
you read Betty Friedan's book *The Feminine Mystique*?"

"I've never even heard of her."

"I think you ought to read the book."

I did, and found it very courageous for Betty Friedan to say
out loud what many thought but were unable to put into words,
that it simply was not enough for a woman to devote her life to
being a wife and a mother. Every argument she made was not
only rational, but captured the sense of what is the essential
struggle in our lives, the two competing demands of family and
work. I grasped her viewpoint instinctively—as did countless millions of other young American women over the coming decades.
We were not inherently less capable or ambitious than the boys
and young men we had grown up with. But until Betty Friedan
spoke out, women as a group were simply expected to truncate
their lives due to their gender, not fulfill their individual talents
or aspirations.

I did not join feminist demonstrations after reading *The Feminine Mystique,* but the book did open my eyes to much wider perspectives, and I was glad to discover a description for my political viewpoint.

Before I left for the College Junior Program that summer, my father offered advice on what would be expected of me in Army training. He had recently returned from Vietnam, and I think he was both proud of and puzzled by my decision to explore the Army. "Work as a team. Organize your time. Memorize your serial number," he said.

Marilyn Gates and I arrived at Fort McClellan in my 1962 Ford Fairlane on a steamy July afternoon. Our milling formation of college juniors was greeted by a no-nonsense contingent of steely-eyed WAC sergeants in sharply pressed Army green cord uniforms, skirts exactly one inch below the middle of the knee, nylon stockings despite the wilting heat, and highly polished black, low-heel shoes.

As the group was broken into platoon-size clumps, Marilyn and I were separated. "Don't say 'ma'am' to corporals or sergeants," I advised her. "Don't say much at all."

But my advice proved unnecessary. She too was a soldier's daughter. Her father had fought in the Philippines early in World War II and had survived the Bataan Death March and almost four years of brutal Japanese captivity as a prisoner of war. Yet meeting Mr. Gates, who was a soft-spoken family man, you never would have guessed his courage. Marilyn had obviously absorbed some of his resilience. She did much better that summer than I did.

I found some of the program, particularly the unbending discipline, to be rather tedious. We lived in cinder block enlisted barracks, three women to a partitioned space, each with her own dresser. Those dresser drawers had to be set up in *exact* order, with shorts and blouses folded a certain number of inches apart, toothbrush and toothpaste tube set in the identical positions as illustrated in the manual we were issued. And another requirement was the girdle display. Every woman had to have her girdle laid out in her drawer for daily inspection. At the time I weighed ninety-nine pounds, less than the skinny British model Twiggy, and I certainly did not wear a girdle. But my girdle was perfectly aligned in my drawer and that made my platoon leader happy.

A few of the homesick young women were miserable and cried for days. They experienced the shouted corrections of the drill instructors as personal insults. Obviously, these girls just were not Army material. After a week or so, senior officers took them aside for counseling, and later culled those from the program who failed to adjust to Army life.

We marched a lot that summer, to and from classes, to the mess hall, back to the barracks, and learned to keep in step. And we all learned the words to the WAC song, "Duty Is Calling You and Me," set to the tune of the "Colonel Bogey March."

Classes focused on military organization, customs, traditions, and skills such as map reading and first aid. We learned the proper way to address seniors, how to salute and to stand at attention in the heavy Alabama sun.

For me, the Army held no great mysteries; I'd been raised with an understanding of its values, its traditions, and its expectations of leaders and soldiers. I also understood the Army's structure. A platoon of thirty soldiers was led by a lieutenant. There were four platoons in a company, commanded by a captain, and four companies in a battalion, whose commander was a lieutenant colonel. Traditionally, three or four battalions formed a brigade, commanded by a full colonel. The next largest unit was the division, a formation of three or more brigades. Divisions were composed of Infantry or Armor with their own organic Artillery and Combat Engineer battalions. Combat support branches—Military Intelligence, Signal Corps, and combat service support branches Quartermaster Corps, Transportation Corps, Ordnance, and so on—all had units assigned to these divisions (see Glossary).

In the 1960s, the WAC's 10,000 enlisted women and 1,000 officers serving in the United States and overseas officially performed "essential" duties that freed up men for assignment to combat units, from which women were barred. That had been the purpose of women in the Army since World War II. In 1942, Congresswoman Edith Nourse Rogers, an early champion for women's equality, introduced a bill for the Women's Army Auxiliary Corps, a quasi-military group of volunteers who would fill noncombat Army jobs, mainly clerical and administrative, so that men could be assigned to fighting units. The WAAC was created on May 14, 1942, without official military status. Its members wore Army-style uniforms, but had their own enlisted and commissioned ranks and insignia, and were not governed by Army regulations or the Articles of War.

A year later there were 60,000 enlisted women and officers serving in the U.S. and overseas in a variety of assignments that included military administration, personnel processing, clerical work, vast and complex globe-spanning military post offices, and maintenance jobs in motor pools. WAAC officers were also in charge of huge military payrolls and ultrasensitive code rooms. For these positions, they were trained to use the Army Colt .45 caliber pistol, a fact that was not widely advertised during the war because the concept of armed women in uniform was anathema to many conservative members of Congress and traditional military leaders. I find this rather ironic, considering that Rosie the Riveter and other women defense workers had become collective national heroes by the second year of the war.

Despite the undeniable contribution the WAAC made, the deep-seated resistance to military women found expression in an ugly and persistent slander campaign that seemed to crop up at many posts. According to those spreading the slander, the women soldiers were disreputable. From the perspective of the late 1960s, I considered such an attitude, especially in wartime, as outrageously untrue as it was grossly unfair. But the history of the Women's Army Corps showed that the pervasive slander campaign that extended into 1944 had a definite negative effect on women volunteering for service.

Nevertheless, in 1943, Chief of Staff General George C. Marshall requested that Congress convert the WAAC from auxiliary status to a full military branch of the Army. The Women's Army Corps was created that year. Enlisted WACs would now have military grades from private through master sergeant, and officers from second lieutenant through lieutenant colonel. The Director of the WAC would be a full colonel. The women of the Corps served under Army regulations and the Articles of War.

During World War II, WACs were assigned to all theaters of operations, from Europe to China, from Australia to the islands of the South Pacific. By the end of the war, over 140,000 women had volunteered for Army duty; some had been wounded in action, and a few decorated for courage under fire.

WACs were allowed to marry if they received proper authorization. But if a WAC serving in the European Theater of Operations married an American military man, one of them was immediately transferred to a distant station. The transfer was meant to discourage romances resulting in pregnancy. In the Far East, a WAC could not marry unless she was pregnant. Any WAC who became pregnant was expected to announce her condition and quickly be processed for discharge on grounds of medical disability.

Remarkably, these stringent conditions, first imposed at the height of World War II, still prevailed in the Women's Army Corps in 1968. A WAC could marry with permission, but not become pregnant and remain in the service.

Nevertheless, I began to think that a few years in the Army would be just the kind of experience I wanted. Still in my early twenties, I expected to be married and a mother eventually, as did many of my peers. But I found the familiar and straightforward military institutions, the comforting certainty of the Army's values, and the unabashed patriotism of such traditions as pausing each afternoon at Retreat to salute the flag as the color guard lowered it for the day, to be more inspiring than the 1960s world of dissidence and negativity. The Army took a lot of guesswork out of life.

And I didn't harbor illusions that the Army was a tranquil refuge. Toward the end of that month, we were bused over to

Fort Benning, Georgia, to observe a live-fire exercise at the Infantry School. This famous "Mad Minute" reminded me that the purpose of the Army was fighting and winning battles, and to do so soldiers had to kill the enemy. As we sat in the bleachers behind the sandbagged model battalion defensive position, however, the effect of U.S. Army firepower was overwhelming.

Helmeted soldiers filed into the trenches before us to occupy the bunkers. They began firing with crackling .223 caliber M-16 rifles, first on semiautomatic, then on rippling full-automatic bursts. Then the heavier blast of 7.62mm M-60 machine guns firing slashing orange tracers toward the distant sand hills joined in. Suddenly the cacophony was pounded by the deeper roar of .50 caliber heavy machine guns from the bunkers. Soldiers fired 40mm grenades and 60mm mortars that exploded louder than any Fourth of July fireworks. All the while, the rifle and machine gun fire continued. Then 105mm howitzers cut loose behind us, and the shells ripped by overhead with a metallic groan. Their distant explosions sent out shock waves that struck us like invisible boxing gloves.

Around me the young women were silent, absorbed by the spectacle. I tried to picture what enemy soldiers would experience, advancing against such a heavily defended position. Then my mind shifted to American troops ordered to attack bunkers like these in Vietnam.

The WAC only gave us a few weeks to decide on the student officer program after we left Fort McClellan that summer. Flying into Southport, North Carolina, where my father now commanded the Army ammunition terminal, I was certainly attracted to the idea of becoming an Army officer, but still wasn't sure about accepting a two-year commitment.

And there were other, much deeper principles in weighing this decision. All around me young men were being required to fulfill their military obligations during wartime. I firmly believed that women were due the rights and opportunities of citizenship equal to men. And along with these equal rights came equal responsibilities, including military service. Personally, I considered it important for both men and women to accept the responsibility of military service. The obligations of citizenship should be without reference to gender, just as they are without reference to race.

As I considered whether to join the WAC, I weighed several factors: the length of the obligation after college, the symbolism of serving my country, and the practical advantage of having a record as an Army officer on my résumé. Before making my final decision, I consulted friends and family.

My brother, Andy, certainly had no qualms and gave me the decisive push: "Only two years? Do it."

In a way two years of service would show a kind of solidarity with the men who were drafted, even though I'd be an officer. Besides, the $200 a month the Army would pay me during my senior year would certainly help my parents a lot, as they had two other children in private college during my senior year. "Well," I told Andy, "I guess I will."

But when I discussed this decision with my father, he was quite thoughtful. "Are you *sure* you're interested in this, Claudia?"

My internal debate continued, but I became surer that applying for the student officer program would be a good idea.

"Yes, Daddy, I am."

I mailed my acceptance letter and called Marilyn. She too had decided to accept.

Back at school, Marilyn and I decided to keep our decision fairly private. We would not bring it up, but would tell anyone who asked. Antiwar sentiment had reached a high point. Now even the faculty at this Southern college were becoming strongly opposed to the war in Vietnam and to the Army. Several of the professors I needed for references harbored antimilitary feelings, but they honored my requests for their support. To any who persisted, I gave the oversimplified answer, "My father's in the Army," which seemed to satisfy them. Maybe it was a lost opportunity to persuade them, but I didn't feel like getting into long ethical debates about the responsibilities of citizens in a democracy, knowing how entrenched the popular position against the war had become.

When my Army paycheck of $200 a month began, most went for tuition, but I could now make a monthly splurge at McDonald's, feasting on a small burger, small fries, *and* a small Coke.

Most of my friends did not know about my Army plans until just before graduation in June 1969. They were puzzled. The concept of women becoming Army officers at that time seemed utterly alien. I might just as well have announced plans to become an astronaut.

On June 2, at the local congressman's office, my father read the oath commissioning me a second lieutenant in the Women's Army Corps. I swore to "protect and defend the Constitution of the United States against all enemies, foreign and domestic, and to obey the orders of the President of the United States and of the officers appointed over me."

2

Persistence

*I*n August 1969, I began the four-month WAC Officer Basic Course at the WAC School at Fort McClellan. One hundred and twenty women were divided into three platoons in our class. We lived in concrete officers barracks now, two women to a room, two rooms sharing a bathroom. There was air-conditioning indoors, but outside we endured the humid Piedmont summer heat.

The level of discipline was dramatically higher than the previous summer. There were almost none of the early homesick dropouts we had seen then. We were expected to keep the barracks and our uniforms spotless, using vast amounts of Johnson floor wax on the linoleum and Brasso on our insignia. Once more the drawers of our dressers had to be maintained at museum-quality perfection. I quickly learned the expedient of setting up my inspection display, but keeping all of my other possessions in my car. Some women went so far as sleeping on the floor to save time getting ready in the morning.

There were two levels of consequences for accumulating demerits: restriction to post and restriction to barracks. But I found the abject and unreasonable fear of demerits very funny, as I did a lot of the seemingly deadly serious arbitrary discipline. We were, after all, volunteers; they could have turned us into soldiers without so much huffing and puffing. I kept my mouth shut, of course, but inside I was laughing half the time. Nobody was going to scare me into sleeping on a hard linoleum floor. It was much easier to get up ten minutes early and make my bed properly. Anyway, there was always a way to beat the system: It was called teamwork. That was what was impressed upon us. "Cooperate to graduate," we were told. No one could meet every requirement individually, but we could all do it if we organized both personally and as a group and worked together.

We stood inspection every day, which made sense because it took a few of us a little while to learn the simple fact that wearing a uniform meant that the clothing in question had to look exactly the same day after day. The principle involved was that every woman in the group matched the others' appearance, that we marched in step, stood in formation in equally spaced ranks, spoke when spoken to, in short, that we surrendered something of our individual civilian identity.

But our officers certainly were not trying to transform us into robots. In fact, one of the rituals of the longer, more intense Saturday morning inspections was close individual questioning by senior officers from the WAC Center and School. Often a major, possibly accompanied by the Olympian presence of a lieutenant colonel, would pause before a second lieutenant and quiz her on any of a wide variety of subjects, ranging from current events to American history, the purpose being to measure the young woman's poise under pressure and also to get to know her.

One Saturday morning, the battalion commander strode down the ranks and turned to stop in front of me. "What are you reading these days, Lieutenant Kennedy?"

"Isaac Asimov, ma'am," I replied, having planned for this contingency.

I think she had heard of him, but wasn't certain about his work. "Enlighten us, Lieutenant."

I launched into an exposition of Asimov's speculative theories on artificial intelligence that I had read about the previous weekend. But this was only a short while after the Apollo 11 moon landing, and the world's technical frontier seemed virtually limitless. The lieutenant colonel listened for a minute or two, and then nodded in satisfaction. I had passed muster.

In these early weeks, the senior officers focused on the weakest of the trainees, the women who simply seemed unable or unwilling to adjust to military discipline. In each platoon, there were about three such lieutenants who were obviously marginal. But the WAC Center and School's senior officers wanted to know them as well as possible before making the decision on trying to "train them up" to class standards, or to discharge them from the Army.

These senior officers had devoted their lives to the WAC. Many had served overseas in World War II and during the Korean and Vietnam Wars. They loved the Army and were proud of their branch. Although none of us young lieutenants knew at the time, and I would only learn five years later, our senior leadership realized that the U.S. military was on the verge of dramatic change. Under recently elected President Richard Nixon, the conversion from the draft to an All-Volunteer Army would occur more quickly than anyone had anticipated. The WAC would undoubtedly expand, and women officers would be assigned to fill men's jobs in branches and Military Occupational Specialties (MOSs), from which they had been long excluded. This was why the leaders of the Basic Course found it imperative to turn out the best young WAC officers they could.

At the time, however, these changes were still far over the horizon. And we accepted the drudgery of the Basic Course classes. Like so much Army instruction of the period, they were too specific, often utterly boring, and required unimaginative rote learning. In our case, instructors might lecture their required fifty minutes on some obscure piece of personnel that one of our enlisted clerks would one day use, then fill the next hour on the details of a similar personnel form. A few weeks into these classes, I hoped I had not made a mistake in joining the Army.

But I did enjoy meeting other young women from around the country whose backgrounds were completely different from mine. A few had quite exotic backgrounds, having led independent lives that I found fascinating. Anne Heurer, for example, had been a blackjack dealer in Las Vegas. But most had more traditional work experience: One or two had been nuns, and several had been teachers.

As the classes continued, it became apparent that assignments in the Women's Army Corps would be restricted to routine administrative and personnel duties, with the possible exception of securing "permanent detail" status in another Army branch such as Quartermaster Corps, Military Intelligence, Military Police, or Finance. But any interesting job outside the WAC required specialized training, and I couldn't expect that for at least a couple of years after the Basic Course. Once more, my original plan of staying in the Army for only two years seemed to be my most probable option.

Then one cool October morning Colonel Maxene B. Michl, commander of the WAC Center and School, addressed the course on the theme of "becoming comfortable in your uniform." She meant this both literally and virtually. Colonel Michl, who had served in Saigon at the same time as my father, was a slight, gray-haired woman with thick-rimmed glasses and a quietly precise voice. She was probably the best-informed WAC officer at Fort McClellan about the changes looming in the Army's future. I was expecting the normal discussion of leadership or our performance as a class when Colonel Michl took the rostrum, but her first words signaled a very different theme.

"All of you women are a little bit behind the West Point graduating class of 1969," she said. "They've had four years to prepare for their futures in the Army. But you can catch up and focus on your careers if you pay attention very carefully in the next few years."

For the first time since coming to Fort McClellan, I was excited about our future assignments. Colonel Michl had compared us to the Army's elite officers, the graduates of the U.S. Military Academy at West Point. She had also suggested that we would have careers that would run parallel to those of our male colleagues, a prospect I had not considered. Here was this veteran, no-nonsense WAC officer telling us to carefully prepare ourselves for a career path that might in fact lead as high as that of our West Point peers, many of whom would no doubt become generals. I was enthralled.

* * *

When I meet civilians, I often find they have very little understanding of the rank and branch structure in the U.S. Army. This comes as no surprise at a time when a small and declining minority of our population has had prior military service. So I think it's important at this stage to present a brief primer—"Army 101"—that explains the building blocks of Army life.

The Army manages its people differently than do civilian employers, bringing enlisted soldiers and officers into its ranks only at the entry level (no middle or executive level accessions for those in uniform). Enlisted ranks start as privates, officers as second lieutenants. The Army also manages its officers by "year group," the year a person is commissioned. Since I was commissioned in 1969, I was in "Year Group 1969" the rest of my career.

There is a fairly structured path for Army officers. The specifics vary by branch, which the officers are assigned on commissioning: Infantry, Armor, Artillery (the combat arms); Engineers, Military Police, Military Intelligence, Signal (the combat support arms); and Adjutant General, Transportation, Ordnance, Chemical, and Finance (the combat service support arms); Judge Advocate General and Medical (special branches).

Each branch has particular tactical and technical skills that it teaches its officers through a mixture of specific Army schools and assignments. The variety of experience that a young officer acquires in the first ten years in the Army builds the record upon which she or he is evaluated in the second twenty years when officers are either selected for the command track or, alternatively, are assigned to staff duty. Traditionally, earning command was viewed as most desirable and is still informally referred to as the "fast track."

But in recent years, as a new officer personnel management system has been put into place, officers in specialties outside the command track who performed very valuable work for the Army—such as Foreign Area Officers (the Defense Attachés serving at embassies abroad)—have been able to earn promotion. These kinds of reforms have been slow in coming, however, because the Army's promotion process and advancement is deeply rooted in the tradition in which command is revered.

Once second lieutenants are assigned to a branch such as Infantry, Ordnance, or Transportation on commissioning, they attend a basic officer course in that branch. (When I enlisted in 1968, of course, women officers were limited to the Women's Army Corps or the Army Nurse Corps.) Army lieutenants might then lead a platoon of roughly thirty soldiers. Their first command would be a company of about 200 troops, which comes after promotion to the rank of captain. On promotion to major, officers can serve on a battalion staff or in a larger command. About one third to one half of all promising majors of each branch are chosen for a year in residence at the Command and General Staff College at Fort Leavenworth, Kansas. A very small percentage of lieutenant colonels are selected to command a battalion, usually composed of three to five companies. This command is of pivotal importance in an Army career. It is often followed by increasingly responsible staff positions in a division or one of the regional joint headquarters. The next critical hurdle is attending senior service college, usually the Army War College at Carlisle, Pennsylvania. Promotion to full colonel occurs at the rate of about 44 percent of lieutenant colonels eligible. A very select number of colonels are chosen to command a brigade, composed of several battalions. Less than 2 percent of colonels are promoted to brigadier general (one star) and higher command, or staff positions of greater responsibility. Of brigadier generals, fewer than half are promoted to major general (two star). Selection to lieutenant general (three star) and general (four star) depend on specific senior leadership positions that require those ranks.

People outside the Army sometimes ask if I had the unofficial help of benevolent senior officers during my career who ran interference for me, thus assuring I received promotions and coveted assignments. The answer is no. The Army doesn't work that way; in fact it's about as close to a meritocracy as you'll find.

The actual Army promotion process has changed little over the years. All officers' performance is rated by their supervisors on formally structured Officer Efficiency Reports (OERs) that must be submitted at least annually, more frequently if the officer or her rater is transferred. These OERs are then reviewed by the rating officer's own rater, called the senior rater, who fulfills the critical role of distinguishing the most exceptional officers from their more average peers. After review, OERs are entered into the rated officers' personnel files and copied onto microfiche.

These are reviewed by the scores of Army promotion boards that meet each year, a human pyramid with a vast base for the junior officer ranks and a narrow apex for brigadier and major generals, the highest ranks to be chosen by board. A promotion board considers a file containing microfiches of all an officer's OERs, previous assignments, a full-length photo in uniform to show "military bearing" taken by an Army photographer—no PR department glamour shots—and other evidence of career progress, such as military or civilian education. There is also commendatory material: awards and decorations, or, in some cases, records of courts-martial, letters of reprimand, and less serious nonjudicial punishment (Article 15). All this material goes into the mix when the board considers which officers to promote. Any significant derogatory information in a file will trigger a process by which an officer must "show cause" why the Army should retain him.

At the conclusion of the voting process, when a board's order of merit list has been completed, a statistical analysis is conducted that compares the selection results by gender and race. When minorities and women are selected at a rate less than the rate of majority men, an affirmative action review is conducted. If this review reveals, for example, that the selection rate for black women is significantly less than that for white men, then the first record of a black woman below the cut line is compared to the record of officers at the cut line. Should the board find that her record is no different than the records of those at the cut line, the board has the latitude to move the woman above the line. In almost all cases, these reviews result in no change because the records are arrayed in order of merit. The next level of review by this board is to determine whether institutional discrimination has taken place. This judgment is based on a review of all records of those minorities and women not selected.

This procedure is an affirmative action program that avoids the politically charged issue of establishing quotas on the one hand, and yet provides institutional review of treatment of women and minorities.

Today, the promotion percentages are roughly the same as they were when I joined the Army. In the junior officer ranks, 98 percent of first lieutenants are promoted to captain. The rate of captains making major is 87 percent. Sixty-four percent of majors become lieutenant colonels. That's the rank where most officers retire, usually after about twenty years' service. The percentage of lieutenant colonels reaching full colonel drops about 44 percent. Then the real triage occurs. Only 1.5 percent of colonels are promoted to brigadier general. About half of brigadier generals make major general in their allotted five years in that rank. And half of the major generals are promoted to lieutenant general, a rank at which they can usually serve for two years before retiring, unless they are extended, appointed to another assignment, or promoted to general. No woman in the Army has ever worn four stars because that rank has always gone to men from the combat arms, from which women remain excluded. But that situation could change in the future.

* * *

In the years that followed the colonel's lecture that morning at Fort McClellan, I came to realize just how little discretionary time any person who is planning their future truly has in her or his professional life, be it military or civilian.

While in the Army, I knew exactly what the expected career progression would be in terms of promotions, command assignments, and school selections. This progression not only guided us, it gave officers and NCOs a clear sense of how they were doing in comparison to their peers. There was little latitude for stagnation or drift in a successful Army career. Then, an officer either was promoted above lieutenant colonel or retired after a few years at that rank. In fact, most officers retired as lieutenant colonels. During times of shortages, there are provisions made to retain highly trained majors who wish to remain up to ten years in that rank serving in their specialties. But when I was a young officer, you were either promoted or you left the service.

This does not at all mean, however, that a young officer could ever plan with certainty every discrete step of a successful twenty-year career. There are simply too many variables involved: unanticipated changes in organizational policy, culture, mission, size (downsizing rocked the Army in the 1970s and 1990s), and budget. To succeed, I believe a person needs to have innate talent and be willing to devote one's full energy to each job for many years. I also think that most success stems from one's basic work ethic and emotional makeup (resilience and adaptability), rather than from the sole intentional activity of planning and setting distant specific goals.

Today, when I speak to ambitious young people, especially women striving to succeed in traditionally male-dominated professions, I remind them of the lesson I learned as a young Army officer: If a position of high leadership is your goal, you must lay the groundwork early and not waste time. In the military, that means choosing your branch of service carefully, so that you have the opportunity to attend professional schools and earn command. In this regard, the Army's "fast movers" are every bit as energetic and dedicated as their civilian counterparts in professions such as medicine and the law, which also have demanding apprenticeships, but successful military officers face an even steeper and narrowing pyramid.

Until recently, the first important "gate" in a civilian career was the choice between graduate school and direct entry into the marketplace. Now increasing numbers of young people, including women, are forgoing a full university education and moving directly into Information Age entrepreneurial ventures, especially Internet initial public offering companies. A few succeed. Many more have to return to employment in a more traditional industry. I think it might be better for these entrepreneurs to have a university degree to fall back on. And I think it is especially unfortunate that these young people miss the opportunity to enrich their lives through a liberal arts and science education.

For people who do take a more traditional route to professional success, persistence is probably their strongest fundamental attribute. The years of hard work of law school inevitably follow the long library weekends of prelaw; years of drudgery as an associate precede partnership. In medicine, the schooling and apprenticeships are even more rigorous and selective.

In this increasingly competitive world, the basic attributes of diligence and persistence will only become more important as factors in success.

*   *   *

As a twenty-one-year-old second lieutenant in 1969, of course, I didn't understand much of this. But after Colonel Michl's lecture, I did have a glimmer that a fully realized Army career might just possibly be an option in my life.

With that in mind, I anxiously awaited word of my first assignment as the end of the Basic Course approached that fall. Coursemate friends like Carol Hoffman and Anne Heurer had already figured out the unseen dynamics of the assignment process.

"If you're near the bottom of the class, they'll keep you here at McClellan," Carol said. "They don't want to send the duds to other posts. Bad publicity."

"But if you're at the top of the class," Anne warned, "they'll keep you here at McClellan to be an instructor and be a good example for the new students."

The prospect of staying at Fort McClellan for two more years did not appeal to me. I had joined the Army in part to travel. My class grades were good, I knew, but my military uniform was not the very best: I never could get my brass insignia and shoes as shiny as some of the women. Maybe I'd fall in the middle ranks and be assigned an interesting job. My stated preference was New England. I had never been there, but I liked the New Englanders I'd met in the Basic Course.

Just before Thanksgiving, I got my orders: Fort Devens, Massachusetts, a medium-size post in the foothills west of Boston. I was very happy. Boston was an exciting, sophisticated city, and the shore and mountains of New England were an easy drive from the post.

Then my platoon leader, Lieutenant Mary Spring, called me in. "Your orders have been changed," she said, glancing down at a form on her desk. "You're staying here at McClellan."

"No!" I blurted out, a very unmilitary response.

She was startled, and then broke into a grin. This was a prank, instigated by Anne and Carol, Lieutenant Spring confessed. I was on my way to Fort Devens.

* * *

When I arrived at Fort Devens, I was interviewed by a Major Landry and assigned as the assistant administrative officer to the Director of Personnel and Community Activities.

Initially, I found this, my first adult job, quite exciting. But after a few months, I came to realize that the DPCA—the Army is addicted to acronyms—often entailed the boring housekeeping duties of running the post. Major Landry, a laconic, chain-smoking former enlisted man, pragmatically assured me, however, that even if the assignment were sometimes frustrating, it was a collection of tasks that were necessary for the smooth functioning of the post.

One of my jobs involved routing the school buses. Parents whose kids overslept and were late for classes called me to bitterly complain that the bus had passed their stop too early and left little Billie or Judy standing in the cold. I was also given the task of directing the contest to choose a slogan for Fort Devens ("Fort Devens, Gateway to Route 2," a popular but ultimately rejected entry).

Whenever I wasn't handling calls, I was shuffling a steady flow of paperwork: endless disposition forms, guard roster forms, duty rosters (important in organizing blood drives), supply requests, a bureaucratic avalanche that heaped my in baskets every morning and kept my two enlisted clerks rattling away on their IBM Selectrics the entire duty day.

My jobs were in fact considered normal lieutenant's work at that time. But in that period, women filled most administrative positions, both in the military and in the civilian world. The vast majority of women employed in the American private sector were either secretaries, teachers, or nurses. And, like me, so many girls that I had grown up with saw their professional horizons limited to either teaching or nursing or this kind of nine-to-five office work.

In the Army, women were thought to be capable of handling little details—the sheet-counting, the paper-pushing, the tweaking of school bus schedules—but not of shouldering more challenging responsibilities outside the all-female ranks of the WAC. From the Corps's creation in World War II, there were firm statutory prohibitions against women commanding men. These still prevailed when I began my service at Fort Devens in 1970. I could and did have men working for me, but I did not write the NCO Efficiency Report on the master sergeant in my office, since it was viewed as demeaning to him to have to work for a WAC lieutenant.

And although I was in no position to issue orders to men soldiers, one of the duties Major Landry eventually gave me was briefing the Field-Grade Officer of the Day (FGOD) when that major or lieutenant colonel reported for his periodic twelve-hour stint as the post's senior leader during off-duty hours. The FGOD rotated among the various commands, so that each of these senior officers might serve once every three or four months. The duty was hardly demanding, requiring the officer to be on call at post headquarters in the event of an emergency, at which time he would follow a detailed set of Standard Operating Procedures (SOPs) found in a thick, three-hole binder, which Major Landry and I had to update and use in briefing each day's FGOD.

But the tasks of the FGOD became increasingly detailed and many officers found them irksome. For example, they had to inspect the public address system at both Reveille and Retreat to make sure the recorded music could be heard far and wide.

Then the garrison staff sent out a rather unusual directive.

"One of the things we're now doing, sir," I said, keeping a straight face as I handed an officer the SOP book, "is writing down the serial numbers and locations of all the Dempsey Dumpsters."

"You're *what?*"

"The Dumpsters, sir, at all the mess halls and the workshops. We need the serial numbers and exact locations noted every day to make sure they're all accounted for. And you need to find the ones *other* than those already on the list."

The officer scowled as he read the neat block paragraphs of the mimeographed SOP that bore the signature of Major Landry and his boss, Lieutenant Colonel John Morrissey. There was no arguing with an SOP.

But that diversion was short-lived. I was soon back to my endless round of less exotic work. Then one day a man lieutenant platoon leader in the Personnel Management shop came by my office and asked if I would consider swapping jobs with him. He was leaving the Army within a year and wanted as many varied assignments as possible on his résumé. He particularly thought the community affairs part of my assignment would be good preparation for work in the civilian world.

"Are you interested, Claudia?"

"You bet."

I went to see Lieutenant Colonel Morrissey. To me, the idea of the job swap made perfect sense: I was dying to lead a platoon. And the other lieutenant would have gladly taken on my multiple jobs. But Morrissey was opposed to the idea.

"No, no," he said, shaking his head. "Your job would *kill* a man's career."

I was amazed. *What about my career?* "Sir," I argued in a reasonable tone, "he's not planning an Army career. He wants the job on his civilian résumé."

Colonel Morrissey shook his head. "Out of the question, Lieutenant. You're in the right assignment."

What he meant, of course, was that I was only a woman, a WAC. Yet I knew he appreciated me and respected my work within the cultural blinkers of his generation. I decided to take a chance and persist in my argument. You cannot be insubordinate in the Army, but with a reasonable senior officer it's always possible to present a logical rebuttal. "Sir, I just don't think my job is very meaningful. I'm no longer learning anything. That's why I'd like to take over that platoon in Personnel."

Colonel Morrissey thought a moment. "Lieutenant, make a list of everything you do and we'll look into it."

I listed the thirty-odd tasks assigned to me, some of them definitely odder than others. But all of them could have been done by a corporal or junior sergeant with a modicum of training. When Colonel Morrissey read my list he tried to enhance the assignment somewhat. But basically he was satisfied that I was indeed in the right job. After all, this was the kind of work WAC officers were *good* at—always had been, always would be.

* * *

As a new lieutenant in my twenties, I didn't see any way out, but I did make the best of the situation. My assignment was like most entry-level positions. It's best just to use the experience to learn as much as possible while recognizing that the frustration will end and that you'll get more challenge in the next assignment. Recently, I had the chance to talk about this issue with my cousin Lele, a smart young woman with a degree in business who is interested in advancing into a management position in retail fashion sales. Lele currently works as an assistant manager for a nationwide retail chain, having risen from a salesclerk after graduation.

But she had a problem and called me for advice. Her current store manager is not very competent. She makes a lot of professional mistakes that ultimately reflect on her staff. In comparison to Lele's previous manager, this boss is much less efficient, and Lele does not see the situation improving. Although she would like to stay with the company, Lele does not want to remain working for her current manager.

"How can I get out of this?" she wanted to know, seeking a graceful way to be transferred. If she couldn't find any, she was prepared to resign.

I suggested she look at the problem in a different way. "Maybe it's better to ask, 'What can I get out of the situation?'"

Obviously, Lele's position is not ideal. But she should consider her entry-level job an apprenticeship, as she knows the stages of the company's career ladder she will have to climb as she gains experience: assistant manager to associate manager to full store manager. The current job, while often frustrating, gives her the chance to work hard, show her competence, and to learn everything about retail management she can while the actual responsibility of management rests on someone else's shoulders.

Before coming to me for advice, she had raised the issue of her dissatisfaction with a higher-level manager in hopes of being transferred to a different store. But she had been far too tentative in her comments about the problem out of a sense of loyalty to her store manager. The discussion was inconclusive and left Lele even more frustrated. Her reticence and sense of professional isolation are typical, I think, of many young women who lack the cohesive social bonds of clubs and after-hours sports camaraderie that their men colleagues often enjoy. On the golf course and the racquetball court, for example, these men receive informal but invaluable feedback on their job performance. But young women often lack such support networks.

Regardless, I told her, now was the time to find out the specific professional skills she needs to acquire before promotion to associate manager. I told her not to miss this opportunity by continuing to remain reticent. Go back to that senior manager (or other knowledgeable people in the store) and ask him to help you learn the business. Don't worry about your mixed feelings toward to your current boss. Just focus on the work, the daily tasks, the myriad skills that go into your profession.

The important lesson here is that young women can act in their own self-interest while remaining loyal to their organizations and their values, if they discuss the professional situation dispassionately and without personal reference to others involved.

* * *

As a young WAC lieutenant, of course, I was yet to learn these lessons. In fact, I wasn't sure what my professional goals were. And the WAC Branch assignment officers weren't much help. The conclusion of my two-year minimum service obligation was approaching, and as much as I enjoyed the New England lobsters and winter snowfalls, I was seriously considering leaving the Army unless I got a more challenging assignment. The branch suggested a transfer that would have freed me from my administrative job a few months early, but then I asked if the new job would require training. I had requested a course in personnel management because at least that training would indicate that the subsequent assignment would be more demanding. But the new job required no special training.

"I'm not interested."

Next came an enticing proposal to be interviewed for an assignment as the junior aide to the Commander-in-Chief-Pacific. "It's in Honolulu, Lieutenant," the captain at Branch told me on the phone.

Now *that* did sound exciting. "What about training?" I asked.

"Not necessary."

"Why did they pick me?"

"Well," the captain said in a confidential tone, "they saw you in the LSD file."

"What's that?"

She explained that the Little Sexy Doll file contained just the photo of junior WAC officers—no records of professional attributes—a system that was sometimes used to choose women for prestigious positions as aides to senior officers solely on the basis of their looks. I was not interested in the job. And I was also disappointed that the Women's Army Corps enabled such an obvious assault on professionalism. How were the men leading the Army ever going to take us seriously if we undermined ourselves in this way?

This period was one of those low points in which one either leaves the Army to start over or one digs in and tries to make the best of choices that are imperfect. I simply did not see how any future in the Army would work out, but I thought I had to pursue two alternatives simultaneously: one, see what the civilian world had to offer; two, press on to examine where the Army might lead. If I had known then just how deeply and how rapidly the Army was going to be transformed in the coming years, I would not have felt the anguish I did in my final months at Fort Devens. But I didn't own a crystal ball. The future was uncertain, and uncertainty often creates negative emotions. But I've since come to understand that just because uncertainty about the future—especially our professional future—makes us feel uncomfortable, these negative feelings do not mean the future itself is bleak. That too is important information for a potential leader considering major decisions that will impact one's career. Learn to be comfortable with uncertainty.

Exercising my options, I went to Boston, and bought a good civilian suit to wear at a job interview for a corporate administrative position. Alternatively, if I decided to enter law school, I knew that after two years of the Army I had the discipline to make it through.

But I wasn't ready to leave the Army. Despite my impatience to receive more responsibility, I had made friends at Fort Devens; there was camaraderie, a shared sense of duty that had become passé in the cynical civilian world. In the end, I decided to remain in the Army.

I was promoted to captain, and learned of a potentially interesting assignment. Army recruiting command had regional positions for WAC officer recruiters open in Buffalo, Syracuse, and Concord, New Hampshire. It was an independent style of working, making the rounds of college campuses. The New Hampshire office also covered eastern Vermont and Maine, beautiful country.

And, deep down, I always hoped the Army would work out for me. I accepted the recruiting assignment and moved to Concord in June 1971. My boss at the recruiting main station was Major Robert Smith, an Infantry officer who knew the service well. He was an energetic leader who wanted the transition to the All-Volunteer Army, which was rumbling toward us faster than anyone had imagined, to proceed as smoothly as possible. But WAC officer recruiting had not been going well.

"We hope that you will make mission," the major told me. "The officer you're replacing started strong but has had a slow year."

"Making mission" was one of those ubiquitous Army recruiting catchphrases. The phrase meant recruiting a minimum number of WAC officers from a rather large number of campuses. After looking at my district's demographics and the colleges in the area, I simply knew, *There's no way I can't make mission.*

But when I made my first college visit, I discovered that the recruiting brochures meant to attract college seniors to the Army listed a pay scale of only $223 a month, a figure years out of date, and certainly not competitive with civilian salaries of that time. No college graduate would be interested in that kind of pay. Later that winter, after I had replaced the old brochures, my first campus appointments in Maine coincided with the season's worst blizzards. I found myself driving the underpowered government sedan with no power steering (and a tiny steering wheel) through whiteouts, smack dab into fender-deep snowdrifts. Farmers kindly pulled my car out of the snowbanks with their tractors. I had been at the job several months and I could count the number of recruitments on one hand.

At that stage, needless to say, I was not enjoying my work as a WAC recruiter. I'd be twenty-six before my Army obligation ended. Would there be a life for me outside the Army? Driving my lonely rounds across the bleak tundra of northern New England, stretching my limited per diem at bargain motels to save money, I felt mounting unease. But I persisted. My parents had taught me to complete an obligation once I'd accepted it. And that was what I intended to do.

Then one snowy January afternoon at Bowdoin College in Brunswick, Maine, I met with some seniors who seemed interested. They'd read all the official material, but obviously needed a kicker to clinch the deal.

"If you join the Army," I told them honestly, "you'll meet a lot of good-looking guys." Then I looked out the stained glass windows of the student union at the drifting snow. "And we'll train you in a nice warm climate."

Eventually several enlisted. After this victory, my standard approach was not just to give facts, but also offer a glimpse of the type of *life* the Army created for women.

Within a few months, persistence began to pay off. I recruited women at almost every campus I visited. Not only did I make mission, but I was recruiting so many that I was filling more training "seats" than my district was allocated and Branch gave me a ceiling. But I kept recruiting because so many women wanted to join the Army. Instead of turning them away, I called my colleagues in other districts and offered them my approved applicants for their credit and their seats. They were more than pleased to accept them on their books.

One contributor to this success was Sara Zuretti, a runner-up in the Miss New Hampshire contest, whom I had recruited in her last year at a local university. She was a January graduate and had six months to wait before beginning the Basic Course. But I convinced Branch to swear her in as a second lieutenant and let her wear her uniform while accompanying me on my campus tours. Sara also was a real hit in a local TV publicity blitz we launched promoting the All-Volunteer Army. When she met the governor of New Hampshire in her well-tailored green uniform, the people in our public affairs office joked she'd gotten so much airtime that she'd land his job in the next election. I couldn't have been happier.

I suppose this is the kind of pleasure a successful salesperson derives from a job well done. But for me, there was more. I had persisted for over two years, learning the apprenticeship of an entry-level officer under sometimes tedious conditions. But now I was perfectly happy to complete the recruiting assignment and I looked forward to my next Army job.

In my last year of that assignment, our recruiting station at the Federal Building in Concord received an impossibly complex manpower survey, one of the bureaucratic legacies of some earlier Pentagon dynasty. The crux of the report was to document how all the civilians and soldiers had used their time during the previous year, divided into labyrinthine blocks of one-quarter hour. The survey would have been laughable had our future budget and allocation of people not depended on completing every box, subparagraph, and column of numbers in the multipage document. The task remained incomplete for several weeks, casting a pall like an unexploded bomb over all who wanted to avoid dealing with it. One morning when Sergeant Major Calais stopped by my cubicle to see me, he warned, "It may be you that has to do it, Captain."

"Oh no, Sergeant Major," I said adamantly. "I've got to make mission, and I don't know a thing about manpower surveys."

He suggested he knew a civil servant who might help if I got stuck with the job.

But about a week before the dreaded report was due, Major Smith reassigned the survey to me. "You're going to have to do this. We don't have much time. But we will give you all the help you need."

That amounted to three typists and two crusty civilian budget specialists from the Army Reserve center. "Just make sure the numbers total accurately," one advised me. But there were literally thousands of figures that had to be added. On the next to last day of the ordeal, which promised to be a long one, Major Smith put on his coat and hat to head home for dinner with his family. He paused before my desk, noting the heaps of legal pads and half-completed budget forms, and the three typists pounding away furiously.

"It's a real nightmare, isn't it?"

It certainly was. But we completed the job. I felt good about getting it done even though it had literally been dumped in my lap. There is an Army tradition of giving junior officers quick reaction challenges, and it probably didn't matter that I was a woman. My persistence in completing the irksome, bureaucratic labor of the manpower study raised my stock in Major Smith's estimation.

A few months later, toward the end of my assignment in Concord, a colonel from the recruiting district visited the station. Major Smith had spoken to him positively about my work.

"You've been here two years, Captain?" the colonel asked.

"Yes, sir."

"It's time for you to command a company."

I thought he was a mind reader because that was exactly the

next assignment I was hoping for. But I told him I didn't see any way I could go from an obscure job in recruiting to company command without some interim step.

"No, Captain," he insisted. "It *is* time for you to command a company."

I'll never know how much of a role Major Smith played in all this—perhaps because of my diligence in making the WAC officer recruiting objectives and completing the manpower survey—but the colonel apparently put in a good word about my work with the WAC staff advisor to First U.S. Army, Lieutenant Colonel Doris Caldwell. In June 1973, I received orders to report back to Fort McClellan to take command of a company.

* * *

The United States had officially withdrawn combat forces from Vietnam, but we kept a large covert paramilitary presence in Indochina, waiting to see when the communists would renew their long war of "national liberation." In principle, the North Vietnamese had repatriated all living American prisoners of war, although many doubted that all of our missing in action had died. Like many others, I kept a copper bracelet with the name of a missing-in-action American, a young Army helicopter pilot who never returned. But at least American troops were no longer dying each night on the *CBS Evening News*, and the nation's political and emotional wounds could begin to heal. As I would learn, however, that process in the Army would take a while.

When I arrived back at Fort McClellan that summer, the post was buzzing with activity. The Army's "draw down" from its high Vietnam War troop levels had returned hundreds of thousands of young draftees with up to a year remaining in uniform from Southeast Asia to America. Fort McClellan, like other stateside posts, had absorbed its share of these soldiers, some of whom were directionless and undisciplined, and others who had never made it overseas. Many had acquired drug habits in Vietnam or elsewhere in the Army. They'd been assigned to Fort McClellan because the post had one of the better drug and alcohol treatment programs in the Army.

Simultaneously, the Army was racing to finish preparations for the All-Volunteer Force, as the draft had officially ended on June 30, 1973. The Women's Army Corps was straining to expand its ranks almost 80 percent in order to provide officers and enlisted women to fill the thousands of jobs that the Army Chief of Staff's personnel planners in the Pentagon envisioned would be otherwise unfilled in the All-Volunteer Army. That meant the WAC officer-training program at Fort McClellan would have to expand and additional enlisted women Basic Training courses would be established at Fort Jackson, South Carolina.

I hoped to be assigned command of a training company. But when my Basic Course friends Captains Sara Parsons and Lenita Sterry and I arrived for assignment interviews at the office of Lieutenant Colonel Virginia L. Heseman, the WAC School Commandant, the colonel saw Sara and Lenita before me. They both received training companies.

"I'm assigning you command of Staff and Faculty Company, Claudia," Colonel Heseman said.

I didn't hide my disappointment. To me, this seemed like performing a support function rather than the primary mission of the training center. I envisioned clerks and supply corporals issuing endless disposition forms, counting mountains of sheets and pillowcases, making sure the fans were turning and the toilets flushing in the three-story cinder block barracks where the instructors were housed. This was hardly the kind of company command I had envisioned.

"Is it because my brass isn't shiny enough, ma'am?" I asked rather despairingly. I had just arrived the day before, and my cord uniform was not as flawlessly pressed as those worn by everyone around me, hardly a good example for the commanding officer of a training company.

Colonel Heseman smiled. "I've given you this assignment for a reason and it has nothing to do with your insignia. I believe you'll find this a *very* challenging command."

When I reported to my office in a small building near the big concrete barracks in the WAC Training Battalion Area, I quickly learned what kind of challenges Colonel Heseman had in mind. My first sergeant, Betty J. Benson, a career WAC and one of the wisest soldiers I've ever served with—who had just been the first WAC graduate of the Army's prestigious Sergeants Major Academy—presented me the company roster. Of the 230 soldiers assigned to me, one third were men. And more were reporting for duty to the company weekly. The practice prohibiting women officers from commanding men had just been changed. My predecessor, Captain Mary Morgan (who would go on to retire in 1998 as a brigadier general), had been the first woman officer to command a significant number of men, and I would be the second. The proportion of men in my company would rise to over one half by the end of my two-year command.

Historically, almost no men had served at the WAC Center and School before 1970, aside from an occasional cook or the chaplain on permanent duty. And most of the men in my company were far different from those who had served in the past. One of the first duties of a new commander is to inspect the company's barracks.

"Ma'am," First Sergeant Benson cautioned, "you can't just walk into the men's barracks. It's too dangerous. We have to get MPs to accompany us."

I looked at her doubtfully. But the first sergeant explained that the cooks, administration clerks, and supply specialists living in the men's barracks, located across the post in the Headquarters Company's area of the U.S. Army Garrison, were dominated by a small, violent, antiauthoritarian clique who had so far managed to flaunt their disregard for basic military courtesy and discipline. They blatantly used drugs in the barracks, brought in women from the nearby town of Anniston, and held all-night parties. Racial tension compounded this already serious discipline problem, with fierce antagonism separating blacks, whites, and Hispanics. Fistfights occurred almost nightly in the barracks, which were more like a cell block than Army housing.

The majority of the men were not rebellious, but they were easily dominated by the bad apples, and were understandably afraid of them.

As I sat alone in my office reviewing the situation that first afternoon, I felt a sense of deep unease, but I also recognized that my senior officers had in fact given me the most demanding command because they thought I could handle it. There was going to be a test of wills. Either I was going to reimpose Army order through the application of leadership and discipline or that mob was going to usurp my legitimate authority. And I did not intend *that* to happen.

Colonel Mary E. Clarke, commander of the WAC Center and School, came to my company on the day I was scheduled to make a courtesy call on her. She was an inspiring leader who did not stand on ceremony. She strode directly into my small office and informally suggested, "Let's take a walk around your company area."

As we walked, she asked what I saw as the company's immediate priorities. I told her about the state of discipline and an issue my battalion commander, Lieutenant Colonel Harrison, had brought to my attention: a problem in the supply system.

Given the rapid expansion at the Center and School, tons of barracks and office furniture, ranging from bunks and dressers to desks, tables, fans, and typewriters, had simply been dumped on the ground floors of our barracks. We now faced dusty, jumbled heaps of equipment and furniture, much of it obsolete or broken. Most of it should have been junked as unusable surplus, and the worthwhile pieces either retained or sent to units that needed them. But the property books that Staff Sergeant Macon, my supply sergeant, had inherited were virtually useless. Few of the entries matched the stenciled serial numbers or faded and torn decals on the desks and mimeograph machines. A property book in the Army, however, was a sacred document, and it was also legally binding. If I had blindly signed those books on taking command, I would have been responsible for thousands of dollars of property that might or might not have been in the area. Fortunately, I hadn't signed. Despite good intentions, Staff Sergeant Macon had not been able to prod any of his contacts in the three property book offices into helping him cut this Gordian knot.

I explained some of this to Colonel Clarke. She listened patiently for a moment, and then nodded decisively. "Take care of the problem as you see best, Claudia. I'll back you up with assistance visits by teams from the Director of Logistics."

Even though I really didn't care about the difference between a single and a double pedestal desk, I tackled the supply situation first because I recognized that in the military if you don't have accountability for property, you don't have authority. And I was not going to abdicate my responsibility as company commander by signing off on property books I knew were inaccurate. Had I done so, word would have quickly spread among the men and women in the company that I was a leader who didn't maintain Army standards. I learned another valuable leadership lesson: One's authority is undermined by lack of adherence to institutional values.

But once it was clear that I was serious about straightening up the mess, Staff Sergeant Macon became less discouraged. First Sergeant Benson helped by getting enough soldiers in to provide the heavy lifting. For several sweaty weeks in the Alabama summer sun, we moved that mountain of junk out of the barracks and rearranged it into coherent foothills, which could then be identified and inventoried. The result was a truck convoy to the civilian salvage broker, a small, neat stack of usable equipment at our own supply room, and three correct company property books, which I duly signed after closely inspecting each serial number decal.

At the end of that year, a major in the WAC Center received the Legion of Merit, a high Army decoration, for "solving" the logistics problem at Fort McClellan. On the surface, this episode was about fixing a company's property management problems and the resulting cleanup of related supply functions. But to me, the exercise was not entirely about logistics. It was about leadership and integrity, and establishing a healthy command climate.

* * *

But I faced challenges with the company that were much more intractable than the supply situation. On any given day, it was likely for the mess hall to be short-staffed because men would be Absent Without Leave (AWOL).

One morning when one of the cooks failed to report for duty, First Sergeant Benson called his home and spoke to his wife.

"I just shot him," the woman announced. "He's fooling around with another woman. He's been stealing meat from the mess hall and tires from the motor pool."

"Did you call the ambulance?" Benson asked.

"He's out in the backyard. I called the police."

The cook lived and returned to duty. The wife was never charged.

Some of the cooks were drunks and gamblers who insisted on taking their pay in cash rather than in direct bank deposit, so that their wives in town couldn't get their hands on it. First Sergeant Benson did her best to intervene and was often successful in making sure the women at least had some food money for their families. But every payday we could count on a minor crisis in the mess hall when some cooks went on a bender and were reported AWOL.

If First Sergeant Benson couldn't locate them at the usual after-hours clubs or sleeping it off, she began calling the local hospitals and jails. The police were generally understanding about minor drunk and disorderly charges, since Fort McClellan was a major local industry. But the sheriff's deputies would not release my arrested soldiers to my control until I came back "with a man." So I began taking my executive officer to escort the soldiers back to the post where they faced their Article 15 (company punishment), a step below court-martial. We never resorted to physical violence.

But the male commander of another company was old school. As soon as he got his drunken soldiers out of jail, he would slam them up against the brick wall a few times. His first sergeant asked me, "Why do you mother your men, ma'am?" He believed illegal beating of soldiers was an effective control measure. I did not.

He had his methods. First Sergeant Benson and I had ours. My plan was to reestablish Army standards in my company and lean hard enough on the marginal performers through legal means to modify their behavior.

With the cooperation of the Military Police, I kept up steady pressure on the unruly men in the barracks. It was simply unacceptable that there could be a housing unit on a U.S. Army post in which the company commander and senior NCOs could not enter without fear. First Sergeant Benson and I were determined to resolve this situation. We staged the first of many unannounced inspections while still working on the supply problem.

It was late at night and what I found was shocking. Normally the second-floor troop bay would have been divided by partitions into equally sized living quarters. But the dominant, most violent men had pushed the partitions back, usurping the space of the weaker soldiers. The barracks were filthy, with cigarette butts stubbed out on the floor, dirty latrines, and curtains hanging askew from the windows. Even though I had once chafed at the rigidity of barracks inspections in my early training, I realized the importance of establishing physical order as a precursor to more subtle but profound personal and professional order.

The MPs moved ahead of me, enforcing the first sergeant's commands.

"Stand up when the commander is in your area," First Sergeant Benson ordered a soldier lounging on his bed.

From the other end of the poorly lit barracks, we heard a woman's grumbling voice as she hastily departed. Someone moaned from that direction, "Give us a break. We're off duty."

"Yeah, First Sergeant," the man on the bed echoed, "we've been working all day."

The big MP corporal glared at the soldier.

"You won't stand up?" First Sergeant Benson asked.

"On your feet," the MP echoed.

"Hey, man, I told her. I'm off duty."

I nodded to the MP. He dragged the soldier to his feet and handcuffed him. We had a paddy wagon waiting downstairs. Now the rest of the MP squad covered the doors and I searched the area. A short time later we had a pillowcase heavy with drugs and knives. First Sergeant Benson's notebook contained the names of over ten men to appear for Article 15 hearings or face court-martial charges for drugs and weapons possession.

As we walked out into the hot night, the men on the second floor went back to their cubicles, still defiant but now subdued.

The next week we were back. And the week after that, never on the same night or at the same time. Slowly, the message was getting out. This new captain seemed serious. We kept up our nighttime barracks inspections so that the men would be present and witness our resolve. The paperwork forwarded for courts-martial on repeat drug and weapons counts was solid. Convicted soldiers went to the stockade to serve three or six months.

Article 15 punishment included reduction in rank, extra duty, and restriction to post. A few men didn't seem to care. Soon after I arrived, I processed my first Article 15 against a private first class named Hall, who clearly had little use for the process. When I read the charge, using the exact Uniform Code of Military Justice (UCMJ) formula, I missed a couple of words. Private Hall corrected me from memory, having been down this path before. Later, when the first sergeant was absent and the orderly room outside my office was uncharacteristically empty, Private Hall tried to physically intimidate me, striding in to plant his fists on my desk and glower over me.

"Private," I said coldly, "you come to attention and you stand two feet back from this desk."

He did as he was ordered. I told him to return later when it was convenient for the first sergeant to see him about the new charges he faced.

Our inspections of the men's barracks continued, but were becoming less arduous, as some of the men began joking to First Sergeant Benson that they'd see her later that night. We could sense the relief among many that we were regaining control of the barracks from the hard-core troublemakers. On the whole, my company had the highest number of courts-martial and Article 15s of any unit on the post during the first year of my command. But we were making progress. The men's barracks now looked like part of the Army. Men stood at attention when I entered. They had also learned that all of them faced restrictions unless the quarters were kept clean. And the all-pervasive scent of marijuana did not hang in the air day and night. Still, drugs were readily available, if less evident. However, discipline in one area carried over to productivity and discipline in other areas. AWOLs decreased. Drunkenness was reduced. More soldiers completed their GED high school equivalency training. And there were reduced levels of domestic violence among the married soldiers, and of violence in the barracks.

About a year into my assignment, two events occurred that gave commanders more options. The Army introduced the Expeditious Discharge Program under which perennial problem soldiers could be more easily separated from the service. If a soldier had a marginal discipline record, but did not deserve a Less Than Honorable Discharge, we could use the program to discharge him. I assembled the company at a hasty commander's call to explain the new process to them.

"If you don't want to stay in the Army," I said, looking at some of the really marginal soldiers, "I'll put you in for an Expeditious Discharge. You don't like it here, and we certainly don't like having you."

But, to my amazement, when faced with the prospect of civilian life, many of these would-be renegades pulled up their socks and began acting like real soldiers.

Others didn't. One I'll never forget was a private named Ramirez, a member of a gang who were more like street thugs than soldiers. After I had preferred court-martial charges against him, he'd gone AWOL. Then the Criminal Investigation Division (CID) called to inform me that Ramirez and his group had a hit list of company commanders and my name was on it. "We're pretty sure he's trying to kill you and the first sergeant," the investigator told me.

The CID taught me how to search my car for a bomb. I accepted the threat as one of the risks that came with the command.

Early one morning that week, my clerk, Specialist Gomez, called my off-post apartment and announced, "Ma'am, the office is on fire." Someone (later it was determined to be Private Ramirez) had thrown a firebomb through the window, setting the interior ablaze.

"Have you called the fire department or the first sergeant?"

"No, ma'am."

"Well, get off the phone and call the fire department. I'll call the first sergeant."

The orderly room was a mess. Although it was connected to a barracks, at least no one was injured.

The incident did not slow us down in our effort to restore discipline. We kept up the pressure on the less disciplined soldiers, now using the leverage of the Expeditious Discharge.

One day I got word that Major General Joseph R. Kingston, the commander of Fort McClellan, wanted to see me and the acting battalion commander in one hour at my office. The first sergeant was at post headquarters, so I flew into action. "Gomez," I instructed, "mow the lawn." One of the clerks, Specialist Allen, had just turned on a huge pedestal fan, scattering papers around the office. "Get all those papers in one place and hide them," I told him. "The general is coming." I wondered why he was coming to see my company.

When General Kingston, a decorated Infantry officer, arrived, he got right to the point.

"Captain, your company has the highest number of courts-martial, Article 15s, drug referrals, and Inspector General complaints of any outfit on this post," he said sternly.

"Yes, sir." I swallowed. The office was hot and I was flushed. I knew he was going to fire me. I'd just had too many courts-martial. It looked like I was running a prison colony over here, not a company. *Here it comes,* I thought, *the request for my resignation.*

"I want you to keep it up," General Kingston said. "If you've got good cases on these people, see them through. I'll support you with anything you need. My entire staff, IG, JAG, and Personnel will handle all the administrative work expeditiously."

I could hardly believe his words. "Sometimes it takes so long to push through a discharge, sir. There've been so many cases, so many rehabilitation attempts. I've had to give so much justification on each of these cases."

"The Army is getting serious about the quality of its soldiers, Captain," General Kingston said. "Let's just do our duty and get these bad apples out of the service."

Like all good leaders, General Kingston kept his word. He made sure the Judge Advocate General (JAG) processed all of my requests for court-martial quickly and fairly. Once more word spread through the ranks: Screw up bad enough and you'll be punished. During the second year of my command, the number of courts-martial and Article 15s each dropped by one half.

* * *

In the fall of 1974, the civilian social revolution of the women's movement resonated throughout the military. Rather than simply assigning WACs on permanent detail to other branches, the Secretary of the Army and the Chief of Staff took the monumental step of opening up Military Occupational Specialties to women in every branch except the combat arms. It had only been five years since the Basic Course, in which I felt we were being trained for separate support roles rather than being fully integrated in the Army. Now we had a wide variety of branches and specialties to choose from.

Like all of my WAC colleagues that fall, I completed a form, listing in order the three branches I preferred. My first choice was Military Intelligence (MI), followed by Military Police and Transportation Corps.

In April 1975, just before the fall of Saigon, I got my orders to report that summer to the MI Officer Advance Course at Fort Huachuca, Arizona. I was leaving the Women's Army Corps. The Army I was entering was hardly the same institution I had known when my father had sworn me in on that June day in 1969. Now all women officers were authorized to command men as I had. We could serve in every branch except the Infantry, Armor, and Artillery and in every MOS except those involving direct ground combat. Combined housing units for men and women, with privacy strictly maintained—an innovation I had introduced out of necessity when my company was forced to move into tight quarters at Fort McClellan—had now become standard Army-wide. Women no longer faced mandatory discharge with pregnancy and parenthood. And within a year, the U.S. Military Academy at West Point would accept its first women cadets.

As I prepared for my new assignment, I felt a sense of satisfaction that six years of persistence had borne fruit. And I was optimistic about my future as a soldier.

3

Devotion to Duty

*T*he optimism I felt about my future Army career was tempered by the tension underlying my personal life. In November 1974, I had married a man I'd met at Fort Devens. He had just returned from Vietnam, where he'd served a year in combat as a platoon officer and company commander conducting long-range reconnaissance patrols with the 1st Infantry Division. He was an Airborne Ranger Special Forces–qualified captain who had earned two Silver Stars for valor. While I worked as a WAC recruiter in New England and commanded a company at Fort McClellan, he was discharged, finished his university degree, and was ready to pursue a civilian career when he joined me in Alabama.

But now we found ourselves in an awkward situation. He was a highly decorated Vietnam veteran, prepared to get on with life outside the military as the traditional breadwinner. Yet I was a partner in the marriage and already had a profession. I was an Army officer, a career that soon required me to uproot to an empty corner of southeast Arizona to attend the seven-month Military Intelligence Officer Advance Course (MIOAC) before moving on to my next assignment, whatever that would be. It was impossible for us to reconcile our joint personal and professional needs.

This put an unusual strain on our relationship. Before the mid-1970s, there were relatively few married women career Army officers. In the past, the Army wife had been the partner in the marriage who surrendered her professional aspirations to accompany her husband on the frequent moves that were a normal part of Army life. But when I completed my training at Fort Huachuca, I would have to ask a man who came from a traditional background to accept the socially uncomfortable and professionally uncertain role of an Army spouse for at least the next thirteen years, assuming I would complete a twenty-year career.

After the Military Intelligence Officer Advance Course, I would have spent seven years in the Army. I would then need an overseas assignment, a tour of duty where I could gain the operational experience vital to a successful officer's first ten years. And my choices of overseas assignments were limited. Tours in Europe—where my husband could join me at Army expense—were three years. But he had no job prospects in Germany. Alternatively, I could request a one-year, unaccompanied assignment in Korea, which would entail a twelve-month separation. And I'd be practically guaranteed a three-year tour back in the States afterward. Then my husband and I could live together and build a more conventional home life. If I chose this course, my husband could begin work with at least a guess that I would be reassigned to the East Coast of the United States after my tour in Korea.

I'd been told the workload in Korea would be heavy, but that I would be sure to learn a lot, so I knew the assignment would help me fill in much of the professional MI background that I'd missed as a WAC officer. When I did manage to think optimistically, that seemed the best plan: trading the emotional pain of a year apart early in our marriage for greater stability later on. But that optimism still masked the prevailing conflict inherent in reconciling a woman's marriage and her career, an issue that has still not been successfully resolved for military and civilian women professionals who are required to move frequently in order to advance in the decades since the 1970s.

And there is a lesson that this issue has taught: The higher a woman aspires in the leadership pyramid, be it military or civilian, the greater the sacrifices she must make in her personal life. This dilemma no doubt stems from the traditional paradigm of a single working spouse in a family. If a woman sought to advance higher in her field, she was often on her own. Fortunately, as we enter the Information Age in which work is being radically redefined, and workplace policies are becoming more family-friendly, the formerly rigid choice between family and professional achievement is resolving.

In the Army today, this situation is still quite dynamic. But change is moving in a positive direction. For example, in 1969 when I entered the Army, less than 1 percent of all lieutenants who were commissioned were women. Today, 19 percent are women. When I was commissioned, less than one third of all enlisted soldiers were married; today, more than two thirds are married. Almost 15 percent of the Army's officer corps are women. For the past twenty years, the Army has been energetically responding to this cultural change by introducing such programs as Army Family Team Building and Army Family Action Plan (a comprehensive plan to improve life for soldiers and family members of all ages). The Army Joint Domicile Program is a fledgling effort to keep married Army couples assigned within fifty miles of each other.

But when I was a young captain, none of these programs existed, nor was there support for such an effort. As with other officers, the Army required that I move frequently. Even though I was assigned a stable three-year tour of duty after my year in Korea, like all married military couples we could only look forward to a continual pattern of disruption and displacement that would preclude my husband from finding any meaningful professional work. In other words, from the beginning of our marriage, our situation would require him to play down his ambition and take lesser jobs, just as similar conditions had imposed themselves on countless Army wives over the years. For that reason, those wives who did choose to work concentrated on the most portable professions and skills—nursing, teaching, and secretarial work. But even if an Army wife were teaching, and she had her own children in school, her husband might be abruptly reassigned, and she and the family would be expected to follow him dutifully to the new post. Leaving Fort McClellan for Arizona in August 1975, I was aware that I was embarking on a difficult journey that would challenge the romance of a young marriage with the unyielding realities of our situation.

*   *   *

As I noted, however, more than twenty-five years later, the prospects for military women having both a successful career and a civilian (or a military) husband seem better. This is due in part to the sheer increase in the numbers of married military women and is also partially due to the evolution in our attitudes about "men's" work. With the Information Age, a small but increasing number of men have chosen to remain at home where they can combine telecommuting over the Internet—anything from day trading to managerial consulting to scientific research—with child care. This frees their wives to assume full- or part-time positions in the traditional corporate workplace. Because there is slightly less pressure on men to take the dominant career path than there was in the 1970s, there is more flexibility in the possible combinations of work patterns married couples can devise, so that both partners can pursue satisfying careers. Just as the spread of e-commerce has allowed a growing number of men to leave traditional corporate life for self-employed consulting, where they can work at home and become better domestic partners with their wives, many women professionals have chosen flextime work arrangements that allow them more hours each hectic week with their husbands and families.

Unfortunately, the plugged-in professionals who can profit

from the Information Age still represent just a small minority of the executive workforce from which America's civilian leadership is selected. Today, any woman or man who chooses to remain physically remote from the power center in order to devote more time to their marriage and family is virtually excluded from the company's rapid promotion consideration. Loyalty to the organization—as opposed to one's family—is still seen as an indispensable virtue; a senior leader, whether woman or man, is expected to be available to devote her- or himself unequivocally to the company when called upon, just as military officers were and are required to go where they are ordered.

As Suzanne Braun Levine has insightfully written in her recent book *Father Courage: What Happens When Men Put Family First,* the "second half" of the feminist revolution never happened; women went into the workplace, but men did not become equal partners at home. In an interview with columnist Judy Mann, Levine cited data on the "insidious forces" that are aligned against men who try to break the traditional mold—simply by leaving work on time, by requesting their legal paternity leave, even by playing with their kids in the park on a weekday morning when people think they should be at work. The message is clear: Real men don't act like women. And that message doesn't come just from the boardroom. Levine found widespread impatience with surrendering control to their husbands among working women who had perfected the difficult task of managing both a job and a household. She found that these women had struggled so hard without the man's help that they were sometimes loath to tolerate his inefficient attempts at doing laundry, shopping, or cooking when he finally did decide to leave work at a decent hour and become less of a stranger to his wife and kids.

Perhaps some of the resistance that Levine has documented in her admirably frank book stems from the fact the women recognize that men are still elevated to positions of leadership far more often than women simply due to their gender. And the fact remains: It is still difficult if not impossible for a married woman to rise to the very top of her profession while devoting the time and emotional energy required to nurture a fulfilling marriage with children. But this is not the time for pessimism; it is the time for creative solutions to how we structure our lives at work and at home. I firmly believe that finding these solutions is not just the responsibility of individual men and women, but rather should be shared by their employers' policymakers. The 1993 Family Medical Leave Act set the national stage for a sweeping cultural movement that continues to improve the lives of American children and families. Subsequent government and private sector programs, the Adoption and Safe Families Act of 1997 and First Star, a civil rights foundation for children created by film producer Peter Samuelson, are two such efforts.

If women are ever going to assume positions of leadership in more than just token numbers, the private sector will simply have to make work more accommodating to families. Flextime is certainly a good beginning, so are shared partnerships in which two professionals can spend part of each week at home and part at their firm. In that way, they retain their professional identity while their children are young and are ready to move on to higher leadership challenges when the children have flown the nest. Quality child care in the right location—near or at work, or near home—is of vital importance as well.

But such successful experiments are not yet widespread. I hope that the younger generation reaching high executive levels in the private sector and senior command in the military will remember the conflict inherent to the role of being a successful professional woman who is also a wife and a mother when these executives themselves make important decisions. Men who have already accepted household responsibilities will have no trouble remembering.

Yet many men military officers and civilian professionals *appear* to integrate successful careers and marriage with ease. In virtually every one of these success stories, it has been the wife who has dutifully performed her traditional supporting role, subordinating whatever ambitions she might have had for the good of the marriage and the family. But times are changing.

Army personnel managers, for example, now recognize the need for greater stability in the lives of couples in which one spouse is in the military and one is a civilian. The Cold War is over; the Army itself is much smaller, and the number of possible permanent assignment locations has been greatly reduced so that it is somewhat more likely that a dual-career couple can establish a quasi-permanent home base for the family. Army couples are buying permanent homes in communities near posts where their branches have large contingents and they can anticipate frequent assignments. If the husband is the soldier, he can expect to rotate back to that post throughout his career, so that his civilian wife can pursue her profession in the area. Deployments create a new source of instability.

For women soldiers, either NCOs or officers, married to civilians, the balancing act between the Army's need for mobility and their husband's professional requirement for stability still presents a dilemma. If she wants to be on the promotion fast track, she must take reassignments as frequently as they come, no matter how inconvenient. The alternative is to remain on what we call the "due course" promotion track. These people are certainly not plodders, but it's well established that they will never rise to the very top. One way to stay in the middle of the pack is to be unwilling to move whenever and wherever the Army dictates—often because of the inconvenience this imposes on family life. The trade-off for less family disruption has been and remains less career success.

An old Army joke is a case in point. An officer complains that a reassignment poses a dramatic upheaval in the life of his high school senior son. His assignments officer replies without sympathy, "If the Army had meant for you to have a high school senior, we'd have issued you one." As humor often does, this joke reflects an underlying reality. There was a cultural maxim in the Army until the time of the post–Cold War force reductions and the emphasis on retention of highly qualified officers and NCOs: Go where your duty sends you no matter the personal cost. Now the Army and other services are making a real effort to accommodate their career management to a more stable family life.

Another significant factor is the growing number of men officers who have civilian wives whose careers demand greater stability. The Army wants to retain its best officers, especially combat leaders and those trained in technical fields who could earn double or triple their military pay in today's booming civilian economy. So the service is proving to be more flexible in trying to help married officers weave together the competing aspects of their personal and professional lives.

* * *

There remains the controversial issue of Army captains leaving in ostensibly high numbers. The year 2000 retention rate for captains was allegedly at a record low since the dramatic Army downsizing of the 1990s. Captains were said to be leaving the Army because they had been deployed overseas too frequently on peacekeeping and humanitarian relief operations and their family life consequently suffered. Since the end of the Cold War, there have been over forty Army deployments for the full spectrum of military operations, including combat, peacekeeping, and humanitarian efforts. Soldiers have been involved in almost every one, from Mogadishu, to Bosnia, to Haiti, to Kosovo. Often these soldiers were sent from their home posts in the States as individual "augmentees" to serve for six months or more with a unit deployed at an overseas trouble spot. Some of these soldiers completed their overseas assignments away from their families and returned to the United States only to find their home units deployed on another peacekeeping or humanitarian operation.

Without doubt, this pattern of repeated unaccompanied overseas assignments negatively affected family life. And many soldiers found their careers disrupted when they could not train in their specialties or attend courses needed for professional advancement.

The Army worked hard to rectify the problem, principally by

drawing on the reserve component (Army Reserve and the Army National Guard). As these Reserve and Guard units assume increasing responsibility, the burden on the Active Army and its individual soldiers has been somewhat relieved.

I personally do not believe that the repeated deployments of the 1990s were the principal cause for junior officer attrition. Young captains who were already ambivalent about an Army career would have found the deployments a convenient pretext for resigning. On the other hand, some of these very captains might have discovered much deeper meaning in their profession during their operational duty overseas, and in the process strengthened their commitment to an Army career. It is more than likely, I believe, that many of the captains the Army lost in the 1990s would have resigned a few years later as majors. Conversely, the more deeply committed captains who have honed their leadership skills in the often frustrating operational conditions of Haiti, Bosnia, and Kosovo will make committed and experienced majors and lieutenant colonels.

Interestingly enough, the "record" attrition of Army captains in the year 2000 may have been a politically motivated fantasy. The facts reveal a different story, which has not been publicized. In 2000, 12.5 percent of Army captains did resign, undoubtedly a high figure. But that figure is misleading because, for the past eighteen months, the total pool of Army captains has expanded and now includes first lieutenants who were promoted six months earlier than in the past. In reality, the attrition rate for both lieutenants and captains taken together has remained stable. But few Americans will learn the complete and accurate story.

* * *

One of the first challenges I faced was entering Military Intelligence as a former WAC captain with seven years' service who knew virtually nothing about my new branch. Some of my male peers at the MIOAC at Fort Huachuca had completed the MI

Basic Course as lieutenants and had served in the branch since then. There were about sixty of us in Class 76-AA-1, all captains. Six of us were women, three of whom were married. With the exception of Carol Martini and Katie Van Tilburg, who'd had some MI background, the other women in the course knew as little about Military Intelligence as I did. The Army expected us to catch up quickly in our professional knowledge. Traditionally, any junior officer changing branches between the Basic and Advance Course did the required remedial work individually. And the Army didn't provide supplemental training for women entering MI or any other branch from the WAC in 1975.

Fort Huachuca itself was hardly an accommodating location in those days. Once we turned south off Interstate 10 just east of Tucson and the narrow highway wound into the dry mountains, the landscape took on an almost lunar aspect. The Advance Course orientation had warned about the hazards of car breakdowns in the baking desert heat and the danger when wandering off the road that rattlesnakes and getting lost posed. I wasn't concerned about snakes, but it was clear that the post was about as isolated as any could be and still remain within the continental United States. In fact, the post and the nearby little garrison town of Sierra Vista were only a few miles from the Mexican border and an equally desolate range of high desert mountains.

It was an old post, having been established as a provisional cavalry camp in 1877 to cut off the escape route into Mexico of the Apache leader Geronimo. The black troops of the 10th Cavalry, the "Buffalo Soldiers," were stationed there before World War I. And it was a training post for Infantry units during World War II and the Korean War. The U.S. Army Strategic Communications Command made Fort Huachuca its headquarters in 1967. Four years later, the Army established the Intelligence Center and School on the post.

When I drove into town that first day, I found the main street, Fry Boulevard, paved only the seven blocks from the post entrance to Seventh Avenue. After that, the roads were hard, rutted dirt and some gravel. Conditions on post were slightly better. As a married Advance Course student, I was assigned what was officially known as "substandard" housing, a unit that badly needed renovation, but which would not receive it until more money was one day made available for repairs to family housing.

This has long been a troublesome issue for the Army: There is always a greater need for housing repair than there is money available. Today, we keep track of this funding shortfall in a category called Real Property Maintenance (RPM) Backlog, a figure that totals $17.8 billion to bring all our facilities up to "green" status. This is an elusive figure, however. The dollar amount of the shortfall exists; the dollars themselves do not. Although the Army has the accounting category, it is empty. In other words, the reason the Army still continues to have substandard housing is because it is forced to spend its very limited budget on other priorities, such as soldiers and weapons.

One of the more notable features of our little 1950s-era bungalow was that we could see daylight around all four sides of the splayed entrance door. When we had guests, one of my first tasks was to sweep the sand out of the little hallway and living room before they arrived. There was a chugging swamp cooler evaporation air conditioner on the roof.

My initial apprehension that the men in the class might be unreceptive to the women proved completely unfounded. They couldn't have been more welcoming. Unlike many officers who had served only with men, most of my classmates happened to have spent their early careers in the Defense Investigative Service, an assignment in Counterintelligence. They were used to working alongside women. And since we were all low-paid captains stuck out there on the far side of the moon, our social life occurred at one another's quarters. Pot luck dinners and barbecues that our two social chairmen, Steve Conrad and Jerry De-Money, organized became the focus of our weekends. Steve and Jerry were very creative in presenting "awards" such as the Rip Van Winkle award (Third Oak Leaf Cluster) for Ben Elley, who had fallen asleep yet again during a particularly scintillating lecture on land navigation. He certainly wasn't the only one to fall asleep. Bob Murfin and Lynn Silvious suffered their share of SIFLs (Self-Inflicted Frontal Lobotomy). No school I have attended since then has been so much fun, either during duty hours or off-duty social life. This was probably because in the Advance Course we were all in our twenties and livelier, most were raising young families, and all of us had no money, so we had to provide our own entertainment.

Duty time was devoted to the classroom. I intended to do my best, both to learn my new career of Intelligence and because I wanted to be a credit to women in the Army. But the first few weeks were hectic and confusing, trying to familiarize myself with the broad dimensions and multiple subdisciplines of my new branch and its elusive jargon, all the while keeping up with classwork.

* * *

Because I retired from the Army as the Deputy Chief of Staff for Intelligence (DCSINT), a position that involves access to some of the nation's most highly classified information, I am legally prohibited from discussing many details of my work. As with other organizations in the U.S. Intelligence community, current and former members of Army intelligence do not reveal the sources, methods, procedures, or targets of their operations. So any description of my work as an Army intelligence officer is based on unclassified sources. The basics I learned about Military Intelligence at Fort Huachuca have certainly evolved in the last twenty-five years, but have retained many of their past features.

The elements of Military Intelligence I studied in the Advance Course initially seemed rather complex, but I soon learned them thoroughly. Military Intelligence is a highly structured discipline, not to be confused with the romanticized cloak-and-dagger view of civilian espionage made popular in spy novels. As I told Sandra McElwaine when she interviewed me for *USA Today Magazine*, "I am no Mata Hari."

The major formal disciplines of the branch are Signals Intelligence (SIGINT), Human Intelligence (HUMINT), Counterintelligence (CI), Imagery Intelligence (IMINT), and Measurement and Signature Intelligence (MASINT). The combat arms also rely on Long-range Surveillance and Scouts and Calvary units for battlefield reconnaissance. Electronic Warfare (EW) and Information Operations (IO) are not Intelligence disciplines, but are often supported by MI operations.

My specialty was cryptology or Signals Intelligence. SIGINT is information we derive from monitoring and locating enemy communications and noncommunications electronic systems. Radios and radars are the most common examples. We call intelligence derived from monitoring enemy communications—such as voice transmissions, Morse code, teletypewriter, or digital data—"communications intelligence." The information we obtain from monitoring enemy noncommunications emitters, including radars, transponders, and radio beacons, is called "electronic intelligence." Since the modern battlefield is a virtual electromagnetic blizzard, with units from the squad level up emitting all manner of signals across the spectrum, SIGINT becomes an extremely important asset for the war-fighting commander in identifying the enemy forces arrayed against him.

The subspecialty of signal security is an invaluable tool in protecting friendly forces from equally effective electronic surveillance by the enemy. (In the Army of the future, which is currently under development, every soldier on the battlefield will be equipped to send and receive information about themselves and the enemy across this electronic spectrum.) The demanding, often arcane, but vital military specialty of SIGINT would occupy much of my professional life.

Human Intelligence is probably most familiar to people outside the military. HUMINT involves the interrogation of enemy prisoners of war, civilian detainees, and refugees, as well as translating captured documents, to learn the composition of enemy forces, their intentions and morale. The discipline requires some to be skillful linguists with an excellent sense of the adversary's culture.

Counterintelligence protects American forces by evaluating the enemy's total intelligence-gathering capabilities. CI detects, evaluates, and prevents enemy intelligence collection and sabotage. When needed, CI specialists can mount effective deception programs to mask our military operations.

As the name implies, Imagery Intelligence acquires and exploits visual representations of the battlefield that reveal the deployment of forces, aids weapons targeting, and produces more effective battle damage assessment so that targets that are already destroyed are not shelled or bombed unnecessarily. Modern IMINT systems cut across the spectrum and include infrared and radar imagery.

The newest MI discipline, Measurement and Signature Intelligence, is a response to the effectiveness of technical countermeasures to traditional intelligence-gathering techniques that have evolved over the years. MASINT involves the use of sensors to sample air, soil, and water for telltale evidence of biological, chemical, or nuclear weapons.

The raw information that is gathered using these collection disciplines is converted into intelligence. The process by which information becomes intelligence is called the intelligence cycle, which has multiple steps: collection, processing, analysis, distribution, presentation (reporting), evaluation, and collection management. In general, the higher up the chain of command, the more intelligence the war-fighting commander requires for decision-making. For example, a company commander might only need to know that enemy tanks approaching his unit would most likely be bogged down in a marsh before reaching his defensive perimeter. This information could be obtained from a traditional reconnaissance patrol. But it is essential that the division commander, four echelons (levels of authority) higher, understand that this armor probe is only a diversion and that the real attack will come in another sector. That type of intelligence can be derived most readily from "all source" collection that includes all the major disciplines.

The echelons that intelligence supports are called "tactical" for division and below, "operational" for regional commands, such as the Central Command that fought Operation Desert Storm, and "strategic," which is at the national level and supports the Secretary of Defense, the Secretary of State, and the President.

The targets of intelligence are military, economic, and political. The armed services, individually and collectively through the Defense Intelligence Agency, are responsible for military targets. Economic and political targets are the responsibility of the Central Intelligence Agency. The National Security Agency supports all of these efforts.

*   *   *

When people hear that I am an intelligence officer I am sometimes asked for "inside" information about UFOs. Recently, one newly introduced acquaintance at a college football game was just certain that I had the real scoop on the phenomenon. None of my denials that UFOs existed or protests that Army intelligence had *any* information (much less secret information) could dispel her impression that I was just following orders to keep the lid on the true UFO story, and thus furthering the suspicion of a juicy conspiracy. But, for the record, I know nothing of UFOs and suggest that anyone with questions about spaceships and aliens should call the U.S. Air Force and not the Army.

Another common misperception about my work in Intelligence was that I "had files" on people and knew "the gossip" about their personal lives—possibly through the use of listening devices planted in their homes. Army intelligence is absolutely prohibited by law from ever targeting U.S. entities (persons, businesses, or groups). And such information would not serve to meet any Army intelligence requirement. During the tense years of the Vietnam War, however, the Johnson administration pressured Army intelligence to conduct questionable surveillance of antiwar protesters, an unwarranted diversion of Army resources and a threat to civil rights. Our resources are scarce and thinly spread over many competing needs. So we are careful to use these limited resources efficiently and we never act outside the law. It is fundamental to Army culture that we support and defend the U.S. Constitution, and further, as powerful a tool as intelligence is, it is even more important to act within all legal and ethical restraints.

* * *

As I entered the new world of Military Intelligence, I certainly felt more like a part of the Army and felt that many more career options were open to women. And the fact that my classmates accepted my women colleagues and me as equal was especially heartening. All the women were serious about the course, I guess because we needed to catch up on the profession of intelligence. Many of the men in the class needed to study as hard as the women, because they had been exclusively in counterintelligence and had not served in tactical assignments. We were all motivated to learn the course content. But a few were a bit too intense: One captain became famous in our class for writing down every fact our instructors presented on Rolodex cards and spending hours each night alone in the room off his carport, flipping the cards as he memorized the facts for the next test. That was hardly necessary. In tried-and-true Army fashion, the instructors stamped or slammed their desk with their fist for emphasis to drive home each point they were going to include on that week's test.

It didn't matter that the instructors made no effort to bring the former WACs up to speed. You would have had to be asleep to fail the course. And none of us were dull. I did learn a lot about MI by listening to the nonstructured give-and-take of informal classroom discussions that many instructors encouraged. Since our colleagues had served in so many different units as young officers, they brought a wealth of experience to the practical problems presented in tactical exercises. And they weren't afraid to state their opinion. "In the 25th Division we did it this way . . ." "When I was stationed in Germany, we always did it like this . . ." Over the weeks, my notebook pages filled with concrete solutions to problems that I would never find in field manuals. I later realized MI was trying to evolve a new doctrine, a method of operations and procedures that best fulfilled its role within the Army, and to do so, the Intelligence School was willing to listen to its most innovative young officers. In effect, the Army school system provides a place where ideas that are developed in the field can be refined and standardized throughout the Army. This was especially important since Military Intelligence had only existed as a formal branch of the regular Army since 1962 and was still establishing its credibility.

But there were other irritants that constantly reminded me we were still women serving in a man's Army. One woman in the class, who was single and very attractive, quickly drew the attention of the bachelors in the course. But she wisely decided to forgo dating among her classmates at this isolated outpost, so a couple of the jilted suitors started spreading rumors about her. She ignored them, but this situation was unfair to her and unworthy of those involved.

Then there were the slides. Before almost every lecture or classroom presentation, our instructors felt it necessary to flash an "attention-getting slide," actually a viewgraph image from an overhead projector. They were always sexually explicit, the mildest being centerfold nudes from *Playboy*. But as often as not the slides were truly crude, pornographic spreads from *Hustler* or cartoons involving women and barnyard animals. I guess the purpose of this allegedly innocent mirth was to snap the male officer out of his habitual stupor to a heightened degree of mental receptivity, so that he could be ready for fifty enlightening minutes on the Table of Organization and Equipment of a Military Intelligence Battalion. Well, I thought, it doesn't say much for the quality of this course if it takes these kinds of pictures to get the guys' attention.

I originally thought the obscene slides were some type of one-time initiation prank aimed at women. But when the slides continued, it occurred to me that the instructors did not even realize that a pornographic cartoon bothered us. Nor did they understand that many men in the course were offended by this as well. My male classmates told me that they'd seen such slides in other Army courses, and my husband confirmed that their use had become widespread in military lecture halls. I believe some of our religious classmates did ask the instructors to tone down the slides, but nothing ever came of their complaints.

And when I repeatedly wrote about my objections to the bizarre and offensive practice in my class critiques, I never got a reply. That was interesting because my instructors always took the time to answer my other written critiques. I guess I touched a sensitive spot by describing the obscene slides as "not relevant to the class, having a deadening rather than an 'attention-getting' effect, and in very poor taste."

Eventually I brought up the matter with a field-grade officer in the School Brigade.

"Sir," I said, "I've repeatedly raised the issue of the slides with my instructors. But none of them will reply. I don't think this material has any place in an Army classroom."

He smiled condescendingly. "Captain, you just don't have a sense of humor."

The slides continued throughout the course.

In the years since then, I've often thought about that situation. Such raw sexual exploitation of women was widespread in the American military in the mid-1970s. Today, it has virtually vanished from our military installations. But twenty-five years ago, nudity and pornography were confined to the fringes of popular culture. Today, however, popular fiction and broadcast and cable television have become increasingly sleazy. I think it is interesting to reflect that we now rarely find this vulgarity in the workplace, while popular entertainment overflows with crude images and language. We have choices in entertainment, but working is seldom optional.

Although the other women officers in my course certainly did not like the slides either, we all had bigger issues to consider: our professional development and our contributions to the Army. Our instructors continually told the class, "Tactical is the only way for a young, hard-charging MI officer to go." By that, they meant a male captain should seek out an assignment as an S-2, the intelligence officer in an Infantry, Armor, or Artillery battalion, then become the G-2, the senior intelligence officer of a division as a lieutenant colonel one day. It was from this tactical side of MI, the instructors all said, that the branch's future leaders would be chosen. That was great for the men. But in the mid-1970s, all those assignments were closed to women.

Today, by the way, the situation has changed: There are women intelligence officers serving as S-2s of battalions and brigades as captains and majors, and G-2s of divisions as lieutenant colonels. Women colonels have commanded tactical MI brigades supporting a corps commander. Wherever women are assigned, they perform their duties admirably.

One day that winter after lunch, I sat alone in my car before class watching the sun and shadow high on the surrounding high desert mountains. Even though the future of women in Military Intelligence seemed truncated at this point, I knew our situation would become clearer later, that things would improve, that the Army was in transition. As an institution, the Army was then like the rest of the country. American women had made a strong entry into the workplace as the 1960s ended, and were now going to seek full membership in the ranks of middle management and, to a lesser extent, in senior leadership in a variety of industries. I did not see this revolution as destructive, certainly not of the Army, which I had come to love, despite its shortcomings. Rather, I saw increasingly greater inclusion of women in the Army as a natural evolution of American democracy, an extension of the impulse I had felt on my college campus in 1968. Thousands of women who had demanded their full share as citizens had shouldered their responsibility and were now serving throughout the military, no longer in separate women's units and branches like the WAC. Traditionalists might not like the fact that we were there, but they couldn't deny the enormous contributions of women and the fact that in a time of recruiting shortfalls, the Army depended on the increasing inclusion of women.

Toward the end of the Advance Course, all students had interviews with a branch career counselor to discuss future assignments, standard practice throughout the Army. And I hoped to have this conversation in the context of how to navigate through the next three assignments. My counselor was definitely of the old school and believed that women should not be in the Army.

I laid my cards on the table. "Sir, I want to think about the next several assignments in MI. I'm having a hard time understanding what the general outline should look like with the prohibition of women in so many assignments."

As I spoke, he nodded complacently. "Your career path is very circumscribed, Captain," he said. "You women will never get anywhere in the Army until the male chauvinist pigs like me are out."

What kind of career counseling is this? I thought. "Yes, sir," I said aloud. I decided he had so little support for women in the Army, it would be counterproductive to argue with him. (He outranked me and one does not argue with one's assignment officer.) I managed to extract a few usable details about possible assignments and we concluded that I would probably go to Korea next. I looked the officer in the eye and thanked him for his time. *You can't run me out of the Army,* I thought. *I'll be here long after you are gone.*

There were a lot of hard cases like that officer. But there were also more enlightened leaders. Lieutenant Colonel Mike Pheneger, one of our class faculty advisors, who became the G-2 of the 2nd Infantry Division in Korea while I was there, was impressed by the dedication and competence of the women officers in the course. "You listen to these women," he told our men colleagues, "because one day you'll be working for them."

I was both pleased and concerned by his comment. One thing the six women in the course did not need was any divisive prodding that would separate us from our supportive peers. But it was a tremendous vote of confidence that forced me to think about why I would want to retreat from such praise.

By spring 1976, I had committed to a one-year unaccompanied tour of duty in Korea. My husband planned to return to New England and find a job. And we planned to spend six weeks together before my departure to Korea. Neither of us was pleased with the prospect of separation. But I was not ready to leave the Army. After completing the Advance Course at Fort Huachuca, I took some brief training at Fort Devens in cryptology—popularly known as code-breaking, but which actually involves far greater technical complexity. Then I packed my bags, my husband and I said goodbye, and I caught my flight halfway around the world to South Korea.

* * *

Seoul was a gritty mixture of ramshackle squatter towns and gleaming new buildings. But the prosperous South Korean capital was precariously near the Demilitarized Zone (DMZ), across which the North Korean People's Army had arrayed one of the world's larger military forces. The noncommunist Republic of Korea (ROK) Army occupied in-depth defensive positions south of the DMZ, which split the Korean peninsula along the curved track of the 1953 armistice line. The United Nations Command (UNC), whose principal ground American combat element was the U.S. Army's 2nd Infantry Division, supported the ROK with over half a million personnel, many in Transportation, Signal, and Intelligence units like mine.

I was assigned to Camp Red Cloud north of Seoul as the operations officer to a signal security detachment that had the mission of protecting U.S. and ROK forces from hostile intelligence services. Our responsibility was to make sure American and ROK forces maintained the highest degree of communications security possible, so that their fixed positions and mobile operations could not be tracked by hostile SIGINT.

This was more than a routine assignment in the summer of 1976. For months, tensions had been mounting along the DMZ. One of the first things I learned on arriving in Korea was that the North Koreans had forward-deployed scores of new divisions, together with their armor and artillery, in the previous two years. ROK forces had also discovered an elaborate system of tunnels, many wide enough to accommodate columns of troops and artillery pieces, dug beneath the mountains of the DMZ. North Korean defectors had confirmed that these were intended as invasion tunnels.

The impression this increased tension had on a newly minted Military Intelligence captain like me was profound and immediate. My unit was on a permanent state of alert. I wasn't even over jet lag when I found myself working sixteen- and eighteen-hour days, often jolting along rough gravel roads in a Jeep, shuttling through the dark hills from one camp to another. Everywhere I went with the officer I was replacing, we noted the serious demeanor of the American and South Korean troops. They knew the situation was precarious. When the soldiers in our section found signal security problems, which they often did, that simply meant we had to spend additional hours discussing the findings and recommending solutions with the leaders of the military organizations involved. When I looked up the steep green hills toward the rugged mountains of the DMZ, I could picture the tens of thousands of North Koreans dug into their reinforced concrete bunkers just a few miles to the north. We were doing soldiers' jobs in support of our fellow soldiers, American and South Korean.

But that didn't make the days any shorter. One night I got back to camp long after the mess hall had closed and went to the officers club to grab a bowl of chili before hitting my bunk. The room was dim, almost empty, but booming with rock music, as always, from a monster tape machine. As I sat over my chili bowl, mechanically spooning in the clotted mixture of beans and hamburger, I felt the long table shaking. *Why do I have to hold on to this bowl?* I thought wearily. Then a bare leg jerked past on the table. I looked up. A bored, naked Korean go-go girl with a flat expression and dead eyes was listlessly bouncing along the top of the tables. The few people remaining in the room hardly glanced at her. This scene was depressing testimony to the poverty of the Korean people who had to take such degrading work and to the Americans who found no more imaginative use of their very limited off-duty time.

* * *

Some of the most aggravating North Korean provocations in the previous year had occurred in the Joint Security Area (JSA) that straddled the Military Demarcation Line that snaked through the middle of the four-kilometer-wide DMZ at its western end near the village of Panmunjom. This neutral zone consisted of conference rooms where the Military Armistice Commission met, a camp for neutral Swiss and Swedish military observers, as well as UNC and North Korean Army guard posts and observation towers, set up on their respective sides of the DMZ.

North Korean guards would often hurl insults at their South Korean and American counterparts, who, like the North Koreans, had full access rights to the JSA under the terms of the 1953 armistice. But by the summer of 1976, the North Koreans seemed intent on pushing verbal harassment toward physical confrontations. The American security guards resisted responding to these provocations, but did not relinquish access rights of the UNC to the Joint Security Area.

One of the problems with maintaining good security in the southern portion of the JSA was a lack of visibility caused by foliage growing between UNC observation posts and checkpoints. When American and South Korean security guards accompanied by South Korean workers arrived to cut down a tall poplar in early August, the North Koreans reacted aggressively, demanding that the UNC leave the tree standing. The United Nations unit complied in order to prevent another confrontation.

But this North Korean order was unacceptable. Unless the UNC observation posts and checkpoints could see each other, they were vulnerable to the increasingly hostile North Koreans. The local American Army commander, Lieutenant Colonel Victor S. Vierra, determined that he could achieve visibility between the posts by trimming branches from the poplar rather than felling the tree itself. His plan was approved by the UNC, and on August 18, a security force of ten U.S. soldiers accompanying five Korean workers left on two trucks to carry out the tree trimming. The unit's commander was Captain Arthur G. Bonifas, with First Lieutenant Mark T. Barrett as deputy. There were five American enlisted men and a ROK Army interpreter.

By about 10:30 that morning, the South Korean workers began cutting branches. Soon, North Koreans, led by a notoriously aggressive officer, Senior Lieutenant Pak Chol, arrived and demanded to know what the workers were doing. When he was told they were only trimming branches, he proclaimed, "That is as it should be."

But within a few minutes, Lieutenant Pak demanded that the work stop and the UNC contingent leave immediately. Then North Korean reinforcements surrounded the smaller UNC unit. Suddenly, Lieutenant Pak yelled, *"Chookyo!"* (Kill!). He delivered a martial art kick, toppling Captain Bonifas.

Photographs taken from the nearest UNC observation post revealed what happened in the next terrible minutes. The North Korean guards surrounding Captain Bonifas wielded pipes and pick handles. Others used axes they had seized from the work party. Captain Bonifas was beaten to death on the ground. Lieutenant Barrett was seen fleeing, with club-wielding North Korean soldiers in pursuit. The melee lasted four minutes before an alert American driver managed to swing his truck out of the area past the wall where most of the unarmed Americans and South Koreans had taken refuge. Lieutenant Barrett was not among the survivors who safely reached a UNC position, battered but not seriously injured. Later in the day, the UNC recovered the bodies of both American officers. They had suffered massive and repeated head injuries. Neither officer had had time to use his personal weapon.

The implications of the murders were clear and ominous. For months, the North Koreans had been provoking incidents along the DMZ. In the Joint Security Area, their guards had repeatedly threatened Americans with death over trivial perceived slights or loss of face. On the morning of August 18, they followed through with those threats. North Korean defectors had spoken of their dictator, Kim Il Sung's, plans to invade the South. Was this bloody incident and the anticipated American reaction to it the final provocation that Kim needed to unleash that invasion?

The UNC commander, U.S. Army General Richard D. Stilwell, could not afford to take any chances. He requested and received permission from Washington to raise the DEFCON (Defense Condition) for the Republic of Korea from the normal level of 4 to 3 on a scale of 1 to 5, with 5 being the lowest (no perceived threat), and 1 the highest (attack imminent).

I learned of the emergency at about noon, when word was flashed that a "full-bore" operational situation was underway. All leaves were canceled. Security was visibly increased. With DEFCON 3 in effect on the second morning of the emergency, I was in steel helmet, flak jacket, and web gear on my way with another officer and a driver up to the 2nd Infantry Division's area of operations just below the DMZ. As we passed South Korean camps, I saw field artillery units hooking up their howitzers to trucks and loading ammunition. American and ROK Huey helicopters thumped by overhead. I passed armored personnel carriers (APCs) and M-60 tanks in staging areas on our way north. For a moment I recalled the terrible cacophony of the "Mad Minute" firepower demonstration years before at Fort Benning. If the situation deteriorated along the DMZ, firepower of unimaginable magnitude would be unleashed among the pine groves and fields of millet stubble I was passing. Thousands would die. I was just a minor cog in a huge machine, but my job was to provide the best signal security support possible and be prepared for additional ad hoc missions. In a crisis there is always uncertainty. It was the job of the leader, even a junior leader such as a captain, to reassure her soldiers by making sure they were well briefed on the biggest possible picture as often as feasible.

When the other officer and I met with our counterparts in the G-2 section of the 2nd Infantry Division, they were pleased with the signal security that the soldiers in my unit would be able to provide during this operation. No one wanted an inadvertent mistake over an open telephone line or radio circuit to be the source of a breach in op sec (operational security), should the standoff escalate to violence. This work was not particularly glamorous or demanding, but it was complex and important in the overall scheme of our military operations following the axe murder incident. I felt the deep satisfaction of devoting myself fully to my duty, knowing that in doing so I was making a vital contribution to the American military's effort.

And that effort—Operation Paul Bunyan—was impressive. General Stilwell and the United Nations Command staff had devised a detailed Operations Plan that balanced the full superpower might of the United States with suitable restraint. The goal of the plan was to demonstrate to the North Koreans our resolve, to intimidate them militarily, yet not to provoke any further bloodshed along the tripwire of the DMZ.

The action was to be centered on the Joint Security Area where the murders had occurred. As General Stilwell told his staff, "That damned tree must come down!" He intended to demonstrate to the North Koreans the UNC's authority in the zone in the form of lightly armed security forces, backed up by enough visible in-depth ground and aerial firepower, including infantry, helicopter gunships, tactical fighter-bombers, an aircraft carrier task force offshore, as well as nuclear-armed B-52 bombers, to give Kim Il Sung serious doubts about his aggressive actions.

H-Hour for Operation Paul Bunyan was 0700 on Saturday, August 21, 1976. While the waves of American warplanes offshore lit up the North Korean radar screens, UNC ground units swung into action. In the Joint Security Area, a United States–ROK guard unit drove directly to the poplar tree, as UH-1 Huey helicopters and AH-1 Cobra gunships of their heavily armed infantry support landed just south of the zone. Part of the unit blocked the North Koreans' approach avenue, while the other element went to work on the tree with chainsaws. Then a UNC engineer team entered the zone and ripped out barriers the North Koreans had illegally placed over the years.

The North Koreans, caught by surprise, finally responded by assembling a guard company armed with AK-47 rifles. But faced by the large and well-supported UNC contingent, the North Koreans made no effort to enter the southern section of the zone. By 0830, the U.N. soldiers had sawed the poplar trunk into sections, thrown them onto trucks, and departed the Joint Security Area. The communist troops made no attempt to interfere, possibly because they faced the awesome presence of the Cobra gunships.

(Those interested in learning more detail of the murders in the Joint Security Area and the subsequent Operation Paul Bunyan can consult the "Extract of the Annual Historical Report, UNC/USFK/EUSA, 1976" and the related report, "A Daily Sequential Listing of Events Between 18 August and 22 September, 1976 Involving Armistice Affairs Division and the U.S. Army Support Group–JSA Which Were Precipitated by the 18 August, 1976 Incident in the JSA." Copies of these documents are available through the U.S. Army Center of Military History, Washington, D.C.)

But the crisis atmosphere remained palpable over the coming months. Although I managed to get a little more sleep each night, I was still working six or seven days a week, just like the other American soldiers in Korea at that time. I began thinking about my duty as a professional soldier differently during this period. In order to do my job well, I saw that my commitment would have to be all consuming. Conventional concepts about business hours taken from the civilian world meant nothing in such an operational military situation. There was work to be done; once a soldier identifies that work, the amount of effort or time required to accomplish it is not a consideration.

By fall, the level of tension following Operation Paul Bunyan was reduced and the local DEFCON was returned to level 4. I went to my next assignment, executive officer to the commander of the U.S. Army Security Agency Field Station, Korea, in Pyong-taek, south of Seoul. Even though the worst of the crisis had abated, working for Colonel Charles S. Black, Jr., was every bit as demanding as my first six weeks in Korea.

In 1976, Military Intelligence had two operational head-quarters, the U.S. Army Security Agency, a signals intelligence and signal security organization, and the U.S. Army Intelligence Agency, which incorporated counterintelligence and HUMINT work. Because I was a woman captain, I was considered a good candidate to become Colonel Black's executive officer (XO).

Colonel Black, aka "the Prince of Darkness" to us (albeit well behind his back), was one of those officers for whom the term perfectionist was minted. When he did not receive absolute per-fection from his subordinates, it was an unhappy time for all.

For example, the unit had several remote sites along the DMZ, which by standard operational procedure were to be evac-uated in the event of North Korean invasion. Colonel Black in-sisted on visiting each site by helicopter to personally observe the soldiers rehearse their evacuation within the prescribed time limits. To prepare for these inspection trips, the operations officer had to lay out meticulously detailed maps showing the chopper's ingress and egress routes with exact timing, commu-nications, and alternate routes should weather problems divert the aircraft. The colonel would hunch over his wide desk, study-ing these maps intently. If he perceived the slightest error, he would fling the sheets onto his carpet and stamp on them with both boots, howling in rage. "Get them out of my sight!" Once he became so livid that he knocked over an intricate, multitiered metallic ornament that a Korean Army officer had presented him, scattering gleaming brass leaves from the coffee table across the entire office.

On another occasion, when the unit sports officer had the temerity to admit that he didn't know when the next softball game was scheduled, Colonel Black had him and me report to his office, delivered a blistering reprimand, and told him, "You're fired."

Black turned to me. "Captain, take care of this. I want this officer replaced immediately."

"Yes, sir," I said, and hustled the lieutenant back to my office. I told him to sit down and try to be calm, and I reluctantly returned to Colonel Black.

Did he mean for the lieutenant to be removed from his job, from Korea, or from the U.S. Army? Such was the power of Colonel Charles S. Black, Jr., that we sometimes wondered. It turned out the lieutenant in question was simply relieved from his position as sports officer.

Once, Colonel Black ordered Captain Chet Baker, our unit S-3 (staff officer in charge of plans and training, but in this case, not in charge of operations), to report immediately on a Friday afternoon, after furiously questioning his "manhood" over the telephone concerning some minor infraction. Chet reported outside the colonel's office door as ordered and proceeded to sit there all day for each of the next three days. We brought him sandwiches from the mess hall. But no one dared suggest he leave the colonel's anteroom that weekend.

Colonel Black delighted in dominating his analysts during each highly structured morning briefing. The officers and NCOs would present their detailed reports, and Colonel Black would fire off increasingly demanding questions until each analyst in turn had been reduced to answering, "I don't know, sir."

We had one senior NCO, Staff Sergeant Denny Preshoot, who prided himself on knowing more about the North Koreans than anyone else in the unit. And this staff sergeant was in fact extremely good. One day, he almost got the best of Colonel Black. Then the good colonel scowled, leaned across the conference room table, and demanded, "Now, tell me about that wart on Kim Il Sung's neck."

Being the XO to a perfectionist like Colonel Black meant my average duty day lasted from seven in the morning to after eight at night. The camp at Pyongtaek offered few diversions, so I hardly missed the loss of free time. Despite his demanding personality, the colonel knew absolutely every aspect of the Military Intelligence profession, and I learned a lot about leadership and management from him. From his deputy, Lieutenant Colonel Larry Runyon (later a brigadier general), and Operations NCO Sergeant First Class Odell Williams, I learned the complex substance of the SIGINT business.

It was obvious that the modern battlefield was rapidly evolving into a complex electromagnetic web in which communications such as voice and automatic data links as well as electronic warfare such as target acquisition and counterartillery radar—and the jamming and *counter*jamming of all these emissions—would play a major role in our future war-fighting tactics and strategy. The more I could learn about this challenging discipline, the more I caught up after having missed the first six years of MI service when I was a WAC. So the hours Colonel Black demanded of his staff were proving to be an apprenticeship well spent.

I began to realize he had an important professional goal. The Army was in the process of consolidating its Security Agency and Intelligence Agency into a single United States Army Intelligence and Security Command (INSCOM), which would have units stationed around the world. Colonel Black's mission was to create a plan to forge the two disparate commands into the newly established 501st Military Intelligence Group (Provisional), which would be formed in Korea in 1977. It's a compliment to his vision and thoroughness—his critics would probably say his single-mindedness—that he did earn that command. Just as Colonel Black, like a shrewd chess player, planned far ahead for organizational change, he intervened personally in the careers of selected young officers. This close attention was often as painful as it was helpful, but the colonel was determined that we would learn as much as we possibly could while under his command.

Colonel Black had fought in the Korean War as a young officer and had experienced the bitter seesaw fighting across those bloody mountains. He wanted all of us and his unit to be ready for the brutal reality of combat, should war erupt again.

For myself, the first half of my Korean tour taught me that I did indeed want to specialize in SIGINT.

* * *

Having made this important decision, I met my husband over Christmas on the West Coast. It was not a happy reunion. The time apart had made us both realize that we were unsuited for each other. It was a difficult two weeks. Despite seven years of trying to work out a life together, we decided to divorce.

* * *

Back in Korea that January, the 2nd Infantry Division had scheduled an elaborate war exercise (WAREX) in its sprawling mountainous training grounds south of the DMZ. Given the ongoing tensions, the American and ROK forces they supported would be deployed in complex mobile operations for a week, simulating a response and counterattack to a North Korean invasion. "Go on up to the WAREX, Claudia," Colonel Black said. "It's a great opportunity for you to get some tactical experience." Another reason for my participating in the exercise was to permit the one woman who worked for Lieutenant Colonel Mike Pheneger's G-2 section to go to the field. She had not gone on an exercise previously because she was the only woman in the section. The Army was still at that transition stage in which a woman in the field was an exception and never would be sent alone on such an exercise. Today, at least 15 percent of the 2nd Infantry Division's G-2 section are women, and they routinely deploy on field exercises.

But then I found myself on a frozen plain between the mountains, leaning into a gale sweeping down from Siberia, listening to Lieutenant Colonel Pheneger explain the developing situation while the tanks and armored personnel carriers (APCs) of the mechanized infantry around us belched diesel smoke as they churned through the thin crust of wind-blown snow, enveloping an "enemy" salient. I wore two sets of longjohns, fatigues, a black turtleneck, a heavy GI wool sweater, and a parka with fur-lined hood, a wool hat, a helmet, double gloves, two pairs of green wool socks, and rubber galoshes over my combat boots. But still I've never been so cold in my life.

There were several evenings when another officer and I accompanied Lieutenant Colonel Pheneger in his open Jeep, jolting over the icy roads, charting the progress of the WAREX. The brief time I spent inside the heated G-2/G-3 vans was a welcome respite. But then we were back outside, coordinating with different elements of the 2nd Division.

Meals were C rations; you got a can that had been heated in boiling water and tried to open it without burning your fingers. By the time you'd removed the lid with the little GI opener, the contents were tepid. An indispensable ingredient of every Army meal is Tabasco sauce. It is the key to edible eggs, meatloaf, potatoes, everything except cake and hot chocolate.

The second night as the clerk and I got back to our tent, longing for a few hours' sleep beside the diesel stove, a sergeant greeted us in the muted red glow of his blackout flashlight. "Well, ma'am," he said, shaking his head, "your stove blew up. So we moved your stuff into our tent."

I stuck my head into our originally assigned tent. This wasn't some prank. The notoriously unreliable oil stove bulged near the stack pipe and was streaked with reeking soot. Our sleeping bags and personal equipment had been removed.

The men's tent was a general purpose medium with an insulated outer cover and a wooden floor. Their stove was working perfectly. The temperature inside must have been around 40 degrees. Even though, at the time, it was highly unusual for men and women, officer and enlisted, to share their sleeping quarters, I can assure you nothing untoward took place. We were all half-frozen. No one could bathe. No one would undress regardless of the mixed-gender tent. My washcloth froze after the first use. I slept in my full uniform inside my sleeping bag. In the morning, my feet were so cold, I couldn't feel them, and I thought I might be jamming my numb toes into my boots crooked. I used the enlisted latrine—a wooden seat over a frozen hole, surrounded by a wind-whipped tent—because the officers' latrine was too far down the road.

Today you hear a lot of nattering among critics of the military, including many in Congress who never served in uniform, about excluding women from the Army's core activities, which by definition involve field deployment. Since that WAREX in Korea in 1977, I've certainly noticed no greater hardship for women than for men in field conditions and no damage to unit cohesion when women and men serve together.

* * *

This issue has given rise to ongoing confusion about "gender-integrated" training, which has been intentionally exacerbated by politicians with strong biases against women in the military. Their reasoning is based on a false premise: that the Army has been "feminized" and subsequently weakened, starting with Basic Training, where physical training standards are allegedly lowered to accommodate women. The ostensible result of this process is that the Army is training weaker, less qualified soldiers for the combat arms: Infantry, Armor, and Artillery. These critics often resort to the argument that the Army should emulate the Marine Corps by training men and women enlistees separately.

As a three-star general, I joined other military leaders to testify on this issue to a congressional commission. It was surprising that so many in Congress were not aware of—or chose to ignore—the true state of Army training. These are the facts: Sol-

diers enlisting in the combat arms, who are by *regulatory* definition all men, undergo both Basic and Advanced Individual
Training in gender-segregated (all-male) units, in what is known
as One Station Unit Training. Therefore there are no women
trainees to "weaken" the combat arms as political critics persist
in implying. Their argument is without merit.

Soldiers enlisting in the branches other than the combat
arms, both men and women, train in gender-integrated Basic
and Advanced Individual Training. They train side by side because that is the way they will serve in the combat support arms
and the combat service support arms.

As to the critics' call for the Army to copy Marine Corps patterns, the Marines have too few women to be able to integrate
men's training units. Concerning the Army developing an elaborate structure of gender-segregated training units, the cost of
this effort would be enormous in this time of scarce resources.
And an unwanted and unavoidable consequence of such segregation would be to erode the cohesion of units in which men and
women trainees will eventually serve together.

* * *

I was working as Colonel Black's XO when the approval for
my Regular Army commission arrived at the unit. A traditional-
ist, the colonel insisted on personally commissioning me. For all
of his eccentricities, male chauvinism was not one of them. Every
day, he'd use equal vigor chewing out both my men and women
colleagues. But I was his XO, and I did learn a lot, probably because of the variety of tasks and responsibilities he gave me.
After the brief ceremony, Colonel Black and his deputy commander, Lieutenant Colonel Larry Runyon, insisted on christen-
ing my commission in proper Army fashion.

"Come on, Claudia," Colonel Black said. "We're going to the
club."

We rode in the commander's gleaming sedan, driven by Mr.
Yee, the short distance from the headquarters to the officers club.

As soon as we entered the room, my colleagues at the surrounding tables looked self-conscious and avoided eye contact, lest Colonel Black seize the moment to task them with additional work.

But the colonel was in a benevolent mood. He and Lieutenant Colonel Runyon were sincerely interested in my future career, especially now that I had a Regular Army commission. I felt bold enough to relate what I had learned at Fort Huachuca: MI officers needed tactical experience to advance, but that path was closed to women. This was the dilemma I faced.

Colonel Black considered this. "What do you think, Larry?" he asked his deputy.

Lieutenant Colonel Runyon explained that SIGINT was evolving rapidly on the strategic level and that many future leaders of Military Intelligence would have well-developed careers in that discipline, which *was* open to women officers. "You should attend the Junior Officer Cryptologic Career Program," he said.

Colonel Black concurred and allowed his deputy to continue the discussion.

Lieutenant Colonel Runyon explained that the National Security Agency had developed the JOCCP in 1971 to give young military officers three years of intense training and on-the-job experience at the super-secret agency at Fort Meade, Maryland. The Army, Navy, and Air Force provided ten 0-3s (Army captain level), and the Marines, one, to the program. These officers rotated through six jobs over a three-year period. The assignments involved the major subdisciplines, including traffic analysis, collection management, and reporting, as well as challenging special projects.

As they described the program, I knew this was exactly the type of challenge I wanted. The program would be an ideal way to learn cryptology in depth. If, at the end of that time, I didn't see a realistic future for myself as a military officer, I'd still be young enough to seek a fulfilling civilian profession. Colonel Black said he would recommend me for the JOCCP and would seek the support of Brigadier General Jim Freeze forwarding my application.

He took command of the new 501st Military Intelligence

Group, and I spent my final months as an operations officer in the Tactical Support Element of the Intelligence unit of U.S. Forces Korea, based in Seoul. Since this was an "all source" (using all sources of intelligence: SIGINT, imagery, and HUMINT) operation, and tensions along the DMZ remained high, the long workdays that I had experienced after arriving in the country continued. Further, just before I returned to the United States, another major incident flared up in the DMZ when the North Koreans fired on an unarmed U.S. Army CH-47 cargo helicopter, causing it to crash among the minefields between the two heavily defended demarcation lines. Although certainly not as severe as the axe murders, the situation kept us all on alert right up to the day I boarded my flight.

It took me a little while to decompress from the tense atmosphere in Korea to the calmer, more relaxed life of late 1970s America. It seemed strange to wear civilian clothes again after fatigues and combat boots for twelve months. But the work and classes in the JOCCP at Fort Meade were engrossing.

The ultrasensitive NSA—sometimes referred to as "No Such Agency"—remains one of the most secret organizations in the U.S. government. My colleagues and I were instructed to simply tell anyone who asked that we worked for the "Defense Department." That seemed like a practical expedient. But when my friend Irene Sanders, an NSA civilian, couldn't find her driver's license while trying to cash a check at a nearby store, she used that ploy with the clerk. "Oh," he said, "you work at the NSA. Just show me your badge." So much for airtight security.

Once inside the huge building, however, security did reign. Formal classes were part of the curriculum of the National Cryptologic School. One of my favorites was a course on intelligence reporting, taught by an admirable and brilliant white-haired lady named Vera Filby, who had been one of the legendary codebreakers at Bletchley Park near London during World War II. She used both historic cases and immediate developing incidents to teach us what and how essential intelligence elements had to be reported.

One day I got a call from a friend. "Claudia, your name's on the promotion list."

I couldn't believe it. This meant I'd been promoted to major "below the zone," one year early, ahead of my year group. "Read me the full name," I asked warily. She did. "Read me the Social Security number." She did. My name was on the list, no doubt about it.

* * *

When I finished my three years at the NSA, I was a major and what we call "branch qualified" in Military Intelligence. It had been just over ten years since I had driven my old Ford Fairlane to Fort McClellan to begin the WAC Basic Course. Now my plan was to spend ten more years in the Army, to reach the rank of lieutenant colonel, and perhaps even to earn command of a SIG-INT battalion as my last assignment. For a woman soldier at that time, this was quite an ambition.

But by this point, I had come to love the Army and its mission as the ultimate peacekeeping force in the precarious Cold War world. And I loved my fellow soldiers, both men and women, because of the camaraderie we had shared, and because they did their jobs so well, often under difficult conditions. We stayed in the Army not because it was just a job that we tolerated, but because it was an exhilarating adventure. You'll often hear people who served a term of enlistment in the Army when they were young yearning for the comradeship and adventure, the sense of purpose greater than one's own self-centered life they knew as soldiers. This was the intensely satisfying experience that devotion to duty in the Army brought me. But I didn't enjoy just a brief time in uniform. I was fortunate enough to spend thirty-two years as a soldier.

4

The Art of Mentoring

uring my long military career, I learned more practical leadership skills from the experienced noncommissioned officers I commanded and from my senior commissioned officers, who took it upon themselves to mentor me, than I did from any formal military school I attended. This lesson undoubtedly also applies to my colleagues who earned their commissions from the U.S. Military Academy at West Point, through the ROTC, or the Officer Candidate School program. Once commissioned, we were often like junior executive graduates of business schools in the civilian world, who somehow feel they have been endowed with innate leadership powers and do not realize that leadership consists of a complex combination of acquired skills. But I soon learned otherwise.

The most fortunate path for any aspiring leader to follow is to be consistently mentored by the junior and senior leaders in her or his organization at the critical junctures of the developing leader's career. For this process to work, of course, the person being mentored has to set aside arrogance, be willing to learn, and be receptive, especially when it involves being guided by

people who are junior in rank. It is essential for leaders to realize that they are always works in progress, in continual need of
guidance and development, even as they reach senior positions.
Once a person decides she is complete, she is announcing her
growth is ended and her potential is fulfilled. This signals to
everyone the end of her progress in that field.

There is a personal component to this issue beyond professional considerations. I firmly believe a person's life involves
much more than achieving distant career goals. In other words,
the process of "getting there" is more fun and personally rewarding than the ultimate "being there." When I was a young
lieutenant in the WAC Officer Basic Course, a chaplain addressed our class, explaining that the ambition of completing a
twenty-year Army career should not be the most important factor in our decision about staying the Army. Equally, in the civilian world, the search for job stability at any cost often stultifies
personal and professional fulfillment, and ultimately quashes
leadership potential.

We all can profit from advice. But the flow of guidance moves
up and down the hierarchy. Civilians sometimes get an inaccurate picture of the personal interaction between commissioned
and noncommissioned officers in the Army. Just because a senior
NCO uses military courtesy and addresses a lieutenant or captain as "ma'am" or "sir," it doesn't mean that the respect between
them is not mutual. In reality, the partnership between officer
and NCO is mutually supportive, especially at the company
level, where junior officers first learn their leadership skills. That
was certainly my experience.

When I took command of the Staff and Faculty Company at
Fort McClellan in 1973, my first sergeant, Betty Benson, became
my first important mentor in the Army. She was a career soldier
who spoke in the clipped, 1940s radio show inflections of Eve
Arden. But she was a serious professional. After a few days in that
unfamiliar orderly room, I took First Sergeant Benson aside for
a frank discussion.

"What is it exactly that I do, First Sergeant?" I asked, genuinely trying to understand our respective roles.

She summed up the difference in our functions this way: "Basically, ma'am, you command the company, and I run it."

She was reinforcing what I had heard from my senior officers at WAC Center, who all advised us: "Listen to your NCOs."

But First Sergeant Betty Benson was far from the uncertain leader that had become too prevalent among Army NCOs in the years after the Vietnam War. She believed in the future of the All-Volunteer Army, and she knew she could play her role in building it, even at the company level. From her I learned that the commander set the course of action—reestablishing Army discipline in our barracks, for example—and that the first sergeant would implement it. She led the effort in restoring discipline to the barracks. And she had her own connections to the Military Police that allowed us to implement that policy on a practical basis. As we struggled week after week to solve this problem, I came to realize that, despite our differences in rank and years of service, we were forming a tight-knit team that stood shoulder to shoulder to regain control of the company. We were working toward a common goal, and she was the more experienced soldier, so I was learning valuable lessons from her. Decades later, I have often reflected on this effort. When faced with tough problems, young executives in the civilian workplace with degrees from prestigious business schools might do well to forget about their MBAs and seek advice among their organization's equivalents of Betty Benson, whom they can find on the shop floor or among the anonymous line engineers' cubicles.

Certainly First Sergeant Benson taught a priceless lesson about the value of decisiveness. In October 1973, the Women's Army Corps underwent a dramatic expansion with the creation of a training center at Fort Jackson, South Carolina, and related reshuffles and organizational upheavals at Fort McClellan. With no warning, I was ordered to move my company out of their old barracks and into newer quarters in concrete buildings that had formerly housed WAC student officers. First Sergeant Benson attended the organizational meeting about this move on a Friday and came back to the company office to announce that we had until the following Friday to move all our people, furniture, and equipment, while, of course, maintaining our normal duty schedule.

"Actually, ma'am," she said. "We've got a very good deal."

We'd been allotted a modern three-story building in the area of the post known as WAC Circle. All three floors were identical, with each two comfortable bedrooms sharing a family-style bathroom. There were none of the open, bunk bed troop bays and multicommode latrines that gave normal barracks life such an institutional atmosphere. The barracks were more like a college dorm than traditional military housing. "The soldiers are going to love it," the first sergeant said.

There was only one problem. When we sat down and counted bedrooms against our roster, it immediately became obvious that we would have to make our new barracks co-ed. To my knowledge, we would be among the first units attempting such an experiment. But we weren't about to lose these splendid new quarters based on this point.

We informed WAC Center that we intended to move the entire company, men and women, into the new barracks. Word soon came back that such a move would be considered "inappropriate." But First Sergeant Benson knew how to jingle the bells of Army bureaucracy. The post needed room for incoming WAC trainees; that's why they needed us to consolidate. "If you want more room for your new trainees," First Sergeant Benson informally told her counterparts in WAC Center, "let us move."

I trusted her and thought the idea of a co-ed barracks was quite sound. This was probably the classic case of a junior officer thinking she was in charge when in fact it was the NCO calling the plays. In any event, we heard nothing further from WAC Center. Apparently, there was no regulation *against* quartering troops under the same roof, provided men and women did not sleep in the same room or share the same bathroom. But how could we make this experiment-cum-expedient work on a practical level? Once more, she advised me well.

She knew our people, and I trusted her judgment. Her plan was simple but based on thoughtful consideration. During phase one, the men would stay in their own barracks while we intensified the effort to weed out the most ill disciplined through the Army discharges available to us. In this phase, we would assign the younger, less experienced women to an all-female top floor. Then, in phase two, the younger, less experienced men would be assigned to the all-male bottom floor. The older soldiers, both women and men, generally NCOs with good behavior records, would share the second floor.

"What do you think WAC Center will say about this room plan, First Sergeant?" I asked.

"They're the ones who ordered us to move, ma'am," she said with certainty, closing the subject. In fact, she had good contacts among the NCOs at headquarters and correctly guessed that our senior officers would support us after receiving a thorough briefing on the rationale for the room assignments in the gender-mixed barracks and making certain all standards of propriety had been met. The move made a lot of sense. In the new barracks, people would have greater privacy and dignity. They could lock the doors of their bedrooms and bathrooms. This provided much greater security for their possessions, and many of the soldiers invested for the first time in expensive stereos and record collections. Having this privacy also gave them a greater sense of autonomy, which came in large part through the knowledge that the Army trusted them to act maturely.

I addressed this issue directly just before we began the move. "We're being given the chance for a big improvement in quarters," I told the soldiers. "So, I'm expecting you to act in an unusually mature manner."

As they enthusiastically loaded up the trucks with their footlockers and furniture for the unprecedented move to the co-ed barracks, I felt good, in part because First Sergeant Benson was there every step of the way. "You've done the right thing, ma'am," she assured me. "People act differently when you treat them better, when they have their own room. They won't let you down."

She was right about that, as she was about so many things. Predictably, a few at WAC Center made some noise about the controversial move, but did not try to rescind it. As a young commander, I was fortunate to have First Sergeant Benson as my mentor.

* * *

She taught me a lot about assuming the responsibility of command. Another senior noncommissioned officer, Master Sergeant Davenport, with whom I worked at the All Source Intelligence Center at Yongsan near Seoul, Korea, in 1977, was probably the most skilled teacher of analysis I had as a young officer. Unlike so many American soldiers who had served fleeting one-year assignments to Korea, Master Sergeant Davenport had accumulated multiple tours of duty there. He knew the tactical and strategic situation intimately and had a rich base of personal experience—his own living memory—on which to draw whenever a single source of intelligence suggested yet another crisis along the DMZ was at hand.

Again, the fact that I was an officer and he held enlisted rank meant nothing in terms of our comparative professional expertise. I was the student and he was the expert teacher. I learned a lot simply by watching him work. We had a young private first class ELINT analyst named Barringer working in the shop. One day his task was to type up a simple administrative disposition form. But the young PFC made repeated typing errors. Sergeant Davenport, however, let PFC Barringer make his mistakes and learn as he did so. Davenport was right, of course. Within a few weeks, the young soldier had mastered his typing skills. Had I given in to my impatience and asked Davenport to type the form, I would have deprived Barringer of his chance to learn.

Master Sergeant Davenport's mentoring style was friendly

and relaxed. He never explicitly took me aside and said, "Let's do it this way." Instead, he led by quiet example.

I observed him when some complex analytical problem arose, as they so often did involving SIGINT traffic in the region. One of the eager young soldiers would present a solution to the veteran NCO. But Master Sergeant Davenport, a Marlboro 100 dangling from his lips, would rise slowly from his desk with a sleepy expression on his face. "Well now," he'd drawl, "let's see about all this."

He would go to his filing cabinets and retrieve several reports from similar past incidents, then spread them on our worktable. Speaking slowly and deliberately, and using his cigarette as a pointer, he would patiently walk us all through the proper analysis of the current situation. What he was showing us, of course, was that there was always much greater complexity and significance to the "take," the raw material of the professional intelligence analyst. Above all, Master Sergeant Davenport gave us perspective, something I would never have learned in school.

Whenever I wanted to submit what he considered a premature analysis, he'd tactfully advise me to "touch base" with a more experienced officer working on a similar project first, knowing that young captains like myself often viewed the world with narrow, laser-beam vision, and lacked the wider perspective of a more mature analyst. But he never put his own opinion aggressively forward; rather, more often than not, he waited for me to come to him for advice. The lesson in this was to know *when* to recognize I needed to ask him. The goal was not to eliminate the need to ask.

I learned that if Master Sergeant Davenport was not hurried or upset, the situation was not overly serious, although this was a period when some people much higher in the chain of command were understandably edgy about the hostile threat. Again, they had usually been in their jobs for less than a year, while he had served in Korea for much longer. Above all, he taught me that a soldier's true value to the Army was almost never related to a person's rank.

In fact, I came to recognize that each rank has its value. Soldiers should be proud of what they have achieved and of meeting the responsibilities attached to those achievements. A skilled sergeant SIGINT analyst, for example, can fill just as vital a role in meeting her unit's mission as a captain commanding the company. I have never felt the practice of adding the notation (P) after a soldier's rank when she or he has been selected, but not yet promoted to that higher grade, to reflect the Army attitude about rank. Soldiers should do their jobs, take pride in their current rank, and not be focused on status rather than work.

* * *

But I also learned that there were soldiers who unethically exploited their rank and position. When I commanded the 3rd Operations Battalion at Field Station Augsburg in Germany in 1986, I encountered a senior NCO who gave me real cause to distrust him. Contrary to regulations and policy, he kept no duty rosters, but operated instead through a network of more junior NCOs who parceled out work assignments almost as a form of patronage. This soldier and his buddies also controlled the lucrative soda and beer machine concessions located in our barracks. In theory, the money collected from these machines was supposed to go into the battalion account to pay for morale and recreation activities and equipment such as stereos for the dayrooms. But when I finally got him to present me the battalion fund books, there was nothing to show where the money had gone.

"Please explain what happened to the money," I said, shaking my head.

He conceded that the machines made a lot of money, but had no record of where that money went. Possibly as a diversion, however, he took me on a tour of one dayroom that had some secondhand wood trim, which turned out to have been scrounged from another unit, and to another equipped with a stereo that he admitted was on loan.

Convinced that I could not trust him to control a corruption-free system, I put the executive officer in charge of the beer and soda machines. This got the NCO's back up and he began to openly challenge my authority, first in small ways, to be sure. I had made it known that I did not want smoking in my office. But he often came through my door with a lit cigarette either stuck in his mouth or jammed between his fingers. "Whoops," he'd say, "forgot."

Further experience in the battalion revealed there was no formal selection board for NCOs and soldiers, which were necessary for promotion and for the Soldier-of-the-Quarter competition, a prestigious award. This was in the hands of the senior NCO and his cronies. He was like a King Rat, invisibly running the battalion behind the backs of the officers.

I finally went to my brigade commander, Colonel Sam Simerly, to discuss the problem. "These are my concerns," I said, laying out the details, some of which probably could have been serious enough to initiate an investigation.

Colonel Simerly had never been overly close to his battalion commanders, to put it mildly, and I was probably the least favorite lieutenant colonel in his command. But he apparently had already picked this NCO to serve on his staff and didn't want to see a can of worms opened with an investigation. The soldier in question was quietly removed from my battalion. There was a lesson in this unpleasant experience: As conflicts appear, you have to be explicit about your concerns from the outset. You do not refrain from giving full details, so there is no ambiguity.

But for every lazy or unethical soldier in my battalion, there were a hundred who were honest and hardworking. One of the best was Command Sergeant Major Ira Gant, with whom I worked closely after I took command of the battalion. I learned invaluable lessons about a military commander's unique relationship to her soldiers. He was among the most intelligent, thoughtful, and loyal NCOs with whom I've had the honor of serving. He spoke and moved rather slowly, and seemed amused by my interest in running. Fortunately for him, I didn't insist on the NCOs joining me on my off-post runs, only the battalion staff officers, who definitely needed some of this type of training time together. But Command Sergeant Major Gant would often mosey into my office toward the end of a long gray German afternoon and watch me lace up my running shoes.

"What are you doing?" he'd ask in mock disbelief. Outside, the raw Bavarian fog would not have lifted.

"I'm thinking about going out running."

Command Sergeant Major Gant would shake his head. "If you wait a few minutes, you'll probably get over it."

With his large brown eyes behind thick plastic Army glasses, he did not fit the stereotypical image of the square-shouldered Sergeant Rock, but the soldiers loved him, and he lived for them. Unlike the devious NCO who apparently viewed the battalion's troops as a con man assesses his marks, Command Sergeant Major Gant took personal responsibility for the morale and well-being of each member of our command. When a soldier, especially a young enlistee, joined the battalion, Gant would question her or him in great detail about their enlistment contracts, sitting patiently at his desk and reviewing the paperwork to make sure that they had received all the bonus money they had coming. Many of these young soldiers did not fully understand the details of these bonuses and were unaware that all the money due them had not been paid. But Ira Gant always had time for them.

Watching him work with these soldiers taught me a vital lesson in military leadership. I learned that caring for soldiers must be more than a trite slogan. Caring is not so much about emotion as it is about doing the job of a commander to ensure soldiers receive their correct pay, as well as fair promotion and recognition. Although these soldiers were legally adults, they were very young, and in many ways we were their surrogate families. This extra effort paid invaluable dividends. For example, we sent our soldiers' next-of-kin in the United States the German postal address at which the soldiers could be reached by telegram in an emergency. This was because a cable sent to the normal Army post office address only traveled at the speed of mail. We also included Polaroid pictures of the soldiers in uniform in the battalion area as a tangible symbol that they had arrived safely overseas. The return letters we received from the appreciative families were heartwarming. Often the proud parents would relate accounts of their own military experiences and describe their children's accomplishments in school and scouting. Both the soldiers and the Army depended on the bedrock of support these families provided.

Command Sergeant Major Gant also taught me through example the value of diversity in a large organization such as the Army. He believed strongly in separating religion from the Army's official policy, that religion was a personal matter that should not be drawn into military life in any manner. In the mid-1980s, however, the prevailing sentiment weighed toward the politically powerful Christian evangelists who promoted prayer and invocations on Army posts.

"Better to leave all that stuff in the chaplain's shop," he'd mutter, trying unsuccessfully to conceal the fact that he was probably one of the smartest, and certainly among the fairest, soldiers in U.S. Army, Europe.

In December 1986, Ira Gant announced that he'd found a married couple in the battalion who had volunteered to work a seventy-two-hour shift over Christmas.

"That's great!" I said. That would free up two shift workers to be home with their kids. "But why are they willing to work Christmas?"

Gant had a slight gleam in his eye. "They're Wiccas."

"Wiccas?"

"Like witches, Colonel, only the good kind. They believe in the Earth Goddess, that type of thing."

"Oh, my." I didn't know we had any of those in the battalion.

Command Sergeant Major Gant smiled. "Well, that's no stranger than some of you who kneel at an altar and drink wine and think that it's the blood of God."

The couple did in fact serve their seventy-two-hour shift. And they did not perform any bizarre rituals in the operations area. Over the coming months, Gant and I sometimes discussed this issue. From his close contact with the troops, he knew that the Army was drawing recruits from a cultural base much more diverse than I had known as a junior officer. Although the mainstream Christian majority still prevailed in the United States, there was a significant number of nontraditional denominations and sects represented in our battalion, ranging from Mormons and Jews to Muslims to that Wicca couple. Our moral distinction from the Soviet Bloc lay in the fact that we did not impose beliefs either directly or indirectly on our soldiers. It was not my job as a commander to ask my soldiers about their religion. It was my responsibility to work hard for our mission and their welfare every day. Command Sergeant Major Gant taught me that being judgmental was not the same as being moral and ethical. Gant was moral, but not judgmental. It was a lesson I've never forgotten.

* * *

When I commanded a recruiting battalion in San Antonio, Texas, between 1988 and 1990, my sergeant major, Glenn Tutor, was probably the most dedicated soldier I've ever served with. From him and the other recruiters I learned that soldiers, no matter how mentally exhausted or physically depleted, will keep working when their leaders work with them. It was amazing what we could accomplish when we believed in our mission and never gave up.

This was a time of great rebuilding for the Army, after Major General Max Thurman had revamped the recruiting command and the enlistment standards had been raised throughout the U.S. military. Patriotism was flourishing nationwide, the economy was slowing down, and young people were drawn to the military. But processing potential enlistees was a far more difficult matter than simply shuffling paperwork. Enlistment standards were high. Recruits had to pass a battery of mental and physical examinations, and undergo thorough criminal background checks. Because soldiers had the option of choosing their guaranteed training specialties and in some cases locations of assignment, the recruiting offices had to coordinate enlistments with the dates of Basic and Advanced Individual Training and specialized military schools. At the same time, the Army needed large numbers of soldiers in the Infantry, Artillery, and Armor, and we offered recruits to those branches generous enlistment bonuses.

So the ostensibly straightforward task of running a recruiting battalion became a series of Daily Performance Reviews in which we tracked the work of every recruiter and recruiting station. It was during these intense sessions that Sergeant Major Tutor showed me the example of leadership by participation.

As the hour for our conference calls to headquarters approached, I'd often think, *We'll never pull this off.* There'd be too many unfinished medical clearances, school record and criminal background checks, and enlistment options. But Sergeant Major Tutor would sit at his desk methodically manning his own phone while he rallied the troops around him. "What are *you* going to do to get that background check?" he'd ask, prodding a first sergeant. "Who are *you* going to call at the El Paso police to get that criminal clearance?" he'd urge another NCO. Throughout these busy days and nights, the sergeant major worked alongside his soldiers. Meals were Dunkin' Donuts and Whataburgers. Given his relentless dedication, we nearly always made our mission goal. And as battalion sergeant major, Glenn Tutor mentored the first sergeants who led recruiting stations in other cities, spreading the same ethos of unyielding dedication: No matter how hopeless the situation seemed, you keep on working and your soldiers will follow you.

As Stedman Graham says in his insightful book *Teens Can Make It Happen* (which I recommend to parents and teenagers alike), "It is *always* too early to quit."

Since I've left the Army, people often ask what assignment gave me the most satisfaction. They're surprised when I say commanding a recruiting battalion in San Antonio during the late

1980s. But the fact is, it was the hardest job I ever had as a soldier and the one from which I derived the most professional fulfillment. We were building the new Army with well-qualified, dedicated young recruits, many of whom went on to help bring us victory in the Gulf War and serve our country so well under such difficult circumstances in the Balkans.

And once more, I learned from a veteran NCO the true meaning of a leader's duty.

* * *

The noncommissioned officers I served with were not the only valuable mentors who shaped me as a military leader. I also benefited from an unexpected form of peer mentoring when I attended the Military Intelligence Officer Advance Course (MIOAC) at Fort Huachuca, Arizona. As I processed into the course, it became obvious that I was entering unknown territory. Many of the young captains around me in the long lines easily exchanged incomprehensible Intelligence acronyms, swapping stories from their recent days in the field.

Then one of the captains, Jack Varnado, introduced himself. "I've never been in MI before," I confided. "I think I'm going to be lost in this course."

"You'll be okay," Jack Varnado said confidently. "I'll make sure of that."

And he was true to his word. Although he couldn't disrupt the normal flow of classroom activity, Jack always made sure to meet me at my desk during each break to thoroughly explain the material. This selfless act made me feel included. As the curriculum became more complex, Jack was always there to offer help when I needed it. Two months into the course, I was able to stand alone, but wouldn't have done so well had Jack Varnado not mentored me.

He was only one of a number of African-American men officers I've known in my career who stepped forward to mentor their women peers. Perhaps these men detected their women colleagues' sense of isolation and more readily understood the awkward position of a minority person entering a group. This ethos of camaraderie always evoked my loyalty to the Army.

To me, one lesson of this experience is that there is a difference between mentoring and serving as a role model. A successful woman officer or civilian executive might well become a role model for younger women, but this does not mean she shouldn't also mentor men. Too often, however, people think they can only mentor someone of their own race or gender. But I believe the profession of the two people involved in the mentoring partnership transcends other aspects of identity.

Equally, some people feel their mentoring responsibility is narrowly constricted within the vertical professional ladder of those who work for them—those whom they rate in the military. But many take a broader view. As the years progressed, I always kept my eye out for promising younger officers in other units I encountered and engaged them in discussions whenever I could to assess their talents. When I had identified one of these "bright bulbs," I'd pass her or his name on to one of my peers who might be scouting for new talent, or I'd call the sergeant major of the unit to which the promising young officer had been assigned to alert that NCO they had a real potential leader arriving. I would always preface my comments by saying, "He or she doesn't know I'm calling." While senior officers must never get directly involved in the actual assignment process, it is appropriate to share with one's colleagues the names of exceptional leaders who are headed their way.

* * *

It's important to stress that the mentoring relationship is not one of a senior person pulling strings to place a favorite junior in a position of advantage. During recent years, it has seemed that perhaps we overpromoted the concept of senior-to-junior mentoring, so that some people saw it as an automatic entrée to career advancement. In fact, this form of patronage is no longer possible, given the Army's promotion and assignment system. So it would often be more appropriate for junior officers and NCOs to cultivate networks of low-risk, high-trust peers with whom they could share career ideas, professional reading, or school material for mutual advancement. The same pattern should prevail in the civilian workplace. Riding to high executive rank on your mentor's coattails without proving your own merit does little credit to either the senior or the junior person and generally causes irreparable damage to the organization's effectiveness and morale. Again, mentoring is not analogous with favoritism.

I also believe the essence of successful senior-to-junior mentoring is the senior person correctly assessing the junior's strengths and weaknesses and giving key practical advice at the appropriate time rather than diffuse and unfocused feel-good pep talks.

For me, one of the most critical—but unlikely—of these mentors was Colonel Charles Black, my commander at Pyongtaek, Korea, in 1976. The Prince of Darkness had developed a leadership style that involved emulating the stress of wartime, pushing us harder than we thought we could endure to accomplish our mission. By being such a demanding taskmaster, he forced us all to improve our performance and he forged us into a tightly knit team. Other leaders might well have achieved similar results through less draconian methods. But it was obvious that, despite his bluster, Colonel Black cared deeply about his officers. During the Korean War in the early 1950s, he had seen firsthand what lack of readiness meant: dead American soldiers and lost battles. He was determined that his command would be trained and ready to face war again in Korea twenty-five years later.

Colonel Black had been carefully observing my performance as his executive officer, a young captain who worked hard and rarely merited one of his truly blistering verbal reprimands. I was very pleased when he endorsed Lieutenant Colonel Runyon's recommendation that I apply for the Junior Officer Cryptologic Career Program (JOCCP) at the National Security Agency. This was exactly the type of timely practical advice a senior mentor can deliver that has a pivotal effect on the junior person's future.

My relationship with Colonel Black was formal, respectful, and distant. This was his style with all of us. Yet his interest in my future and the specific mentoring he delivered eventually proved to be one of the decisive turning points in my career. This is an important factor to consider: Although mentoring often involves friendly personal interaction, it is not a requirement. In the case of Colonel Black and myself, for example, mutual respect and the good of the service replaced emotion.

* * *

While at the National Security Agency, I also learned that senior-to-junior mentoring need not require a close professional relationship as I had had with Colonel Black. My assignment to the JOCCP put me in the Agency's A Group. I found the work both professionally intriguing and personally fulfilling, by far the most engrossing assignment I'd had so far in my Army career. As the time approached for me to leave the Agency, I approached Joe Amato, head of the A Group.

"Mr. Amato," I said, "I'm considering resigning from the Army and applying to the NSA as a civilian."

He had been a distant supervisor with whom I'd had little direct contact. But like all good senior executives, he had learned as much as he could about those in A Group. And he probably knew more about the aspirations of young captains than they did themselves.

First, he explained, the NSA was not hiring any new people in operations, but if I wished he would check in the logistics division of the Agency. Then he looked at me thoughtfully. "If you decide to come into NSA," he said in an even tone, "you'll be settling down and making a career here. But are you really ready for the Army adventure to end?"

I thought of the thousands of Agency commuters who filled the vast parking lots each day, week in, week out, never leaving this immense facility during their careers. Was that what I truly wanted? Thinking about this question, the answer became clear. The next time we spoke, I told Mr. Amato, "I guess I do want more travel and adventure in my life. And the best way to get that is in the Army."

Before I'd met with him I had interviewed for a civilian job at the Veterans Administration, and even a position with a real estate agency. But his precisely focused questions had made me realize my true preference was to remain in the Army for at least twenty years.

Even though I was just one of several junior military officers working in his area, Joe Amato had insightfully analyzed the dynamics of my personal and career options and gave me critical advice that caused me to focus my thinking clearly on those options. I took that advice and stayed in the Army. About the time we last spoke about my future plans, I learned I had been promoted to major ahead of my peer group.

*   *   *

When I was a junior officer, Colonel Black spontaneously acted as my mentor, and I later requested specific career advice from Joe Amato at NSA, which kept me from leaving the Army prematurely. Since then, I've often thought about the sensitive mentoring relationship that exists between a younger person and an older, more senior officer or executive. Although it might be appropriate for young people to ask for specific advice, they should never approach their seniors and request that they become their mentors. This is the prerogative of the older, more experienced person. Giving a few words of advice is easy; actually mentoring—guiding a younger person over a long period of his or her career—is a significant, time-consuming task that only the busy senior officer or executive can choose to do.

And, in the Army, offering good, honest career advice to colleagues is part of the culture. We all learn to share openly in order to be as strong a team as possible. But I know from civilian friends that this is far from true in the private workplace where people are often individually competitive.

That being said, I still must emphasize the difference between the challenge of mentoring and the task of giving specific advice. After I was promoted to general officer, friends and colleagues continued to refer young officers to me for professional advice. Whenever the questions were focused and specific, I gladly shared my knowledge and opinion. But I also found that occasionally people went too far to seek me out as if I were some kind of a good-luck talisman who would somehow charm their careers. One example of this was a field-grade officer, a complete stranger, serving in a branch other than Military Intelligence, who had been referred to me by her commander when her questions about advancement became too persistent. She began to inundate me with e-mails and handwritten letters requesting that I "mentor" her. In one message, she blatantly asked: "How can I become a general like you?" Asking it signaled to me that she was an unlikely general officer prospect. Gender is not a sufficient reason for developing this sort of professional relationship.

I certainly believe in giving women and ethnic minorities the equal opportunity to advance that I enjoyed, but I do not feel that gender or ethnic identity automatically entitles a person to a mentoring conduit to any senior officer of their group.

* * *

Sometimes mentoring involves being frank, even bursting someone's illusions. I particularly remember a lieutenant colonel with whom I had been casually acquainted who called me when I was assigned as the J-2 intelligence officer to FORSCOM (Forces Command) at Fort McPherson in Atlanta to say a board on which I had served had passed him over for promotion to full colonel. I had reviewed over a thousand files and could not remember his.

"I can't understand why I wasn't promoted," he said. "I have a flawless record. Maybe you can help explain what happened."

I didn't know the officer well, but he had sincerely requested advice, so I wanted to help him. "All right," I said. "Next time I'm in D.C. I'll come see you and review your file."

I went to an office in the Pentagon where he had the microfiche containing his Officer Efficiency Reports and a microfiche reader. Reading his file, I immediately saw that his record was definitely not unflawed as he believed and that one of his reports as a battalion commander put him directly in the "center of the mass," in the middle of his peer group. Given the Army's current rating system, he had what was called a "2 block," while those promoted to colonel had mostly "1 block" ratings. Yet this officer thought his cumulative OERs were unflawed, mainly because he'd always been promoted in the past and because he had no basis for comparing his record to those of others and seeing truly excellent reports. And it was clear that he believed it was virtually automatic for him to continue this progress and be promoted to full colonel.

I remembered advice I'd received from Command Sergeant Major Raymond McKnight before taking over my recruiting battalion in San Antonio.

"Training is important to the unit, ma'am," he'd said, "but honest counseling is essential to the individual soldier. It's the only time people learn their strengths and weaknesses."

It was now time to tell this lieutenant colonel frankly that his record was not flawless and that he was unlikely to be promoted. To his great credit, he listened intently as I pointed out the weak points in his OERs and suggested areas where he should concentrate to improve his future performance. I'm happy to report that he was in fact promoted to full colonel the next year, an outcome that might not have occurred had he not sought specific advice, had I not been frank with that advice, and had he not been willing to listen and act.

Since then, the Army has changed its OER. Under the new system, only 49 percent of those rated are admitted to the top block, now referred to as "above center of mass." All officers know exactly where they stand after each rating. Some people feel this might discourage those who do not do well, but I believe it is in the best interest of the rated officers to understand their position in their peer group. And this information becomes especially important as officers reach field-grade rank and must decide between continuing in the Army after twenty years and seeking a civilian career. In effect, the new OER allows the Army itself to act in the role of the honest mentor that I filled with the lieutenant colonel who had been passed over for promotion.

* * *

Immediately after the Gulf War, the Army underwent one of the biggest downsizings in history, cutting active component soldiers from over 800,000 to 500,000. I was the commander of a Military Intelligence brigade at Kunia, Hawaii, when one of my best young officers, Major Howard Phelps, sought my advice about a dilemma he was facing. There would be an Army-wide Reduction in Force (RIF) to pare down the number of majors going before the lieutenant colonel promotion board. But Howard had received an unfavorable OER earlier in his career that prevented him from attending Command and General Staff College (CGSC). Although he had been successful in having that OER removed from his personnel file, he did not know if he would be reconsidered to attend CGSC, a virtual requirement for promotion to lieutenant colonel. Now he had to decide whether to take advantage of an "early out" the Army was offering officers as part of the downsizing. This program would entail a substantial incentive, which would provide Howard and his young family more than a year's living expenses while he found a civilian job and reestablished himself.

The crux of his dilemma was that if he waited to see whether he was selected for CGSC, he might still be ordered to leave the Army under the mandatory RIF and lose the generous voluntary early-termination incentive.

"So, Colonel," Howard said, "this is my choice: Get out now with the money or stay and risk having to leave anyway, but without the money."

He was naturally tense discussing this subject, and I needed to understand more about his background and his family and the context in which he would make the decision. I learned his father had been in the Air Force, a fact of which he was very proud. Howard and his wife, Mary Ellen, were very happy with Army life. He loved his work and wanted to be a career officer more than anything. But that prospect did not look good. He had already been passed over for lieutenant colonel once due to that Officer Efficiency Report, and his assignment officer had encouraged him to leave the Army now and not risk being caught in the RIF.

Finally, I said to Howard, "Let's stop analyzing this by trying to *predict* the future. Instead, why don't we try to calculate your degree of comfort with each possible outcome? Then we'll work to *create* the future you want."

At the end of our discussion he decided that he loved the Army and definitely wanted to stay, so it would be irrational to "volunteer" to leave just to add comfort to the less-desired outcome, acquiring more money for the transition to civilian life. He said that he wanted to stay in the Army strongly enough that it was worth the risk of losing the incentive money.

After Howard left my office, I realized I had used the lessons I had learned when trying to sort out my future as a young captain at the Military Intelligence Officer Advance Course to help clarify this young officer's future career.

The sequel to this episode is that Howard Phelps escaped the RIF, was selected to attend the Command and General Staff College, and was promoted to lieutenant colonel and to colonel. He served as the senior operations officer at the Kunia Brigade, commanded a battalion, and completed the Army War College. Colonel Phelps currently holds an important position at the Battle Lab at Fort Huachuca, a part of the Training and Doctrine Command. He and his family remain deeply committed to the Army and to Army life. And we are very fortunate to have him.

* * *

In 1993, after I was selected to the rank of brigadier general, I was assigned as the senior intelligence officer at FORSCOM, one of the largest commands in the Army. I came to the assignment from the strategic side of intelligence and lacked the direct tactical intelligence experience (battalion S-2, division G-2) with the combat arms that my instructors had predicted was an absolute requirement for advancement in my profession so many years before at Fort Huachuca.

So, almost as soon as I took up my new assignment, my commander, General Dennis J. Reimer, became a mentor and began sending me to visit as many tactical Intelligence units at our command's combat divisions and corps as possible. Within six months, I was familiar with the intelligence operations at Forts Benning, Bragg, Lewis, Hood, Stewart, and Campbell. I was on Temporary Duty so much that I often missed senior staff meetings back at Fort McPherson. And when I did manage to attend, General Reimer always ribbed me, "Kennedy, Kennedy. I know I've seen you somewhere before. Don't you work for me?"

One of the truly exciting aspects of my job was the chance to observe the Army's computerized Battle Command Training Program operation that uses simulations to replicate combat operations. As I observed the busy staff of officers and NCOs, which included a large percentage of women, sitting at their consoles and making decisions under tight deadlines, I recalled with a tinge of irony the cynical advisor I'd conferred with in 1976 at Fort Huachuca who had told me there would never be a future for women in the Army until all the male chauvinist pigs like him were gone.

In his own way, he too had been a mentor.

To me the important lesson for women is not to believe all those like him who would diminish our potential. Certainly the odds were against me. In fact, the probability of Second Lieutenant Claudia Kennedy of 1969 becoming a brigadier general in 1993 had been zero. But who has to believe the odds? Every one of us, woman or man, of every race, ethnicity, or religion, represents an individual variable of unlimited potential.

5

Self-Discipline

When I retired from the U.S. Army in the summer of 2000, women comprised approximately 15 percent of the total force. They served in every branch and in every Military Occupational Specialty except those involving direct ground combat. Women aviators fly both fixed-wing aircraft and a wide variety of helicopters. In both the Panama operation and in the Gulf War, women helicopter pilots and aircrew flew hazardous combat missions, often in extremely adverse weather. Army women continue to fly and operate heavy equipment under difficult operational conditions in the Balkans and the Persian Gulf today. In my own branch, Military Intelligence, women NCOs and officers are now routinely assigned on the tactical level and increasingly serve as battalion S-2 and division G-2 intelligence officers.

Although still a distinct minority, the proportion of senior women NCOs and commissioned officers is steadily increasing. There are currently fewer than thirty women general officers in the Army (Active, Reserve, and National Guard). Unfortunately, the "bench" of replacements, that is, the women colonels with brigade command and War College experience, is too thin to guarantee a steady progression of qualified women into the ranks of general officer. But to continue the sports analogy, the junior varsity looks especially promising. For twenty years, West Point has produced outstanding women graduates, as have our college and university ROTC programs. With competition between men and women fair and open, women have more than held their own in the progression from company-grade to field-grade officer.

And it's important to remember that two thirds of the units in the Army are *not* in the combat arms, so women play a vital role in maintaining the effectiveness of the total force. Increasingly, women are commanding battalions and brigades in the combat support arms, such as Military Intelligence, Engineers, Military Police, and in the combat service support arms, such as the Transportation, Ordnance, and Signal Corps.

* * *

As women advance into such positions of authority both in the military and the civilian world, they often discover a close relationship between personal authenticity and leadership power. By authenticity, I mean the leader's ability to draw on her innate character traits and personal history, often involving experiences that lie outside the traditional leadership model.

In "Making Differences Matter: A New Paradigm for Managing Diversity," an article in the *Harvard Business Review*, September–October 1996, Harvard Business School Professor David A. Thomas and Professor Robin J. Ely of Columbia University's School of International and Public Affairs describe the levels of sophistication and effectiveness of three workplace paradigms for managing the talents of a diverse array of leaders. They note that, although efforts to improve effective workplace gender, racial, and ethnic diversity have been underway for decades, it is difficult to identify the actual positive impact of those initiatives in corporate America. This is because those efforts were based on two ineffective paradigms. Models of a corporation's culture can be seen as stages of evolution in its path to using the full range of talent available. Alternatively, these diversity paradigms can be viewed as descriptions of different corporate cultures that may not necessarily be in the process of changing and improving.

The first, the discrimination and fairness paradigm, is the most widespread and the least effective. It stems from the recognition that discrimination is not only wrong, but also generally runs counter to federal Equal Employment Opportunity requirements. The goal of this paradigm is to meet those requirements, and to do so, companies often create mentoring and career development programs tailored specifically for women and minorities. Meeting recruitment and retention requirements to fit this paradigm becomes an end in itself, as does the goal of creating ostensible gender- and color-blind conformism. But the "diverse" employees normally do not rise to positions of leadership proportionate to their numbers. As Thomas and Ely indicate, "The staff, one might say, gets diversified, but the work does not." And individuals' talents are not adequately exploited.

One of the major shortcomings of this model is the myth of the desirability of conformity, which denies all gender, racial, and ethnic differences and assumes assimilation is the goal. For example, three decades ago in the Army, officers discussed seeing only "green" soldiers—whom they viewed by the color of their uniforms, not by their race. Today in the Army and elsewhere, bitterness over supposed political correctness—in which diverse groups exert their own identity and seek commensurate rights and responsibilities—is a product of the false assumption that organizations composed of diverse human talent should desire to create uniform approaches to work and leadership.

The access and legitimacy paradigm takes the opposite tack, celebrating gender, racial, and ethnic differences. Here the goal is to use a diverse workforce to seek access to a more diverse clientele, matching company and consumer demographics. But this paradigm often leaves women and minority employees feeling marginalized or exploited, not truly integrated into the corporate mainstream based on their demonstrated individual personal strengths and potential.

In the third, and in my opinion, more enlightened, approach, the learning and effectiveness paradigm, corporate leaders are proactive in exploiting diversity in their quest to harness employees' strengths and cultural experience. Company leaders make a sincere effort to fight all forms of dominance and subordination (generally based on the presumption that leadership is the prerogative of white men). They encourage people to make explicit use of their personal backgrounds and cultural experience in the workplace. For example, women managers are viewed as soft if they display empathetic support to their employees. In other words, in this paradigm, a woman leader is not encouraged to abandon her authenticity as a woman in order to retain her power as a leader. Equally, members of minorities are encouraged to retain their cultural identity and not split their characters between workplace and community.

Thomas and Ely illustrate this point well in a case study of a large national insurance company in which an African-American woman being groomed for a leadership position faced dismissal just three months after being selected by the manager of her unit, an African-American man. That manager told the vice president investigating the situation he was deeply disappointed with the woman's performance, even though he had been certain she possessed "tremendous leadership skill." It turned out the man knew this woman from church where she was an extremely effective leader in that traditional African-American community setting in which women often fill high leadership positions. When the vice president questioned the woman about the gap between her effectiveness as a community leader and her lack of leadership in the corporate workplace, she replied, "I didn't think I would last long if I acted that way here." She added that her personal leadership style—her authenticity—worked well where she felt free to employ it fully. But she felt constrained, afraid to be herself, in the corporate setting. Having worked for the company for years, she added, "I know this organization, and

I know if I brought that piece of myself—if I became that authentic—I just wouldn't survive here." The vice president, herself a woman who'd had to adapt, recognized the mismatch between this woman's cultural background and the cultural environment of the workplace. She had long seen herself as undervalued in the organization, even though she was a highly valued person in her own community. Both the supervising manager and the vice president began to guide the woman toward drawing on the personal power released by being authentic.

The learning and effectiveness paradigm integrates personal diversity and approaches to work, making explicit use of a person's background and cultural experience. This paradigm's measure of success is how well the company allows employees to draw on their personal assets and perspectives to accomplish their work. People working in this paradigm feel authentic and incorporate their perspectives into the main work of the company.

* * *

As I watch younger women officers assume their well-earned commands, I reflect on my own career and recall the turmoil that accompanied my selection as a battalion commander in the spring of 1985.

I was a recently promoted lieutenant colonel working in a huge office of the Deputy Chief of Staff for Operations and Plans in the Pentagon. About seventy fellow officers and I sat at groups of desks in a windowless maze of gray partitions on the supposedly prestigious E-Ring (but in the inner, less prestigious, part of the corridor), breathing air that, according to Pentagon myth, had been recycled since World War II. In DCSOPS alone, majors and lieutenant colonels numbered in the hundreds, each responsible for a multimillion-dollar "program package." The work was heavily bureaucratic, but filled a vital function in support of the field Army.

I had been a commissioned officer almost sixteen years and could retire four years later as a lieutenant colonel and as a young woman ready to take up a second, civilian career. My professional life was at a crossroads. I awaited a decision by the Army. Selection for battalion command might be next. There was no indication that this splendid possibility was in the offing, however.

Then one March afternoon, I was sitting at my desk after lunch when I got a call from a friend. "Claudia," she whispered, "you've been selected to command a battalion."

I felt a rush of elation such as I had not experienced up to that point or since. "How do you know?" I found myself whispering like a fellow conspirator.

The Department of the Army selection board for fiscal year 1986 for battalion commanders in the combat arms, combat support arms, and combat service support arms had concluded. And my name was on the list.

"Are you absolutely sure?" I asked.

"I'm looking at it," she confirmed.

"Can you get me a copy?"

"Absolutely not." My friend was taking a real chance by revealing this confidential information that had not yet been cleared by the personnel command.

It seemed I would have to wait an indefinite period of time before official notification. But I couldn't help smiling broadly through the rest of the afternoon. And over the coming weeks, I'd feel surges of joy just thinking about this wonderful opportunity. I was going to be a battalion commander, the dream I'd harbored as a young officer ten years before when I'd decided to stay in the Army.

I considered what Military Intelligence battalion the Intelligence and Security Command would assign me. I had experience in Korea, and I'd served as an operations officer at the largest SIGINT operation in Germany—Field Station Augsburg, where a four-battalion brigade was stationed. The unit that most attracted me was Field Station Korea, an independent battalion, still stationed at Pyongtaek. The outfit had its own helicopter detachment and several remote sites along the DMZ. If I got that assignment, I thought I would be well prepared to build on the work of past commanders and to forge productive relationships between tactical and strategic assets.

The actual assignment process after selection for battalion command was called "slating," matching a particular officer's qualifications for the requirements of the command. Officially that process was an objective procedure conducted by Military Intelligence Branch, the Deputy Chief of Staff for Intelligence, and the leadership of INSCOM (Intelligence and Security Command) to determine who fit best where. Since I had previously served in Korea and had spent two years in the Junior Officer Cryptologic Program at the National Security Agency honing my strategic intelligence skills—and much of the responsibility of Field Station Korea was strategic intelligence—I felt I had a reasonable chance of being slated for that coveted assignment. A woman had never commanded that battalion before. In fact, women had commanded only a handful of battalions in the entire Army.

In June, I received word of my official slating. I was to attend pre-command training later that year, before assignment to Field Station Korea. Once more I was elated. The unit was the premier SIGINT battalion in the Army. It had an interesting mission, with a broad range of responsibilities that required unusual operational and logistic skills and I would have much more latitude to lead the battalion.

Then a peculiar event occurred. The lieutenant colonel slated to take command of the Support Battalion at Field Station Augsburg telephoned me one day. "Do you want to trade assignments?" he asked.

I was taken aback by his question. "No," I replied. "I certainly do not."

But he persisted. "Well, if you don't mind, I'm going to make some calls and try to get the trade anyway."

"Look," I said as forcefully as I could, "I *do* mind, and I hope you will *not* try to make the switch."

That was the end of our conversation, which left me uneasy,

even though I felt confident that any phone calls he would make could not upset the formal slating process and deprive me of my assignment to Korea. I was also confident that no change would be considered based on his request without someone calling me and asking my view. In my years in the Army, I had learned that officers operated honorably and didn't lobby for selection to certain assignments when the decision had already been made, unless the other officer affected agreed.

So I was shocked when I called the training people at Fort Devens to review the dates for the pre-command course there, and learned that I would be assigned to Germany, not Korea. "You're not going to Korea, Colonel," an officer insisted. "We've got you down as slated for the Support Battalion at Field Station Augsburg."

I was gripped by simultaneous disappointment and outrage. Somehow, that other lieutenant colonel seemed to have manipulated the system and pulled off this trade against my will. I called INSCOM. They verified what the school personnel at Fort Devens had told me: I was now slated to command a support battalion, not even one of the three SIGINT operations battalions in the Field Station Augsburg Brigade. Further, INSCOM verified that they'd known of this change in slating for some time, but no one had bothered to tell me.

"There's got to be some mistake," I told the INSCOM personnel officer. This was not just denial. I simply didn't believe the Army leadership would become involved in a manipulation of our system.

So I now called the most senior personnel officer in Military Intelligence Branch that I could reach. "Yes, Colonel Kennedy," he verified. "Your slating has been changed to the Support Battalion in Augsburg."

And the phone call confirmed that my fellow officer had indeed secured Field Station Korea. I was disappointed in that officer and in not having been informed by those involved in the decision process, either before or after the change. The time was drawing near for me to begin pre-command training, and it looked as if I'd been undermined by a peer rather than assigned by an objective Army process.

Then a friend, an Infantry officer, called with additional news. He had seen a message sent from Korea to the Military Personnel Center concerning the change in my slating and the reassignment of the other lieutenant colonel to Field Station Korea. The official reason stated in the message was my "gender." Ostensibly, Koreans would not respond to a woman in authority.

"You and I both know that's not fair, Claudia," he said.

"That's for sure."

I'd never had any trouble with my Korean counterparts when I'd served there before. Dealing with Korean officers, they had always respected the mission and our operation, and I had received their full cooperation and complete access to their leadership. My gender had certainly had no negative effect on our professional interaction. And given the mission of Field Station Korea, the battalion probably had the least direct contact with the Korean military of any of the American units stationed in the country. I could have been a green-striped purple gremlin and still effectively commanded the battalion as far as the Koreans were concerned. The issue of gender was utterly irrelevant.

The more I learned about the actual cause for the change in slating, the more unprofessional it seemed. I learned that the officer who had approached me to trade assignments had actively lobbied at INSCOM for the switch and had enlisted the help of some field-grade officers and influential civil servants. This small but powerful clique had acted in a manner not only unfair to me, but to women as a group, and they had certainly not acted in the Army's best interest, but rather on behalf of one individual. My concern only intensified when I considered that the slating process had originally determined that I was better qualified to command the battalion in Korea than the officer who secured that command.

And later that year, I was further disappointed to learn in a phone call to the Military Personnel Center that my slating had been changed yet again, from the Augsburg Support Battalion to the 3rd Operations Battalion. This new battalion had not yet been designated to be assigned "centrally selected" commanders (those chosen by an Army board), but rather by locally designated officers who had not successfully competed Army-wide for selection. Therefore this new assignment was additionally unfair. And, once more, no one had bothered to tell me until I happened to call to discuss my pending transfer.

When I raised this apparently arbitrary slating process with the personnel people in Branch, an irritated colonel told me, "You should feel lucky you've been selected to command."

I'd had it. "You should feel lucky I don't have two lawyers, one on each arm, when I come over there."

The more I thought about these events, the angrier I became, especially as I remembered that happy March afternoon when I'd first heard the news I had been selected to command a battalion. So I decided I could not let these circumstances stand unchallenged. It was too late to redress my own case, but I might be able to prevent this from happening to others by bringing this situation to the attention of my seniors.

In December 1985, I sent a personal, handwritten letter to Major General Harry Soyster, Commander of INSCOM, using this unofficial means of communication not to vent my anger but to make sure that he personally knew the story and that it was not left to just a cabal of colonels and civil servants to make slating decisions. I detailed the events involving my change of slating and did not mince words. Although I cited the official excuse of my gender, I noted that the actual reason was the officer originally slated for the Augsburg Support Battalion had "actively lobbied" among senior military officers and civil servants to have that slating changed. And I protested the manner in which my assignments to Field Station Augsburg had been changed without either consulting or informing me.

"Sir," I continued, "notwithstanding this litany of slating problems, I have always wanted to command and continue to want to command more than any other Army assignment. But I do not wish to command at any cost." I noted that I was an officer who had passed the tests of competence and leadership, but was denied an assignment based on gender, while another received that assignment based on the influence of a clique. I also noted that senior officers who were my raters had offered to intercede, but I had declined their help because I believed officers should serve where they were needed. In this case, however, I concluded, "It is not the Army's needs which have been served, but the needs of a few individuals. And Army values have not been served either."

The letter was a verbal hand grenade with a rather short fuse. It landed on Brigadier General Chuck Scanlon's desk at INSCOM. The officers and civilians at the command knew I'd caught them red-handed doing something outside accepted Army processes. A brigadier general addressed my concerns. "General Soyster got your letter," he assured me. "And I've been assigned to police the battlefield."

In the years since those frustrating months, I've often thought about the dynamics involved in the situation. One lesson has become very clear. Women, including myself, often underestimate the extent to which some men consider institutional or workplace politics a sport, like a hard-played tennis match, or an elbow-digging session of one-on-one basketball. Acing a lieutenant colonel out of her assignment may have seemed perfectly acceptable to this small group, even though they had corrupted the integrity of the Army slating process. Having said this, I should point out that a number of men officers actively objected to the self-serving tactics displayed during my slating process.

My friends in academia and in the private sector tell me there are parallels among their executive colleagues, who often view professional competition as a game in which rules are meant to be bent or broken.

Ironically, however, it is women who have been traditionally seen as forming cliques in an organization, when I think the reverse is probably true. From what I've seen, women value being more disclosing and open at the outset of relationships to provide the largest zone of agreement possible. But this can work against them because the true rules of the game—which may be invisible—might be defined by a very sharply competitive culture in which the other side will take every possible advantage rather than reciprocate openness and honesty. I am certainly not advocating professional women become too defensive. But I do suggest everyone recognize that there are still a lot of men in both the military and private sector workplace who consider them inherently weaker, not just physically, but of softer spirit and character as well.

In the 1970s, there was a cultural debate over whether independent women should allow men to open doors for them. Since then, succeeding generations of young women have matured both with and without the figurative doors of opportunity being opened. But today, women who aspire to high leadership do not find false comfort in the outdated belief that the door to the top will somehow miraculously open. If they want to enter, they will have to open it themselves. However, that door is often blocked, either by implicit institutional policy or simply by inertia. When I attended the Army War College, Jack Welch, then CEO of General Electric, spoke to our class about the importance of diversity in the workplace. His point was that GE embraced diversity—including the advancement of women—because it was good for business, not simply because this was a fair course of action. As more senior corporate leaders adopt his enlightened view, the doorway to executive office and boardroom is certain to open for women.

* * *

I was intrigued by a special report in a November 2000 *Business Week* detailing research that reveals women executives outperformed male peers in a wide variety of categories, including producing high-quality work, goal-setting, and mentoring employees. However, some of the women executives featured in the report with whom I later spoke told me their leadership skills—

especially the empathetic ability to relate well to colleagues and subordinates—had sometimes either been ignored or taken for granted as attributes innate to women.

Women leaders often exercise power differently than men. According to Professor Joyce Fletcher of the Simmons School of Management in Boston, women leaders see their responsibility as having two components, getting the substance of the work done while also creating an environment in which employees can be more productive. But traditional observers usually see these attributes as evidence that the executive is a "nice, thoughtful woman," rather than identifying these attributes as effective leadership skills. But women realize this perception is disempowering and try to avoid the characterization of being too good and considerate. Traditionally, Fletcher says, we confuse women with mothers. "We get *disappeared* as leaders." The problem with this situation is that the definition of competence is very narrow and remains unchallenged in many workplaces. The result is that the "same kinds of people get promoted" and those who were not promoted in the past remain unrecognized.

I agree with Fletcher. From my own experience, preconceived concepts of gender attributes in our leaders color our view of their performance. Here's a small but emblematic example. When I was a brigadier general serving in FORSCOM at Fort McPherson, Georgia, I rotated with other generals officiating at monthly retirement ceremonies. For the retiring NCOs and field-grade officers and their families these occasions—marked by stirring military music—were a tribute to their service to the nation and to the Army we all loved. I always delivered a speech tailored to the careers of the soldiers being honored.

After one ceremony a woman from the audience complimented me on the speech I had just given. "It was so nice that you personalized your speech for each soldier retiring," she said. "A man general would *never* think of doing that."

I thanked her. I did not correct her. But my speech had been written by a man in my office.

Professor Joyce Fletcher recognizes that stereotypes are

slowly disappearing. While old perceptions of gender identity, leadership, and competence went unchallenged for so long, Fletcher and Robin Ely, her colleague at the Center for Gender and Organizations at the Simmons Graduate School of Management, have evolved a fourth paradigm of diversity from the concepts Ely and Thomas developed on the benefits of workplace inclusiveness and diversity. This fourth paradigm is, "What can men learn from women?" By this they mean men executives can become more effective leaders by emulating women. In so doing, the men will have to recognize that effective empathetic skills are not gender-specific. But it's not surprising that many men feel constrained from copying women's skills because in the past men have criticized women who used men's traditional leadership techniques as being less feminine. Those men might see their own use of women's empathetic skills as rendering them less masculine.

For this cultural shift to occur, however, there will, indeed, have to be major attitude changes in the workplace. Traditionally, it was viewed as proper for young men executives to be openly ambitious and their women counterparts to be modest, according to Shirley Ross of the Hagberg Consulting Group. "Women must be seen as working for others rather than for self. To the extent that they are viewed as working for themselves, they are seen as less good, less effective leaders."

There is another important dynamic to consider when comparing women and men leaders. All the women executives I spoke with agreed that women tend to focus more than men on the greater mission and on their own contribution to the larger institution, while men measured their success based on the size of the department they personally controlled. In other words, women set aside their ambitions more readily than men in order to get the job done. Sandra Kiely, Chief Administrative Officer of the National City Investment Company in Cleveland, told me, "Women don't let their egos get in the way of doing what is necessary to achieve the goals." She said that aspiring women leaders "are not very good at tooting their own horns." In the corporate world, this attitude could be viewed as passivity.

But in the Army, we have long fostered a culture in which transparent ambition is not rewarded and teamwork is the norm. Being a good team player is a path that I think civilian leaders, both women and men, can profitably follow and foster in their own organization. Jackie Streeter, Vice President for Engineering at Apple Computer, sees her role as taking a flexible, cooperative approach to achieving company goals. When she saw opportunities to improve team performance, she voluntarily gave up members of her department to other divisions where their functions could be better integrated. She told me that her male colleagues were surprised by her actions. Turf, as assessed by the number of employees assigned to an executive, has long been a measure of corporate success. But this is another of those patterns that will have to change.

"One of the attributes of a leader is to help people realize that change is necessary," she said. "My boss is now very supportive of this attitude. He sees its value and likes it. Now he also has the men shifting people around. This gives him greater flexibility."

* * *

The slating difficulty I encountered in 1985 was well outside the Army's cultural norm. Even at a time when there was still a degree of leadership intervention in officers' assignments, they were not expected to lobby actively for choice positions with the help of a clique. Today, the Army's promotion and assignment boards are so structured that it is virtually impossible for this type of injustice to occur. Officers have to move ahead on their own merits. But I find it disturbing when I meet some who illogically cling to the old attitude that a mentor will manage their careers. This is naive. No one should depend on either a senior woman or man to reach down and pull them up the career ladder. Army officers or civilian executives must achieve power on their own merit, seeking the requisite professional training that entails, and undertaking the assignments that provide the best experience to accumulate leadership skills. Certainly women should demonstrate that they are good team members, but they must manage their own professional lives.

The woman who wants to be protected in the workplace and not fight her own battles when required will never achieve power or be given the chance to demonstrate leadership. For a woman to reach a position of authority, she must show she'll play with the team, but she won't give up when the game gets rough.

During the controversy surrounding my original slating, the major general I worked for, Johnnie J. Johnston, recognized the patent unfairness of the manner in which I had been treated. He offered to intervene on my behalf to have my original slating to Field Station Korea restored. And there is no doubt that his intervention would have succeeded.

"I can call someone and have this fixed," the general told me.

"Thank you for offering to help, sir," I said. But we agreed we would win the battle and lose the war. By that I meant I understood the importance of being a team player with Military Intelligence leadership. Further, I would have, in effect, adopted the same tactics as the officer who had originally approached me for the switch, which I was unwilling to do.

* * *

During my Army career, women friends and acquaintances have often sought my advice on how to deal with challenging or difficult supervisors. But my advice varies on the individual situation. I have often made an assessment that unless the issue involved was a matter of real ethical importance, it was *my* job to adjust to the supervisor. Many times, when I decided to adjust, the decision later proved appropriate, either because my longer experience with the supervisor revealed his strengths (and I acquired important skills I otherwise would have missed) or I became more resilient and internally powerful by deciding that *I* would control my responses even if adversity seemed beyond my control.

I've certainly had my share of *interesting* professional relationships with complex supervisors over the years, ranging from Colonel Charles Black in Korea to Colonel Sam Simerly, my brigade commander in Augsburg. My initial impression of them was that they would be senior officers impossible to please. However, as I forged my self-discipline and met these officers' demands, I grew professionally, and our mission was accomplished better than that of any similar unit because of their leadership. Although their eccentric styles resulted in mission success, however, the cost was high for some people, who gave under the strain and left the Army.

So, in advising both men and women on ways of improving their professional relationships with their bosses (ranging from ideal to impossible), I draw on my Army career to suggest they distance themselves emotionally and consider the following factors:

- Communication: How does the boss prefer to receive and give information? How does this compare to your communication style?
- How work is assigned: Does the boss provide a mission for you to accomplish within a context? Or, rather, does he generate a series of specific tasks?
- Experience: Is the boss experienced in her position and therefore has more concrete views on getting work done? Or is she less experienced and likely to be more flexible and perhaps innovative?
- Personal chemistry: Is the relationship with the boss augmented by friendliness? Or must the two of you overcome lack of personal warmth?

I believe that women more than men often suffer professionally when the interpersonal atmosphere in the workplace deteriorates to the point of animosity and distrust between superior and subordinate. Once, I had presented my views on workplace dynamics to a group of military women, when a field-grade officer approached me. "That really rang true, General," she said. "May I come to talk to you later about a problem I've been having?"

As I expected, the problem involved a personality clash with her boss, who, she said, was trying to exert unreasonable control over her. She had always been used to doing her job independently, roaming freely around her building, where she had cultivated a mutually supportive network of colleagues. But when her new boss arrived, he saw her long absences from the office as a neglecting of her duties. He took away more and more of her responsibilities and autonomy, and an atmosphere of open distrust developed between the two. A bizarre situation ensued. He required that she sign in and out of the office to use the bathroom and go to lunch, although he did not try to exert this type of stringent control over any of the other officers or civilian employees he supervised.

When the situation became intolerable, the officer went to her boss's senior officer, ostensibly to tell him the whole unhappy story. The problem was, however, that she did not relate enough detail and only told him in effect, "We're not working well together."

Like many women, she was trying to resolve a serious conflict (analogous to my earlier slating difficulties) without admitting just how serious the conflict was. I think one of the reasons women do this—especially in cases involving bizarre circumstances such as these—is that they think that they won't be believed, that people will look at them as if *they* are the problem. After all, in our culture, the woman complainer is a pejorative figure of near legendary proportions. In *Men Are from Mars, Women Are from Venus,* John Gray says that men panic when women start talking because they're afraid the women will never shut up. Women learn this lesson young: Don't talk too much; above all, don't complain. Be grateful. Accept what you're given.

But there are often times when a woman cannot accept inappropriate behavior on the part of a supervisor, who, for the sake of this argument, is almost always a man. Too often women think if they adjust, the man's behavior will change. What they don't realize is that his behavior is *not* a reaction to her. The man will act as he pleases anyway, unless he is challenged.

Although they certainly do not like their position, many women silently accept it because they feel they have no control, that men have manipulated events to their own advantage. In reality, I believe it is often that very attitude that keeps women in such a position either in the military or civilian workplace. The lower the expectations, the lower the achievement. If women expect to remain in subordinate positions, everyone around them will expect the same thing.

This diminished level of women's expectations relates to the differences between the sense of professional entitlement men and women experience. Men generally feel entitled to advance as high as a combination of talent and connections will permit. Women usually feel entitled to advance only up to, but still short of, the limit of their talent as defined by the system in which they find themselves.

A telling example of this pattern occurred when I attended a dinner meeting organized by a male colonel who invited me and two field-grade women officers, the purpose of which was to discuss an upcoming leadership conference. Toward the end of dinner, he asked one of the women whether she wanted to attend the conference. Her answer was, "Do you want me to be there?" He explained they needed help with a number of topics, and repeated the invitation. Again she asked, "Do you want me to come?" After a third such exchange, I interrupted, and said, "Yes. He wants you there. We all want you there."

She had been a pioneer in a branch that had long excluded women and had no experience of feeling entitled. It was clear from later conversations that she did not even hear the colonel's repeated explicit invitations to participate in the conference. Although she wanted to advance professionally, her cumulative experience had taught her she had no right to expect inclusion.

But today it is not enough to say to our young women that all they have to do is hold the expectation of advancing to top leadership and they will do so. Both military and civilian institutions have to continue to expand the diversity of their leadership paradigms (as has GE's Jack Welch) to demonstrate that they value women's leadership style equally with men's. As this additional leadership paradigm evolves, a parallel evolution in women's sense of professional entitlement should also occur.

Traditionally, of course, often the reason women are not well represented in the most senior positions is that they, unlike men, have no one to whom to pass responsibility for family life. The negative impact of the Mommy Track on advancement to senior executive has been well documented in business literature. But there is a new pattern emerging. As women acquire valuable and marketable skills, their status as wives and mothers becomes much less important to their employers than their professional accomplishments.

* * *

There is, of course, a productive and fulfilling middle ground for lower-level professional women, both military and civilian, who wish to balance career and family. The library and bookstore shelves are full of advice books on how women can or should walk this difficult tightrope. The reality today is that both these approaches are outdated. Most professional women who have talked to me about their careers also want to find a more balanced life. What they need is practical information on how to manage both.

As a military commander, I began discussing this, after drawing on my own approach as a younger woman thinking about the pivotal choices I faced.

A married twenty-seven-year-old captain with five years' service came to see me to discuss her future. She was an excellent officer with solid OERs who had a promising future in the Army. Married to another well-qualified career officer, she wanted to decide whether to continue in the Army or resign to pursue a civilian career and have children. To make such a decision, it helped her to visualize how she might construct a twenty-year career during which she would advance to the rank of colonel while also raising two children. This was an ambitious objective, and one that would require real cooperation from her husband and self-discipline.

Although they were currently assigned together at Fort Huachuca, it was likely she would be selected for Command and General Staff College at her eleventh year of service on promotion to major. That was an excellent time, I told her, to have her first child. But this might mean she would be separated from her husband during the pregnancy and birth. As we worked further along the timeline, we anticipated she could achieve battalion command as a lieutenant colonel at about sixteen years of service. After that command, it would be appropriate for her to have her second and final child. That baby would then be old enough to comfortably leave in child care during her time at the War College, which was a precursor to brigade command. The timing of these events all fit together so that both her and her husband's retirement as colonels would coincide with the entry of their first child into college.

This, of course, was not easy, especially during a period of frequent deployments when both might expect to be assigned overseas with little notice. Nevertheless, she has chosen a profession that requires unusual levels of self-discipline. And if she is going to succeed in balancing her personal and professional lives, she will have to become a master of timing and flexibility.

* * *

As I was promoted into positions of higher authority, I sometimes found what I consider to be an inappropriate level of curiosity about my personal life among my colleagues and some of my soldiers. It was known that I was a divorced woman who dated men, and I guess that was just too intriguing for the gossips to leave alone. So I completely separated my personal and professional lives because I knew, as unfair as it was, that women lose authority if their personal lives become too openly discussed in the workplace.

We all need a circle of confidants, and I'm no exception. But I cultivated that circle of close friends well away from the people I commanded or in my immediate office. And if there were one piece of professional advice I could give to aspiring women leaders it would be to maintain a clear distance between their personal and professional identities. The popular entertainment industry today has gotten this message dead wrong, with TV shows such as *Ally McBeal* in which a purportedly successful young lawyer who possesses no personal boundaries discusses her most intimate secrets nonstop throughout the office. This doesn't work in real life.

* * *

At DCSOPS in the Pentagon, when I first learned I'd been selected for battalion command, I had felt some apprehension considering the demands of leadership. I was a short, rather slender person. No one would ever mistake me for square-jawed General William Westmoreland or "Stormin' Norman" Schwartzkopf. Army command involves a combination of leadership, considerable intellectual work, and substantive mission knowledge. But beyond this, traditionally there has been required a certain military bearing and presence. Would the soldiers in my battalion respect my authority and be proud of me as their new commander?

In a private counseling session for me as a newly selected battalion commander, I mentioned my concern to my boss in DCSOPS, a highly respected infantry colonel named Steve Arnold, who later retired as a lieutenant general.

"I'm just afraid my troops won't be proud of me, Colonel," I said. "I'm not the usual male leader with the broad shoulders, narrow hips, and the steely gaze you associate with command."

Colonel Arnold smiled. "Once your soldiers get to know you, Claudia, you'll be just fine."

His prediction proved accurate. And when I got to Augsburg, I also followed the advice given in pre-command training on how one introduces oneself to the new battalion. In the first two days I walked the entire area, including the operations floor staffed by my battalion during all three daily shifts, and when the fourth shift rotated onto duty a few days later, I also visited them. All the soldiers had a chance to meet their commander and engage in an informal exchange. In later detailed briefings with warrant officers and NCOs, I learned the full scope of our mission and our degree of success. Meeting with my company commanders, their first sergeants, and the battalion staff, I posed three basic questions: What were we doing well? What were we doing badly? What did they want me, the new commander, not to screw up by changing?

I knew the impression I made on my soldiers in these first few days was extremely important. A leader sets the tone of command unconsciously through appearance, sense of purpose, and communication style. If a new commander is sloppy or disorganized, the unit will follow that newly lowered standard.

A few days after my individual meeting with Colonel Arnold, Major General Tom Tait, another respected Infantry leader, addressed newly selected battalion commanders as a group. "Within three days of your arrival, your battalion will reflect your personality." I found his insight invaluable and believe it's a lesson all leaders, both military and civilian, can apply to their organizations.

* * *

Surmounting the problems of a stressful workplace dominated by a complex and sometimes difficult boss is never easy. But I know from personal experience that it is essential to maintain one's habits of self-discipline during such trying times. In 1986, I was among the first women to command a battalion in

Military Intelligence. The fact that I took command of the 3rd Operations Battalion at Field Station Augsburg under the acrimonious circumstances of the slating controversy certainly did not help the initial relationship with my brigade commander, Colonel Sam Simerly. On the other hand, given our difference, I might have arrived completely free of controversy and still rubbed him the wrong way. Professional relationships within the brigade were convoluted. Although Colonel Simerly was one of the best managers I have ever worked for, and I later employed many of his management techniques when I commanded a Military Intelligence brigade, he was an inconsistent leader.

In my opinion, Colonel Simerly also found it useful to pit his officers against each other, to keep them off balance, rather than try to form a cohesive team. He convened the four battalion commanders (three men and me), and warned us bluntly, "I have to spread my ratings." This was an uncomfortable, one-sided discussion because the Officer Efficiency Reports would have a critical impact on our future careers. We all knew that the Army expected him to distribute his ratings recommendations over a roughly diamond-shaped hierarchy with no more than one in the top block.

But I felt it was inappropriate for him to emphasize the "block check" of the rating rather than the standards against which he would judge our performance. In effect, he was inviting us to lobby for ourselves, to make our personal case to him why each deserved that top rating.

It was not the task of professional officers, however, to put themselves forward to win their commander's favor. I did not intend to do so. Rather, I would do my job to the best of my ability and try not to think about OERs. In this regard, none of the other battalion commanders had an obvious advantage, but the colonel did apparently see me—someone who had complained about the slating changes—as a likely candidate for his average rating. I knew I was the odd "man" out in Colonel Simerly's mind.

Still, the Army had given me this battalion to command, and

once I formed the productive partnership with Command Sergeant Major Gant, we concentrated on the mission. It was a job I knew fairly well, having served in the brigade as assistant operations officer and later operations officer from 1981 to 1984.

To deal with the stress, I maintained the discipline of regular running. And I was pleased that many of the battalion staff officers and NCOs followed my example and ran as the Army advocated. Several months into my command, I'd often see groups of lean young officers and NCOs running for the sheer pleasure of the exercise.

But my professional relationship with Colonel Simerly never improved. Despite the fact that my battalion always accomplished its intelligence mission and met all Army training requirements, I sensed an undercurrent of dissatisfaction. I learned to keep silent and not rise to any bait. When I realized his discontent was more personally than professionally directed, I focused on accomplishing the battalion's mission and making certain our soldiers had the best quality of life possible. Still, Colonel Simerly's reaction to my performance ran hot and cold. This unpredictability was an unpleasant factor in my life for a year.

One of the most egregious incidents between us happened about nine months into my command. The 3rd Operations Battalion had a small, remote site in Schleswig-Holstein in the far north of West Germany, close to the East German border. The inspection of the site was a big event for the soldiers involved because both their battalion and brigade commanders were coming at the same time.

But I had long been concerned about the isolation these young soldiers had to endure in this bleak, windswept countryside near the Baltic. They were far from any other American unit, and their main recreation was beer drinking at the local village Gasthaus. This might seem innocent enough, but German beer has much higher alcohol content than American beer, and is also often served in big one-liter steins. The unit's first sergeant, Becky Hibbs, had told me she was worried that some of the soldiers were showing signs of drinking problems, a situation of which Colonel Simerly was well aware.

The night after our inspection, the colonel, First Sergeant Hibbs, all the troops who were not on duty, and I went to the local Gasthaus for dinner. The food was excellent, as one might expect. And behind the bar, there were several embossed mugs and plaques revealing that some of our soldiers had become champions in local drinking competitions. These were events in which the last person literally standing after hours of swilling beer was the winner. Colonel Simerly thought this was a splendid achievement. I began discussing the problem of chronic drinking, night after night, with the young NCOs at the long plank table.

But the colonel, who was enjoying the beer himself that night, loudly interrupted me. "Claudia," he said, "I don't agree with you at all about cutting back on these soldiers' beer. After all, they don't have much else to do up here."

I was dumbfounded. First, I was the battalion commander and he was publicly undermining my authority, something an Army leader should never do. Secondly, that was a terrible message to give those soldiers, who certainly needed no further encouragement.

But after he spoke out, I saw a hard glint in his eye. I believe he wanted me to start an argument in front of these soldiers. Instead, I remained silent.

Driving back to the quarters, First Sergeant Hibbs told me, "Ma'am, I couldn't believe that Colonel Simerly spoke to you that way."

"Don't worry, First Sergeant," I assured her. "Everything will be fine with the battalion. And don't worry about me, either. I'm tough."

This was true enough. I continued to focus on my job. But as Colonel Simerly had warned us, he spread out his Officer Efficiency Reports, forming a pyramid with a narrow point. In my OER, he skillfully damned me with faint praise, precluding any recourse on my part to have the rating removed based on more objective evidence of my performance. By the end of that year, I was fairly sure I no longer had a good chance for promotion, attending the Army War College, or selection for brigade command.

Although Colonel Edwin Tivol, my new brigade commander, and I had a positive professional relationship and he wrote favorable OERs on my performance, I thought the damage of Simerly's ratings had already been done. One cold gray afternoon in the winter of 1988 when I was nearing the end of my battalion command and thinking longingly of a warm-climate assignment, I called the Military Personnel Center to enquire about openings at the NATO Defense College in Naples, Italy.

"Those assignments are all filled for the next three years," the officer said.

So I asked MILPERCEN what kind of assignment they had in mind for me next. They offered three staff jobs outside my specialty, including an assignment as an imagery analyst.

I had no interest in any of these, but, in the Army, you either went where you were assigned, or you got out. As much as I regretted this option, I had to face reality. "What is the earliest date I can retire?" I asked the MILPERCEN officer.

"Don't worry," he said. "We'll find you the right job. What kind of assignment would you like?"

"I'd like to command a recruiting battalion," I said, realizing the request might seem unusual. But I'd always loved recruiting and recognized its importance to the Army's future.

"That's impossible," the officer said. "We have a shortage of field-grade officers in MI and we have to keep them in the branch."

It looked as if my Army service would end after twenty years.

But a week later, that MILPERCEN officer called back to ask if I was still interested in commanding a recruiting battalion. "We're underrepresented in women and minorities, so we would like to put your name on the slate to compete for a battalion, if you're still interested."

"I'm still interested."

It looked as if I might be staying in the Army after all.

I was selected for command of that battalion and worked harder than I ever have before or since. And while I commanded the battalion, I was promoted to full colonel, chosen to attend the Army War College, and selected to command the 703rd Military Intelligence Brigade in Hawaii.

Reflecting on those roller-coaster years, one important lesson becomes obvious. When I began to be treated in an unjust manner during my battalion slating, I took a stand. Although this action undoubtedly antagonized my first brigade commander, Colonel Simerly, what I had done did not harm me in the eyes of those Army leaders who understood the true dynamics of the situation. And the fact that I served in Augsburg under difficult circumstances with quiet self-discipline undoubtedly did not go unnoticed.

The reason I go into detail about these matters is to make it clear that no one can spend a thirty-two-year career completely free of conflict. And often that conflict poses crippling threats to one's career. We cannot control when those conflicts will arise and which military seniors or executive supervisors they will involve. But we can control our reaction to these serious differences.

One habit of self-discipline that I have cultivated is to maintain a sense of humor upon which I could draw during times of tension, even if only internally. Putting the relationship with the troublesome supervisor in perspective is also another successful tactic: Even though he might seem to loom large at the time, remember that you have literally scores of additional professional relationships that give balance to his one negative viewpoint.

6

Loyalty and Ethics

As I've noted, there were several times in my Army career when an unexpected phone call brought fortuitous news: my early promotion to major and my later selection to battalion command. In late 1979 I also got a call from a friend announcing that I had been selected to attend the Command and General Staff College at Fort Leavenworth, Kansas.

I was working at my desk in the National Security Agency one Friday morning when the phone rang.

"Congratulations, Claudia," my friend said.

"What for?" I asked, puzzled at his tone.

"You're going to CGSC. I just read the list in *The Army Times*."

Attending the Command and General Staff College was considered an important milestone in a young field-grade Army officer's career. Moreover, those majors and lieutenant colonels who did not attend CGSC stood very little chance of commanding a battalion, of reaching the rank of full colonel, or of later being considered for promotion to general officer. Since I started work at the NSA, a succession of assignment officers had told me that I was in the top third of my peer group.

Now I had confirmation that my persistence and hard work had in fact been recognized.

I was glad to be attending the college because CGSC had long been an Army tradition. Although Infantry, Armor, and Artillery officers formed the majority of each class, a much smaller percentage of officers from the other Army branches, from the Reserve components, other services, a few U.S. government civilians, and officers known as Allied Officers from abroad rounded out the student body.

The Command and General Staff College was an integral part of the Army's professional development system. And we knew that the Army was an honorable institution that had weathered the harshly disillusioning years of the Vietnam War and was struggling to rebuild itself on a foundation of professional excellence, discipline, and integrity. These were all Army attributes that had suffered during the long conflict in Indochina, as they had throughout the American government, including the national security system.

I wanted to play my part, however small it might prove to be, in the Army's recovery from Vietnam. Working with my peers at CGSC to increase our level of professionalism presented one such small opportunity to meet that responsibility.

* * *

Fort Leavenworth, Kansas, on the wooded limestone banks of the Missouri River near Kansas City, was an old frontier post, dating from the Indian Wars of the 1820s, and probably best known to civilians as the site of the nearby U.S. penitentiary. The Army had established the School of Application of Infantry and Cavalry at the fort in 1881 to educate officers on modern tactics. But early in the twentieth century, a more formal and complex curriculum, based on the European general staff model, was created with the establishment of the General Service and Staff College, which later evolved into the CGSC. The mission of the college was to form future leaders by educating them through a rigorous program that followed the case-method study technique common to many business graduate programs.

My class assembled to begin the course in early August 1980. There was a lot of discussion generated because this was the college's centennial year. I was one of only fifteen women out of 983 total students. (In the class of 2001, there are ninety-one women out of a total of 1,054 students.) But I'd long grown accustomed to being in the minority in that regard. The class was divided into sections, each containing approximately sixty students. The women and forty-eight Allied Officers were distributed evenly among the sections, which were further broken down into work groups and two-officer teams of tablemates. I was in Section 12. My tablemate was an Egyptian Army lieutenant colonel named Abdel Siam, a soft-spoken, kindly man with a halting command of English, who had the distinction of having been taken prisoner of war by the Israelis twice in the same war. Despite his gentle manner, Lieutenant Colonel Siam held several decorations for valor and had experience as a combat leader.

The curriculum centered on classroom lectures and tactical exercises known as "problems," which might last a morning, or continue for several days. Some of them involved relatively simple map exercises in which work groups had to deploy hypothetical forces in either defensive or offensive operations. Other problems were more elaborate, pitting teams of opponents against each other on wide, three-dimensional tabletop terrain models, over which we maneuvered miniature tanks and artillery pieces, all the while observed by the instructor umpires who had given the requirements of the particular battle scenario and assigned us our objectives and restrictions. This classroom wargaming bore no resemblance to playing toy soldier because we realized our instructors' silent scrutiny and after-action reviews reflected their interest in finding new solutions to old tactical problems and gaining insights into new techniques under development in the field and now displayed in our performance of these exercises. They were interested as much in why as in what we did and continually quizzed us on our intent.

A major purpose of these exercises was to help an officer to think beyond traditional branch limits. For example, an Infantry major might have acquired a great deal of experience commanding a rifle company in the jungles of Vietnam as a captain, but knew little about positioning an armored cavalry troop for a desert defense. I, as a Military Intelligence officer specializing in strategic cryptology, had no firsthand experience of tactics. Yet I had to take my turn with my section mates, one day role-playing as the G-3 operations officer of an infantry division, the next, struggling to understand the ammunition shortages a field artillery battalion might face in protracted mobile combat.

Although the college was meant to offer a well-rounded curriculum, with adequate independent study time and intramural sports such as basketball, running, and soccer, there was a steady regimen of testing and written exercises, much more rigorous than earlier service schools I had attended. And the faculty always stressed that we write in "clear, concise English."

Unfortunately, the spoken and written English of my pleasant Egyptian tablemate, Lieutenant Colonel Siam, was neither clear nor concise. I realized he had not been chosen to attend the college as an Allied Officer, one of three Egyptians to do so that year, based on his command of English. Rather, he was walking, talking testimony to the fact that the United States and Egypt had mended fences since President Anwar Sadat had made peace with Israel and sent the massive Soviet military assistance mission packing. Lieutenant Colonel Siam also proved to be a popular officer at CGSC because he readily shared what he knew about the tactics involving Soviet-built T-72 main battle tanks and BMP armored personnel carriers and associated Soviet Army battle doctrine. This was an invaluable addition to class discussion, and everyone loved to hear this detailed lore, especially because many of the officers had trained for years to face such Soviet forces in the Fulda Gap in Germany. However, he had a propensity for pointing to the red-tinted portions of the map indicating East Bloc forces and saying "We." When he did so, the class rowdies would begin to boo and hiss.

"No, Colonel Siam," I would whisper. "You say 'They.'"

Lieutenant Colonel Siam would often find it convenient to leave the classroom for one of his five periodic daily prayers, which he had informed us were the solemn duty of every devout Muslim. He also told us he would meet with other Muslim officers in a quiet room in the building where they would spread their prayer rugs, perform their ablutions, and face Mecca. But some in the work group began to complain to our leader, a laconic Armor major named Chuck Piker, that Lieutenant Colonel Siam's self-summoning to prayer invariably coincided with some demanding task in the classroom. "We think he's just smokin' and jokin' until it's time for lunch or the end of class," they said.

Chuck Piker, who'd served in the Infantry in Vietnam, was not one to observe diplomatic nuance. The next time Lieutenant Colonel Siam announced he was leaving to perform one of his mandatory daily prayers, Chuck Piker stood up and pointed to the front of the classroom where a chalkboard could serve as a screen. "You knock out those prayers right here," he ordered. Unflustered, Lieutenant Colonel Siam did not again attempt to escape class under the guise of religious devotion.

He had no escape from the inevitable classroom tests and quizzes. Early in the semester, he turned to me with a sweet, rather sheepish smile that had replaced the tangled frown through which he had regarded the test paper before him on the table.

"Claudia," he whispered, "you give me the answers."

I looked up in surprise. The instructors had been very clear about the inflexible honor code that was part of the long tradition of the Command and General Staff College. Our orientation had emphasized the absolute necessity of integrity as a basic principle of military discipline. And that principle was centered on trust and *self*-discipline. Professional soldiers—both officers and NCOs—had to trust each other. Their word had to be based on a core of honor. We did not have time to check up on each other in our profession. We could not tolerate those who lied or cheated.

Now this naive foreign officer was asking me to break the honor code right here in the classroom. "Colonel Siam," I said, "that's called cheating."

His face broke into a radiant smile because I had enriched his vocabulary. "Cheating," he said, testing the new word. "Okay, Claudia, let me cheat from you."

"No," I insisted. "That would not be right."

"Why not, Claudia?" he asked, crestfallen. "You come to my country and you need water, I give it to you. You need food, I give it to you, whatever I have. I open my house for you to sleep. I come to your country, you give me answers."

I managed to resolve this situation with the knowledge of the faculty, who recognized Lieutenant Colonel Siam's language difficulties, and allowed me to act as his unofficial tutor during quizzes. But I always wrote that I had shared answers with him on the top of each test paper on which I had done so. And I always signed that statement, so that there could be no question that I was trying to breach the honor code. In this manner, the faculty had found a way for me to be loyal both to a foreign colleague who did not want to feel excluded from his American peers and to the Army's ethics.

*　*　*

As one of the course requirements later that year, we were all required to write a research paper. This certainly was not a very challenging assignment; the paper only had to be about ten pages, but we were required to follow the standard format, using several sources referenced with footnotes. The instructors made it clear that we had to place any cited verbatim material from the sources within quotation marks and so identify it with our footnotes. Any lowering of this standard, they said, would be considered plagiarism, a breach of the honor code.

The faculty also told us to read the papers on our chosen topic from those written by previous sections, which were on file, so that we could see how those students had treated the material.

As the assigned topics were the same for all of us, this advice made sense. I read a number of the papers and closely reviewed the source material we were all required to use. I had picked up some good insights on how to proceed when I turned to a paper written by an officer from another service. There was something about his language that seemed unusually familiar. On a hunch, I compared his paper to the sources he had used and which I had earlier read.

There were several large sections of his paper where the language had been lifted verbatim, word-for-word, paragraph-for-paragraph, from these sources without quotation marks or attribution. Nor had he made any attempt to indicate that this material was anything other than his original ideas. This was clearly a case of plagiarism, and a clumsy one at that.

My first reaction was vexation rather than outrage. *I wish I didn't know this,* I thought. But my dilemma was that I had, in fact, discovered a glaring example of plagiarism and I had to decide what to do with this information. It would have been so much easier if the instructors who graded the papers had discovered this themselves. But for whatever reason—probably the press of work and the blurring familiarity of the often cited passages—the offense had escaped them. Now the officer who had plagiarized and I were apparently the only two people at CGSC who knew what he had done.

And it also would have been very easy for me to let the situation remain that way. In fact, I was torn. Nobody enjoys reporting a wrongdoing, especially by one of our peers. The person caught suffers professionally, and, like it or not, the person taking the moral stance is often singled out as being overly judgmental. It certainly did not help that I was one of a small handful of women in the class, and the officer who plagiarized was a man from another service. Although I did not view this as a gender issue in any way, I could see how some might see me as being too moralistic.

We women officers were already well aware that some of our classmates, and indeed some on the faculty, tolerated our presence with ill-concealed resistance. They refused to consider the hard work and dedication that had brought us to Fort Leaven-worth and felt we were "taking a man's place" at CGSC. At the Wednesday noon guest lecturer series, almost every speaker found something negative to say about the increasing role of women in the Army even though he could look out and clearly see fifteen women officers in the audience. Sometimes afterward, we would meet in the ladies' room to discuss this situation. One of my colleagues, a tall, slender nurse, always wore her uniform with slacks rather than the skirt and kept her hair short, a con-scious attempt to blend into the male-dominated environment. But most of us refused to surrender our individuality. We were both women and professional soldiers.

While some resisted our presence, others did not. Although most of our men classmates at CGSC did not consider women their peers, they in fact held a spectrum of attitudes. Some clung to the old WAC-era "separate-but-equal" mentality (which never resulted in equality), similar to the racially segregated military before the Korean War. And now, although blacks were com-pletely integrated, many soldiers considered women almost a separate race in the Army. Other of our peers conceded that we had a limited contribution to make in a few branches, such as the Finance Corps, the Nurse Corps, and the Quartermaster Corps. By 1981, I had, however, met many other officers with a more enlightened attitude who believed that if women did well in a branch such as Military Intelligence, why shouldn't they advance in other branches such as the Signal Corps or Aviation? To me, these officers represented the best of the Army's future leaders.

But the future Army we discussed in the classroom would have to have a solid grounding of ethics. In the CGSC orienta-tion lectures of 1980, the faculty stressed themes of professional rigor and ethical integrity. Unspoken in this message was the subtext that the Army's professional standards had fallen during the Vietnam era. After 1969, when America's stated policy was to withdraw its forces and turn the war over to our South Viet-namese allies, discipline among many U.S. units had deteriorated. Incidents of "fraggings," in which soldiers murdered their officers or NCOs with fragmentation grenades, rose in this period, as did drug use; racial tensions and open strife became a problem. Still, American combat troops in Vietnam had to continue engaging a dangerous and dedicated enemy—Vietcong guerrillas or the North Vietnamese Army regulars often dressed in the black pajama-like garb of peasants—whom Americans could not differentiate from civilians. In some brigades strict Rules of Engagement were blurred, and the overuse of artillery and air strikes led to needless civilian casualties, an ethical nightmare that was then compounded when all the dead Vietnamese bodies found at the battle site were listed as enemy combatants, sometimes with a collusive nod and wink up the chain of command from the rifleman grunt in the jungle to the colonel in command. Many historians have indicated that, probably more than any other single factor, this reliance on body count as an indicator of success during a war of attrition—in which the traditional capture and holding of territory meant little—led to the ethical abuses and splintering of leadership that weakened the Army in Vietnam.

During my first ten years of service, I'd met enough combat veterans of that war who had provided grotesque firsthand accounts of illegal acts they had either witnessed or initiated. Some of these stories may have been warped bravado, meant to impress. But other descriptions had the anguished taste of confessional truth: a village shelled because a lone sniper had fired from a banana grove; an unarmed farmer machine-gunned in a rice paddy to avenge a helicopter crewman killed a few days before in another district. While investigations during and since the war have shown that such events were neither systematic nor universal, they were pervasive enough to negatively affect the Army's good order and discipline.

But there was no doubt that the Army was recovering from Vietnam by 1980. Major General Max Thurman took over the Army's Recruiting Command and dramatically raised the educational standards of enlistees in the All-Volunteer Force. Thurman would go on to help build the training center system, where the Army's newly equipped heavy and light units honed their fighting skills to the edge of devastating perfection revealed during the Panama operation (which he commanded) and Operation Desert Storm.

In 1980, however, the Army was still figuratively kicking the mud of Vietnam off its boots, working to form a new generation of leaders. These were my peers in the Command and General Staff College's centennial class. Most of the Army officers had seen combat in Vietnam as younger men. They had endured the unthinkable suffering of war, then been demoralized when the cause for which they and their soldiers had struggled and bled ended with the stampede off the roofs of Saigon in April 1975 as the last American helicopters fled the victorious North Vietnamese tanks. But to me, the most amazing aspect of my peers at Command and General Staff College was not that they had become disillusioned by their experiences in Vietnam and lost their moral and ethical compasses, but how few seemed to have suffered these emotional wounds. They were strong, whole, effective leaders, often mature beyond their years.

As I wrestled with the dilemma of whether to report the plagiarizing, I remembered the famous passage from the anti-Nazi German religious leader Martin Niemoller: "All it takes for evil to exist in the world is for good people to say nothing." Obviously, it was an impossibly long stretch from the complaisant villagers of Dachau ignoring the unpleasant smoke from the chimney down the road to reporting a lazy, cheating student at CGSC.

But then I began to make some connections. Many of the ethical lapses in Vietnam had been passive rather than overt. We had asked our soldiers to fight a cruel and elusive enemy who resorted to terrorism and assassination to control the population. For example, the North Vietnamese Army massacred approximately 3,000 unarmed civilian government officials, South Vietnamese Army prisoners, intellectuals, and clergymen in Hue during the 1968 Tet offensive. Yet we required that our Army not sink to the enemy's methods but instead conduct all its operations strictly according to the Law of Land Warfare of the Geneva Convention of 1949. Nor could they officially punish the pro-Vietcong peasants who planted booby traps or laid land mines along their paddy dikes used as trails. But when individual soldiers did sometimes strike back without authorization, their superiors might abet the criminal act through their silence.

One Army unit faced with the harsh frustrations and hatred this guerrilla warfare engendered, a component of Task Force Barker—C Company, 1st Battalion, 20th Infantry Brigade, 23rd Infantry (American) Division—broke under the stress on March 16, 1968, at a hamlet in Quang Ngai Province called My Lai. On a search-and-destroy operation, the soldiers were ordered to sweep through the multiple hamlets of Son My village and roll up the 48th Local Force Vietcong Battalion, a tough enemy guerrilla unit that had killed five and wounded fifteen of C Company's soldiers with mines, booby traps, and snipers since the Americans deployed for combat that January. The soldiers sought vengeance for their dead and wounded friends. And their officers, Task Force commander Lieutenant Colonel Frank Barker and company commander Captain Ernest Medina, assured them that the only Vietnamese they would encounter in the Son My village complex on the morning of March 16 would be Vietcong from the hated 48th Local Force Battalion.

Human intelligence gleaned from the CIA's Phoenix Program, which relied on the dubious information of Vietcong prisoners and deserters, indicated all the village's innocent noncombatant older men, women, and children would have "gone to market" by the time the Charlie Company troops swept into My Lai hamlet at 0730. Significantly, the later Army investigation revealed Military Intelligence officers in the 11th Brigade and Americal Division discounted this information, but for whatever reason—inertia, disinterest, overwork—did not protest the false Phoenix Program intelligence assumptions on which Task Force Barker's search-and-destroy operations plan was based.

So Captain Medina and one of his platoon leaders, First

Lieutenant William Calley, told their soldiers that the village of My Lai was a "VC stronghold," Medina noting that they should expect "a hell of a good fight," and that they had orders from superior authority to completely destroy the hamlet, including houses, livestock, and any enemy who resisted. Since the soldiers had already been briefed that innocent civilians would have left the village before the Americans arrived, most of the troops believed they would face only the 48th Local Force Battalion and its civilian auxiliaries in the warren of thatched huts and tangled banana and litchi groves.

When Lieutenant Calley's 1st Platoon entered My Lai, they came firing their M-16 rifles on full automatic and pounded bursts of M-60 machine gun fire through the thin walls of the houses. Soldiers threw grenades into the villagers' shallow bomb shelter bunkers. As civilians ran down the muddy lanes, clutching children, ducks, and pigs, they were cut down in their tracks. A number of those who did surrender were herded out of the village to an irrigation ditch, where Calley gave the order for them to be machine-gunned. After about four hours of chaotic murder, almost 500 Vietnamese civilians were dead, all old men, women, and children.

Calley radioed Captain Medina that he had encountered the enemy in a sharp firefight and accounted for approximately 125 "enemy Killed in Action," a very respectable body count.

But before Calley's unit could move on to the next hamlet, Warrant Officer Hugh C. Thompson, Jr., flying a Light Observation helicopter near My Lai, was shocked to see Americans slaughtering civilians. Thompson landed his aircraft and argued with the American troops, eventually hovering to land again and place the helicopter between the cowering Vietnamese and the U.S. troops and ordering his door gunner and crew chief to threaten the Americans with weapons if they continued to menace the civilians. Thompson managed to shepherd the handful of survivors to safety and even retrieved a wounded child from a heap of dead bodies near an irrigation ditch. Effectively, he and his crew's action brought an end to the worst American atrocity of the Vietnam War.

Thirty years later, in 1998, Hugh Thompson and his surviving door gunner, Lawrence Colburn, were awarded the prestigious Soldiers Medal by Major General Michael W. Ackerman (later a lieutenant general and the Inspector General of the Army), himself a former Americal Division combat helicopter pilot, in a ceremony at the Vietnam Veterans Memorial in Washington. General Ackerman cited Thompson's and Colburn's loyalty to the Army's values of courage and sacrifice as having set "the standard" on a day that was "one of the most shameful chapters in the Army's history."

For almost a year after the My Lai massacre, the leadership of the Americal Division tried to cover up the massacre. And it was only when a soldier with firsthand knowledge of the horrible event returned to the States and contacted the news media did the cover-up unravel. Then the Army acted quickly, naming Lieutenant General William R. Peers to lead an investigation commission. The Peers Commission broke open the rotten core of the cover-up. A large criminal investigation ensued, but the only officer ever convicted was Lieutenant William Calley, who served about three years' house arrest of a life sentence for murder before President Richard Nixon pardoned him.

I had read about My Lai and of Hugh Thompson's heroism before coming to CGSC. To me Lieutenant General William Peers, who led the investigation commission, was also a heroic figure. It would have been easy for him to quash the inquiry and effectively spare the Army the protracted anguish of the long court-martial's media circus. But Peers was a decorated combat veteran of three wars who felt a deep sense of loyalty to the Army as a vital, ethical American institution. He knew that the massacre at My Lai had been an aberration so far beyond the scale of smaller illegalities that the act had to be excised from the flesh of the Army like a cancer or it might devour the service from within. Peers was an officer who placed loyalty to the Army and faith in its future beyond Vietnam above all else.

* * *

Civilians sometimes misunderstand the Army's culture of hierarchy, discipline, and authority. Perhaps the cause can be found in clumsy Hollywood depictions of Army life in which the arrogant senior officer swaggers to the conclusion of a monologue delivered to silent subordinates with the words, "And that's an order."

This is just not how command works in the Army. There is a great deal of give-and-take as the course of action is mapped out. Key officers and NCOs with a stake in the outcome play a role as a decision develops. Typically, we identify the problem, gather information bearing on it, develop several possible courses of action with discussions of pros and cons on each alternative, recommend the optimum course to the decision-maker, and await the decision. This is what we call the deliberate decision-making process, which can take weeks to reach conclusion in some cases. The "hasty process" accommodates the need for a quick decision, but also supports the culture in which expert opinion or group input plays an important role. In thirty-two years in uniform, I have never spoken the words, "And that's an order." Nor have I heard them. Except in the movies.

There is simply no need for gratuitous, dramatic emphasis when a senior officer issues an order. We all know and accept the authority of the person in command. In fact, the related principle of unity of command is one of the Army's fundamental concepts. The person of the commander is the central clearinghouse for all information relevant to an operation. It would be disastrous in combat or any other stressful circumstances to have several commanders vying for authority in an operation.

Although my colorful commander in Korea, Colonel Charles Black, often resorted to bluster and flourishes worthy of a Hollywood film director, he never felt it necessary to emphasize his orders. He could have whispered, and we would have felt the hurricane. Still, as I've noted, Colonel Black had a solid motive:

He wanted to make things so stressful for us under tense peace-time conditions that we would be ready for war.

Another widely accepted, and equally inaccurate, myth about the Army is that soldiers are inculcated to "just follow orders." In fact, the opposite is the case. We teach soldiers from their earliest days in the Army (as recruits in Basic Training) that there is a clear distinction between lawful and unlawful orders. A soldier has an obligation to obey lawful orders and *not* to obey unlawful orders. Among the many differences between an Army and an armed gang, this is one of the most significant. Soldiers are personally accountable for their actions and cannot use the defense, if accused of impropriety, that they were only following orders. The international tribunal that convicted Nazi war criminals at Nuremberg after World War II helped make this concept a widely accepted international value. Unfortunately, as we have seen tragically unfold in the Balkans, the Caucasus, across Africa, and in Indonesia in the past decade, this value has not been universally applied. We have witnessed the spectacle of national armies degenerate into murderous gangs that savaged the civilian population they were officially sworn to protect. In these cases the senior officers responsible issued unlawful orders, which their soldiers chose to follow. We in the democratic West can feel fortunate that our armies are firmly rooted in order and discipline.

Part of that foundation of discipline involves a hierarchy of authority, what is often referred to as a chain of command that extends from the most junior private to the President of the United States. It is enormously important to Army culture that we respect the position of the senior person we salute, that we defend the Constitution and the nation, not a particular individual. I salute an officer senior to me (when we are out-of-doors), not as a statement of personal respect, but as a recognition of my oath to "obey the orders of the President of the United States and the orders of the officers appointed over me."

The more powerful an army, the more necessary it is to instill this obedience to civil authority. Not since the tragedy of the Civil War almost 150 years ago has the American military defied the rightful authority of the President. General of the Army Douglas MacArthur assumed that his well-earned status as a military leader of heroic proportions would permit him to question the orders of his commander-in-chief, President Harry S. Truman, during the Korean War. MacArthur was wrong. Truman fired him.

In a formal bilateral discussion with the senior military officer of another country, I was startled to hear him sounding me out about American reaction if his military were to overthrow the weak current civilian head of state. I gave him my very complete and unrelenting view that the United States was adamantly opposed to internal military takeovers against a civilian government, regardless of the sentiments in their military about the civilian leadership. When I finished my year at the Command and General Staff College, I happened to be chatting with an Allied Officer from a developing country about our next assignments. I was on my way to a staff job in Germany. I asked about his assignment. "I'm going to overthrow my government and become President." I waited for the punch line. There was none.

* * *

Thinking back on the time that I weighed my own small decision after discovering the plagiarizing, I consider the most important leadership attributes I look for in my peers and seniors. Integrity and honesty are at the top of the list. The military is not like the private sector, where office politics too often becomes an ongoing intramural tournament in which deception and cheating may be considered acceptable. We in the military simply have to trust each other to tell the truth. For example, when an Infantry captain acknowledges an order to move his company to a ridge to protect the exposed flank of a battalion's advance, the battalion commander has to take the captain at his word that he has completed the movement. We are not in the habit of checking up on each other in the Army because we are taught as career soldiers to act honorably. Our bonds of trust are mutual.

But if this ideal situation prevails in the Army of the twenty-first century, the moral and ethical hangover of Vietnam was still a lingering problem in late 1970s. I had to decide where my loyalties lay, to the ethical compromises that had fostered the My Lai cover-up or to a future Army that had regained its moral and ethical grounding under leaders such as William Peers and Max Thurman. To me, it would be impossible to respect senior leaders whom I could not trust: By definition, a leader was a person of character who earned the loyalty and respect of all.

Certainly we've all worked for people who dominated their subordinates through rigid means of control, often playing one group off the other by unprofessional means and cultivating favorites. But such leaders never earn respect or loyalty because we can't trust them. They cheat and lie out of expedience. At their core is an ethical vacuum. When we see them employ these tactics on someone else, it's obvious that we might be the next to suffer. We obey their orders out of necessity, but they will never inspire us to excel.

* * *

I was uneasy until I made the decision to report the officer who had plagiarized the research paper. But once I had taken that step, my mind was free of doubt.

The faculty thanked me for bringing the issue to their attention and said they would look into it. I was relieved that they handled the delicate situation in a low-key manner and did not overreact. They confronted the officer with the evidence of his plagiarism, but did not bring formal charges against him for this obvious breach of the honor code. Instead they made him rewrite the paper.

As I wrestled with the dilemma of reporting the cheating officer, I again recognized that overlooking an ethical lapse was tantamount to participating in the event. It had not been my intention to personally judge this officer for unethical conduct, but rather to act out of a sense of loyalty to the Army as an institution. I was attending a professional Army school that formed future leaders. That school had repeatedly told us that it had an honor code meant to foster standards of self-discipline and ethical behavior among those leaders. My decision to report the incident had been an act of loyalty to those standards. Having recognized this duty, I had nothing to regret.

* * *

Soon after taking command of the 3rd Operations Battalion at Field Station Augsburg in 1986, I learned important lessons about the complex bonds of loyalty that tie a leader to her soldiers, those soldiers to one another, and the transcendent higher bond that unites them in their loyalty to the values of the Army. Since then, I've come to realize that the insights I gained during a trying episode at that time are also readily applicable to leaders outside the military.

The situation involved my responsibility as a commander to administer military justice, which includes both forwarding cases for trial by court-martial and sitting in judgment in nonjudicial punishment cases under Article 15 of the Uniform Code of Military Justice. In Augsburg, I had far fewer occasions to administer nonjudicial punishment than I had as a company commander at Fort McClellan in 1973–75. This was because the Army had made remarkable progress in improving the quality of its soldiers in the intervening years, because a battalion commander is a step removed from the soldiers in the chain of command and normally leaves Article 15 proceedings to the company commanders, and also because Military Intelligence soldiers go through a far more selective screening than troops who are not subject to the security clearance process.

So, where an Article 15 hearing was a routine part of my week as a company commander during the troubled 1970s at Fort McClellan, it was most unusual as a battalion commander in the mid-1980s. However, when I took command of the unit in Augsburg, I sent a memo to my subordinate commanders announcing my policy of reserving judicial responsibility for certain categories of cases: all charges against officers and senior NCOs, as well as all cases involving assault and drug charges. Among other legal reasons, my purpose in officially stating this policy was to help set a climate in which it was clear to the entire battalion what I considered intolerable behavior. And that behavior included assault of any kind—often a consequence of the heavy alcohol use being systematically reduced in the Army—as well as use of illegal drugs.

Drug abuse posed a particular problem for Military Intelligence soldiers in Europe during the Cold War. We were all potential targets of hostile intelligence services, which were constantly seeking to recruit agents from NATO ranks. Soldiers with a drug problem were especially vulnerable; they could be blackmailed with threats of losing their security clearances, and they needed extra money to pay for their habit.

Fortunately for me and my fellow commanders, the American military had a vital new weapon in the arsenal of defensive measures against illicit drug use: the urinalysis test. As in all units, the test was administered to randomly selected soldiers based on the last digits of our Social Security numbers (this selection included me and the other battalion officers). The U.S. Army installation in Augsburg supported the drug program, which was administered as often as needed to ensure that all soldiers and officers were tested on the average of 1.5 times a year. The success of the test was that no one ever knew when their number would come up and they'd have to immediately report and provide a sample. As one might expect, very few soldiers had tested positive for recent drug use.

So I was concerned when I received a phone call alerting me that a staff sergeant in our battalion had been found to have a positive urinalysis for recent marijuana use. The call was an informal heads-up to let me know that the official results stating this NCO had tested "hot" would reach my desk the next day. On checking the staff sergeant's record, I found he had never been a disciplinary problem. Moreover, further inquiry revealed he was well liked and well respected, a veteran with more than fifteen years' service. My initial reaction was to wonder if there could possibly have been some mistake on the urinalysis, but deep down I doubted this because I knew how carefully the Army preserved the scientific integrity of the entire testing process.

But my personal opinion was irrelevant. Military justice demanded that I initiate disciplinary action. The staff sergeant would be offered an Article 15, an administrative process less threatening than a court-martial, which is a formal judicial proceeding and could result in his having a federal conviction on his record. An Article 15 hearing was nonjudicial—I wasn't a military judge and there would be no jury—but an administrative finding of guilty on the charges would harm the NCO's career even though a notation of an Article 15 in a sergeant's record had not been that unusual thirty or forty years before. The Army had changed since then, however. So the staff sergeant had a lot riding on the outcome of this hearing.

Accordingly, he carefully considered his options. These included consulting an Army lawyer (representing him, not the Army), deciding between a closed or open hearing, and calling others to speak on his behalf both to defend against the charges or to mitigate punishment if he were found guilty. The accused NCO did consult an Army defense lawyer and opted for a closed Article 15 hearing in which he would call sixteen other NCOs from the battalion to speak on his behalf. This was an unusually large number of defense witnesses for an Article 15 case, and the whole process of arranging the hearing took time, which was rather short because there is a prescribed limit to the number of days a soldier can be under charges before receiving a hearing.

As viewers of the hit television show *JAG* know, the Uniform Code of Military Justice contains many protections for both the accused and the military institution. For example, if a soldier demands trial by court-martial, the commander might decide to proceed or to drop the case. And most commanders do not offer the option of an Article 15 hearing to the accused unless their case is strong enough for a court-martial. Part of the strength of the Article 15 is that it isn't a game of bluff. It is a streamlined disciplinary process that is not an overreaction to less egregious offenses, which need not clog up the staff judge advocate's docket of more serious cases.

Everyone realized that the staff sergeant's character witnesses represented his only chance of winning a finding of either not guilty or charges not substantiated. This was because the urinalysis test was so accurate and tightly controlled as to be generally considered a completely objective standard, a factor made even stronger by the random nature of its administration. To counter this seemingly insurmountable evidence, however, the staff sergeant had assembled some of the best NCOs in the battalion to speak in his defense.

And it was a very credible group who took the oath and stood before my desk to speak that day. One by one, each stated how long he had known the accused and talked at length about his good conduct and character. Several had served with him as young soldiers in Vietnam and stressed that even at that time and place, where drug use was much more prevalent than in the 1980s in this battalion, the NCO had avoided the pervasive drug so many GIs had smoked. "Ma'am," a fellow NCO said of his friend in Vietnam, "he didn't even drink much of that Ba-me-Ma beer at night down in the ville." I'm sure he meant well, but that certainly did not help me make this decision.

When all the character witnesses had spoken, the staff sergeant's chain of command testified. To add to the dilemma, they were equally divided as to his guilt. We adjourned for the day. And I was faced with my decision. I had two sets of seemingly immutable and opposing facts to consider: On the one hand, the drug test was considered so tamperproof that false positives were virtually ruled out; on the other, sixteen of the battalion's best NCOs had testified under oath that it was virtually impossible for the accused staff sergeant to be a drug user and for them not to have known it. Although the legal clock was running, I decided to think the case over for a day.

Several facts became clear in my mind. First, a few close

friends of the staff sergeant must have rallied to his cause as soon as the news of the test results became public. In turn, they probably had recruited a looser circle of friends and acquaintances to form an alliance of support, the group of sixteen NCOs who eventually testified for him under oath at the Article 15 hearing. I had absolutely no reason to believe that any of them were lying, but I saw that many might have simply jumped on the bandwagon to help out a buddy, a good guy, who they saw as being unjustly accused. But it was equally possible that the testimony of these witnesses represented "evidence" as valid as the biochemical laboratory results. I simply could not disregard the soldiers' testimony and be a fair commander. I was the leader and ultimately had to sort through the tangled bonds of loyalty that ran in several directions in this case: from the soldiers to their buddy, from me to the soldiers, and from all of us in the battalion to Army values.

I consulted the lawyer for the Army's case to clarify my legal options, based on the evidence. He told me I could find the staff sergeant guilty, not guilty, or charges not substantiated. Then I received a call from a chaplain who knew the staff sergeant.

"This is a very good soldier," he said, speaking of the accused NCO. "I don't see how that test could have been accurate."

I spoke with Colonel Simerly, my brigade commander, about this case. We had to carefully construct our conversation in order to preserve each echelon's judicial distance from influence by the next higher level in the chain of command. For example, if the colonel, as brigade commander, did not agree with what I, as a battalion commander, was doing in the case, he could not tell me how to proceed, but could only take the case from me and handle it himself. He was also reluctant to do this because by so doing he would lose the chance to review the case and thereby relinquish it to a yet higher authority than was appropriate for such an infraction.

At that point I was trying to maintain a frank and honest relationship with Colonel Simerly. And, to his credit, he acted in a thoroughly professional manner, allowing me to proceed to the

best of my judgment, even though he didn't agree with my conclusions. The crux of my argument was that the disciplinary
process was flawed in regard to the urinalysis. If the test were invariably 100 percent accurate, why were soldiers who came up
positive provided either judicial or nonjudicial processes? Why
weren't they simply sentenced? The fact was that my discretion
as a commander *had* entered the equation, and I had carefully
considered all of the evidence presented in the hearing, including the very persuasive sworn testimony of the sixteen NCO
character witnesses in the staff sergeant's defense.

"You're the battalion commander, Claudia," Colonel Simerly
said. "You'll do what you have to do."

Two days later, I reconvened the hearing and formally found
that the charges against the staff sergeant had not been substantiated. I could not say that he was not guilty. In fact, there was
strong evidence pointing to his guilt: the positive urinalysis test.
On the other hand, I noted, if the test were to be treated as an
automatic basis for the finding of guilt, commanders should not
be given such cases to consider and reach a decision on guilt, in-
nocence, and the appropriate punishment. At the end of the
proceeding, the staff sergeant saluted smartly, his face showing
great relief, did an about-face, and left my office. As he walked
away, I felt a twinge of doubt: Was he truly innocent, or had he
somehow beat the system?

My decision caused an immediate uproar among the drug
enforcement staff of the Augsburg installation commander. They
sent word to brigade, which Colonel Simerly delivered to me
during a closed-door conference: Did Lieutenant Colonel
Kennedy not understand the infallibility of these drug tests? Did
she not have confidence in the scientific integrity of the urinalysis processing system? Was she soft on drugs?

Colonel Simerly was initially impatient with this potential
controversy. "Claudia," he said, "I don't think you can say that
you don't believe the validity of this urinalysis. It *is* infallible, you
know."

But again to his credit, he listened to my counterarguments.

I did not think the system was 100 percent infallible, I explained. And I also did not think commanders administering discipline had to necessarily explain where the failing lay.

"I believe the system itself has to show that it's infallible before it can be used to *force* an automatic finding of guilty," I said. I added that I did not completely trust the urinalysis processing because it was a system that has multiple steps and many levels of people involved. There was just enough room for error, however rare that error might be, to cause some doubt. "And no, Colonel," I added, "I am not soft on drugs, nor have I ever tolerated any gray area for drug use in the Army or outside the Army."

Following this incident, the installation hastily arranged a drug education class for all commanders to explain the technical aspects of the exacting urinalysis process, with its multiple evidence safeguards and redundant procedures to rule out positive tests falsely linked to a soldier. Obviously the class had been arranged to educate me and other commanders, but if it had also been intended to single me out so that I would not act independently in the future, I was prepared to endure this period of doubts about my judgment. Eventually the truth would emerge. I felt deeply it was more important for me as a commander to preserve the sense of fair play, to demonstrate that a soldier's defense testimony would be given appropriate consideration combined with the outcome of a drug test. If that defense were as convincing as that of the staff sergeant's character witnesses, I believed the benefit of the doubt should go to the accused.

But I continued to discuss the case with Colonel Simerly. We agreed that a travesty of justice in any direction would not be good for the battalion: whether the man had been innocent and convicted or a habitual doper who had walked free. So we examined each aspect of the case for a strategy to find the truth. Old soldier that he was, Colonel Simerly came up with a sharp insight, "Sometimes truth can best be found by separating it from the legal process."

This was a strategy that we jointly created as a means to determine the truth. About ten days after the Article 15 had been completed, I ordered the staff sergeant to report and submit another urinalysis. The results of this test would not be legally binding because the urinalysis had not been random and there was no probable cause to order it. But its results would give us another test of the NCO's drug status. If he tested negative, this wouldn't have completely allayed my concern about his previous urinalysis, but would partially have supported my finding of charges not being substantiated in the Article 15. My reasoning here was that one could use patterns to discern human behavior. After all, this second sample would only give us information for the current period of a few days. But if he were using drugs at that time, there was a strong chance he had been using them earlier. And if this second test were positive for recent drug use, it would give us a basis for starting him on rehabilitation, even though no legal action could be taken because the urinalysis was a directed test.

Two days later, the results of the second test showed that the staff sergeant had recently used marijuana. His company commander referred the NCO for mandatory drug counseling. Then the captain and I discussed the next step.

"Colonel," the company commander said, "with your permission, I'm going to let every NCO who testified in his defense know the results of this second drug test."

"Have at it," I replied.

Those soldiers needed to learn how their friend had let them down. They had made a mistake involving loyalty. Undoubtedly, he had desperately sought out character witnesses among his closest friends who had in turn sought their buddies of similar rank. But they had made their judgment based on their limited professional knowledge of the veteran NCO as they saw him perform his duty in the battalion, not as the private person off duty, off post, where strong North African hashish and kif (marijuana) were so prevalent among the German counterculture. The staff sergeant was a popular and effective NCO, his witnesses had all testified. How could he also be a drug user? They had judged the man, not the event: the stark evidence of the positive urinalysis.

Their bond of loyalty was closer to their friend and colleague than to the Army. We call such bonds unit cohesion, and they are very important in the Army. Indeed, they are often considered the glue that holds an organization together under the most trying circumstances, the stress of combat. But there has to be a transcendent loyalty to the institution's higher values. Otherwise you have a gang, with little more than brutal, atavistic values, not a disciplined army. At My Lai, the men of 1st Platoon, Charlie Company, certainly were loyal to each other as they took revenge for their dead and maimed comrades, but displayed absolutely no loyalty to the Army's values, the precepts of the Geneva Convention, or to the basic values of civilized behavior.

The principle of transcendent loyalty is also vital in institutions such as the police, where the notorious Blue Wall of Silence, by which few officers ever inform on their peers, contributes to corruption and brutality in departments in many of our largest cities. In these organizations, leaders permit their police to be more loyal to their fellow officers than to the citizens they are all sworn to protect.

After the news that the staff sergeant had failed his second drug test spread through the battalion, the NCOs who had delivered sworn testimony on his behalf were chagrined that he had misused their loyalty. They had put their trust in the wrong person.

* * *

But there was a positive side to this potentially disillusioning experience. This was a case that could have caused sharp divisions in the battalion along which people developed strong partisan feelings for or against the staff sergeant and the chain of command that was prosecuting him. Before the second drug test, I knew it was important to resolve these lingering issues. If the man were truly innocent, his reputation should be restored. But it was also important for the entire battalion to know that soldiers did not receive unfair or arbitrary treatment and that their commander maintained the Army standard of not using drugs.

Weeks later, the staff sergeant came up for a third drug test, this time a random urinalysis based on his Social Security number. He again tested positive. This time he did not contest his Article 15 or even mount a defense. Everyone in the battalion viewed him as a discredited soldier and wondered why he had not used the first test as an opportunity to reform, or why he had not taken to heart the drug counseling resulting from the positive second test. The second Article 15 hearing was brief. I found him guilty and administered the maximum punishment, reducing him in grade and fining him heavily. His career in Military Intelligence had ended.

Years later, I realized that the situation with the staff sergeant might have been one of the irritants that started to sour my relationship with Colonel Simerly. Certainly the colonel was not pleased that the Augsburg installation found it necessary to involve itself in our brigade's business. But the Army had assigned me to command this battalion, not to be the subaltern of my brigade commander. And to be an effective commander, I had to be true to my own values and those of the Army. Ultimately, steady loyalty to institutional values is inherently more important than meeting short-term performance goals—such as quickly disposing of disciplinary actions—by whatever expedient necessary.

As a leader, another important lesson I learned from this difficult episode was not to run roughshod over soldiers' vital bonds of loyalty to one another, but to guide them toward their loyalty to the Army's higher values. And the soldiers of the battalion also learned a lot about the intricate web of loyalty that connects us all. They gained a renewed awareness that there was a process that worked well to build and maintain the institution we all sought: a sober, hardworking, honest group of soldiers whose word could be trusted.

7

Fairness and Equality

*I*n the fall of 1996, I was a major general, serving in the Pentagon as the Assistant Deputy Chief of Staff for Intelligence. I was well satisfied with my professional position and hoped that I would reach three-star rank and be considered for the Deputy Chief of Staff for Intelligence (DCSINT) before retiring. I thought that service in that position would allow me to meet several goals that I considered critical to Army intelligence, including strengthening the foreign language program and helping the Army revitalize its intelligence doctrine and equipment.

My optimism about this productive future stemmed from the professional advice I had received upon being promoted to brigadier general four years earlier. I was one of the most junior colonels on that year's list. The expectation for the list's most senior colonels was that this would be their last promotion. But for those of us who were the most junior, it was probable that we would continue to serve as general officers for several years and retire after additional promotions. With this in mind, I had been asked whether I would prefer my last job in the Army to be Deputy Chief of Staff for Personnel or DCSINT, both three-star assignments.

I was not prepared for this discussion, having hardly adjusted to the news of my selection as a brigadier general. So I simply said that I'd prefer my first position as a general officer to be in Military Intelligence. After that, I would serve where the Army needed me. But when I was assigned as Assistant Deputy Chief of Staff for Intelligence, I had renewed confidence that I would retire as the Army DCSINT.

This would mean I'd be the first woman in the Army to earn the rank of lieutenant general. I couldn't think of a better way to round out a deeply satisfying career than by having the authority to pursue my long-standing goals for Army intelligence.

* * *

That fall, my staff received a call from the office of Brigadier General Larry Smith, who was serving as the manager of the Saudi Arabian National Guard Modernization Program, requesting an appointment when he visited Washington from overseas. The meeting was scheduled for Friday, October 11, 1996.

I had first met Larry Smith when we were colonels serving together on a selection board, but he was no more than a nodding acquaintance at that time. In 1993, when I'd been assigned as the FORSCOM director of intelligence at Fort McPherson near Atlanta, I had moved into the Army quarters next to Larry Smith and his wife, Ann. Larry Smith was an Armor officer and helicopter pilot with combat experience in Vietnam who had served as both a battalion and a brigade commander later in his career. The Smiths were very kind, often inviting me for supper at their house on the spur of the moment; Larry prepared my lawn mower for winter storage in the garage. In turn, I had helped with the arrangements of keeping a car for their son, who was away at school, and had turned it over to him when he returned. This was a typical Army neighbor relationship: One doesn't know the other well, but is ready to help when needed, especially when a family is being reassigned.

So I certainly anticipated nothing unusual during Smith's office call on October 11. Like all professional officers, he was prompt, arriving exactly at the appointed time. We sat across from each other at a coffee table in my office with the door open. The discussion was purely official business, other than a brief initial social exchange about his family. Smith had served in his assignment to Saudi Arabia for over a year and was able to recount a great deal about the military and political leadership, as well as the often complex decision-making dynamics of the region. I found his perspective helpful and planned to have one of our regional analysts call on him and officially obtain his assessment.

Then, when Smith rose to leave my office, he suddenly committed an act of inappropriate contact that two attorneys on different occasions have informed me constituted sexual assault and battery. (In May 2000, the Army Inspector General substantiated that Smith's act was an "assault consummated by a battery.")

I have decided not to discuss in detail the nature of this act. As one might imagine, it is unpleasant for me to dwell on the event. Also, I do not want that incident to become the focal point of this book, which I hope young people will read as they consider their professional options. But it is important to clarify that, even though the incident fell within the legal definition of sexual assault and battery, people should not conclude that I was deeply affected either physically or emotionally.

It is an understatement to say, however, that I was shocked. More accurately, I was very angry. Smith had absolutely no right to do what he did. His act occurred without provocation on my part. The fact that the incident had taken place in my Pentagon office with the door open made his behavior even more inexplicable.

After he had left, I weighed my options. Over the weekend I carefully considered whether to report the incident to Army authorities. I had complained of a similar, though less egregious situation involving another officer several years earlier at Fort McPherson. That complaint resulted in an Article 15 investigation of that officer during which two of his women subordinates had come forward to disclose acts on his part that were far more serious than his actions toward me. That officer had received nonjudicial punishment, was fined, and retired early. So I knew that when someone behaves in this manner once, it often turns out to be a part of a behavior pattern.

In my mind, reporting Smith's actions now did not seem necessary. I outranked him and I could control his future access to me now that I knew he could not be trusted. The matter was something I could deal with individually, so I decided to tell no one in the Army about it either officially or unofficially at that time. Although I had no proof that Smith had acted improperly in the past, I was aware that I might be failing in my duty to protect more junior women by not reporting the incident. What I did know with complete certainty was that he had assaulted me and that I could protect myself from him in the future. Additionally, I was concerned that the Army would not find my report credible and that my complaint would somehow harm the cause of women soldiers of all ranks who came forward to report sexual misconduct.

There was another reason influencing my decision. For several weeks, the Army leadership had been concerned with a growing scandal at the Ordnance Center and School at Aberdeen Proving Ground, Maryland. Although details had not yet publicly emerged, it was evident that NCO drill instructors and one officer were under criminal investigation, charged with multiple counts of sexual abuse of young junior enlisted women trainees. From the reports I had heard, it appeared several drill instructors had systematically preyed on young women assigned to them. When the story broke, I knew the Army would have a serious public relations problem, so I made the decision not to distract from the Aberdeen investigation by reporting the Smith incident.

What had happened in my office was not on the same scale as the situation at Aberdeen. Yet I knew the news media would have found an incident in which one general officer accused another of sexual misconduct to be so explosive that the resulting publicity would have been a major embarrassment at a time when the Army was already engaged in damage control and trying to correct the underlying leadership problem.

There was also little chance I would see much of Smith during my remaining Army career. Although my anger remained, I decided to try to put the incident behind me.

Less than three weeks after the incident with Larry Smith, the situation at Aberdeen burst into the headlines. Army Chief of Staff General Dennis Reimer called a press conference to announce that the Army would thoroughly investigate every allegation of sexual misconduct at training bases. General Reimer also stated that the Secretary of the Army, Togo D. West, Jr., would appoint an advisory panel to examine the prevalence of sexual harassment and abuse Army-wide. He reiterated that the Army had a "zero tolerance" policy toward sexual harassment of any kind and that "consideration of others is a fundamental principle upon which the Army operates."

The Chief of Staff cited the Consideration of Others Program that Major General Robert Foley, the commander of the Military District of Washington, was instituting in his command. General Foley, a Vietnam War Medal of Honor winner, had helped create the program while commandant of cadets at West Point in the early 1990s. A major feature of the Military Academy's four-year curriculum, the program formed an important part of future Army leaders' education and professional development. General Reimer cited it to show the deplorable situation at Aberdeen lay far outside acceptable Army norms.

As the investigation proceeded, other instructors faced sexual misconduct charges. The events at Aberdeen did prove truly appalling. On November 15, 1996, the Army announced court-martial charges against two drill instructors and an officer at the Ordnance Center and School. Captain Derrick Robertson, a training company commander, was charged with rape and other forms of sexual abuse of a female soldier. Staff Sergeant Delmar Simpson, a drill instructor in Robertson's company, faced nine counts of rape and multiple counts of forcible sodomy, assault consummated by battery, and related charges, involving a total of eight young women soldiers. Another drill instructor, Staff Sergeant Nathaniel Beach, faced lesser charges. The victims, whose average age was twenty-one, were provided with counseling through the Aberdeen

Community Health Clinic and the chaplain. In the wake of the revelation, the Army established a toll-free number for military personnel who were victims of sexual abuse. Almost 2,000 calls were logged within days; over 200 were referred to investigators. Of these, fifty-six involved Aberdeen Proving Ground.

By the time the courts-martial were concluded in the spring of 1997, a shocking pattern of sexual abuse of trainees had emerged involving additional defendants. It became clear that a relatively small number of drill instructors had used their authority over young junior enlisted women undergoing Advanced Individual Training at Aberdeen either to rape them or to coerce them into sexual relationships. This coercion was often accompanied by physical abuse and threats, leaving the trainees terrified. The drill instructors went so far as to have contests with each other as to who could dominate the largest number of trainees.

Staff Sergeant Delmar Simpson, the most serious offender, was found guilty of eighteen counts of rape and twelve counts of indecent assault, as well as lesser charges. Army prosecutors proved that Simpson coerced and dominated the young women trainees for whom he was responsible. In one case, where Simpson discovered a trainee was having an illegal but consensual relationship with another drill instructor, Simpson ordered the woman to his office, raped her, and told her if she reported the attack, authorities wouldn't believe her because of her relationship with the other NCO. Simpson received a twenty-five-year prison sentence after the military jury found him guilty of rape and other sexual misconduct charges.

In all, ten Ordnance Center and School personnel had charges preferred against them. The only officer charged, Captain Derrick Robertson, pleaded guilty to adultery and other charges, including conduct unbecoming an officer. He was sentenced to serve one-year confinement, followed by dismissal from the service with a loss of total pay and benefits.

It is fair to say that as the Aberdeen sexual abuse scandal unfolded, it became one of the Army's most devastating leadership failures since the Vietnam War.

Then, in February 1997, another shocking allegation exploded in the media. Sergeant Major of the Army Gene McKinney was suspended from his duties pending resolution of allegations of sexual misconduct a recently retired soldier made against him. Only a moral leader beyond reproach is considered for the position of the top enlisted soldier in the service. The Army investigation of the original charges, which paralleled the Aberdeen investigations and courts-martial, eventually led to McKinney's own court-martial. He was charged with adultery, indecent assault, making threats, and maltreatment of soldiers, allegations involving four women during the 1990s.

During a pre-court-martial hearing in the summer of 1997, McKinney's former public affairs NCO, retired Sergeant Major Brenda Hoster, testified McKinney had forcibly kissed her and made unwanted sexual overtures. Other witnesses, all enlisted women in the armed services, testified McKinney had solicited them for sex or tried to coerce them into sexual relationships. One witness cooperated with investigators who taped a telephone conversation between her and McKinney in which he urged her to change her earlier statements to the Army.

The investigation and court-martial proceedings dragged on for over a year, keeping McKinney's name in the news media and inevitably harming the Army's reputation as an institution that provided a fair and equitable environment for women soldiers. In March 1998, the court-martial convicted McKinney of only one of the nineteen specifications of misconduct with which he was charged, finding him guilty of obstruction of justice related to his efforts to have the witness withdraw her testimony. McKinney was sentenced to a reduction of one grade and was reprimanded. The Army allowed him to retire without further punishment.

I watched these troubling developments unfold with a sense of combined anger and deep concern. Young women who joined the Army had a right to feel safe, to serve as soldiers with dignity, not to be preyed upon by drill instructors who saw them as mere sexual objects they could brutalize. And the Army had the right to expect much better leadership than Sergeant Major McKinney had shown.

I knew, however, that the sordid Aberdeen and McKinney episodes did not represent a true picture of the Army as a whole.

I had only two contacts with the Smiths during this period. There was a Christmas reception that they and I both attended, but I stayed away from Larry Smith, speaking briefly to Ann but not to him. At the end of the reception, I was looking for a place to put my glass down and he appeared from somewhere, lifted my glass and said, "I'll take that for you." I remained silent.

Several months later, I was caught in a receiving line behind the Smiths at a large farewell dinner. I found this situation very awkward. And I could see that both Ann and Larry felt awkward as well. Ann recognized from my silence that a rift had developed between us, and I would guess that she did not know why.

Meanwhile, I had been busy with responsibilities far more important than my individual grievance with Larry Smith. On November 22, 1996, two weeks after General Reimer voiced the Army's determination to thoroughly investigate the situation at Aberdeen, Secretary of the Army Togo West announced formation of the Secretary of the Army's Senior Review Panel on Sexual Harassment, of which I had been appointed a member.

The Review Panel had an unprecedented charter: Conduct a thorough, Army-wide investigation into the perceived and actual levels of sexual abuse, harassment, and discrimination at all levels. Secretary West also gave the Review Panel the mandate to recommend concrete changes in any existing Army policies in order to improve the human relations environment. Finally, he asked the members to determine how Army leaders throughout the chain of command viewed and exercised their responsibilities to prevent sexual harassment, specifically addressing actions that failed to acknowledge the dignity and respect to which every soldier was entitled.

The Secretary recalled two retired general officers to active duty to head the Review Panel. Major General Richard S. Siegfried, an Infantry officer with a distinguished combat record who had last served as acting Inspector General, U.S. Army, was the chair. The vice chair was Brigadier General Evelyn P. Foote, who had been an

Army Deputy Inspector General and commanding general of Fort Belvoir, Virginia. Among the other panel members was Major General Larry Ellis, the Assistant Deputy Chief of Staff for Personnel (later the commander of the 1st Armored Division and, when promoted to lieutenant general, Deputy Chief of Staff for Operations and Plans). Command Sergeant Major Cynthia A. Pritchett, a former drill sergeant and instructor at the Army Sergeants Major Academy, was the senior enlisted woman member.

The Review Panel, which in many ways paralleled the ongoing effort of the Army Research Institute, was backed up by a large professional staff that employed the most rigorous polling techniques to elicit the soldiers' opinions on how sexual harassment or misconduct impacted their lives and their units' missions. We used four methods of collecting data: surveys, focus groups, personal interviews, and observation. In all, we contacted over 30,000 soldiers during our investigation. And the specific data analyses involved a cohort of 14,498 men and women soldiers, selected as the most representative sampling. Then the data was subjected to scientifically verified analysis processes to determine its validity.

Working in teams between January and May 1997, Review Panel investigators fanned out to Army units stationed worldwide, interviewing troops at forty posts in the United States and eighteen overseas. I helped interview soldiers and their leaders at a number of these posts, including Fort Lewis, Washington, Fort Polk, Louisiana, and Fort Clayton, Republic of Panama. The Review Panel visited units forward-deployed in the Balkans, in German garrisons, at training sites on sprawling bases in the American West, and in classrooms at a variety of Army schools. In view of the highly publicized priority the Secretary and the Chief of Staff had placed on our mission, we were given complete access to inquire into the human relations environment surrounding soldiers in every conceivable location, performing every type of mission.

We discovered a number of troubling shortcomings and recommended a number of changes. But we also found a very-well-trained and combat-ready Army, the best that any of us had seen in over 200 years' collective experience in uniform. This Army was far better than the poorly led soldiers suggested by the scandalous revelations of Aberdeen.

But the Review Panel found that the Army lacked institutional commitment to the Equal Opportunity (EO) program designed to prevent sexual harassment and discrimination. Further, soldiers distrusted the EO complaint system and were often hesitant to use it.

We also discovered that sexual harassment existed throughout the Army, crossing gender, rank, and racial lines. But sex discrimination was more common than sexual harassment. It is important to note that sexual harassment is a form of sex discrimination.

The overwhelming majority of drill sergeants and instructors performed competently and well. But there was not enough emphasis on the Army core value of respect in the Initial Entry Training where the drill sergeant worked and through which all new soldiers spent varying degrees of time as trainees before joining their assigned units.

Not surprisingly, the Review Panel found that Army leaders were the critical factor in creating, maintaining, and enforcing an environment of respect and dignity. But too many leaders had failed to gain the trust of their soldiers.

A study conducted a year before the panel's investigation produced interesting and disturbing findings about the extent and impact of sexual harassment and sex discrimination. When asked the question, "Were you sexually harassed in the last twelve months?" 22 percent of women soldiers and 7 percent of men answered affirmatively. This means that in an Army of 470,000 active component soldiers in which 15 percent (70,000) are women and 85 percent (400,000) are men, three times as many men as women are being sexually harassed each year.

When broken down by rank and gender, it became obvious that junior enlisted women were the most likely targets for sexual harassment; 29 percent—almost one third of those surveyed—reported sexual harassment, while 17 percent of women NCOs and 6 percent of women officers said they had been sexually harassed. A much smaller percentage of men soldiers of all ranks said they'd been the targets of sexual harassment, but their complaints were significant in that this showed the problem was not limited to women.

The investigation of sexual harassment revealed that inappropriate behaviors were commonplace throughout the Army. They ran the gamut from crude and offensive behavior (unwanted sexual jokes, stories, whistling, and staring), sexist behavior (insulting, offensive, and condescending attitudes based on gender), unwanted sexual attention (including touching or fondling and pressing for dates even when rebuffed), sexual coercion (which included classic quid pro quo cases of job benefits or losses conditioned on sexual cooperation), and finally to sexual assault that included attempted and actual rape.

Crude or offensive behavior was the most common problem, experienced by 78 percent of the women and 76 percent of the men surveyed. Almost as many of each gender said they experienced sexist behavior. The gap widened in the unwanted sexual attention category: 47 percent of the women, 30 percent of the men. Nearly twice as many women than men (15 percent vs. 8 percent) had experienced sexual coercion. The gap closes on reported sexual assault: 7 percent of women vs. 6 percent of men.

Overall, the Review Panel found that 84 percent of these Army women and 80 percent of these Army men reported experiencing some type of inappropriate sexual behavior. But many, apparently, did not perceive these behaviors as sexual harassment because the number of soldiers who believed that sexual harassment was a problem in their unit was relatively small (10 percent of men and 17 percent of women). This was consistent with the personal perception of 22 percent of the women and 7 percent of the men who reported they had been sexually harassed in the previous twelve months.

In a focus group, a soldier commented that there was "lots of low-level sexual harassment," but it was "just part of the environment." Others described the least offensive behaviors as "noise," "static," or "clutter." Many soldiers were uncomfortable with the situation, but found their exposure to these behaviors inevitable. What the Review Panel found striking was that Army men and women would tolerate such behavior and not state they had been sexually harassed, an indication that, for whatever reason, behavior that fell within the official definition of sexual harassment was accepted as the norm throughout the Army. One soldier noted that inappropriate behavior and sexual harassment was so pervasive, "I'd keep reporting it every day. But I handle it better than most." Another said the official definition of sexual harassment was "too broad now," adding that a newcomer to the unit might perceive sexual harassment, "when it is really only bantering back and forth."

We learned that soldiers were likely to perceive they were being sexually harassed only when inappropriate behavior reached the level of sexual coercion or sexual assault. When this happened, 52 percent stated that they had been sexually harassed. "As long as no one is touching me," a soldier said, capturing a common sentiment, "I don't care."

During focus groups, many of those who had reported they had been sexually harassed described experiences that actually fell within the official Department of Defense definition of sex discrimination. Very often this discrimination involved soldiers being given certain duties solely because of their gender. All these cases involved units in which men and women were serving on an equal footing, with women qualified to perform their Military Occupational Specialty (MOS). The discrimination was often linked to assumptions about sex role stereotypes concerning abilities, competence, status, and roles of the particular gender (either man or woman), which resulted in the disparate treatment or a negative impact on those soldiers. For example, an officer or NCO might have made the arbitrary decision to assign women to "light" administrative-type duty, while men got the dirtier, heavy-lifting jobs. In a full field exercise, this might involve men digging trenches and foxholes, while women set up tents or light equipment.

The Review Panel found examples of such discrimination throughout the Army. When we asked soldiers if they were treated differently because of their sex, 51 percent of the women said yes, and fewer than half that percentage of the men (22 percent) said gender played a role in their treatment. This perception that women were incapable of serving as "real" soldiers had a definite impact on the way they were treated within their units. A group of senior women NCOs heatedly told the Review Panel about having no voice in meetings with their male peers: "We speak, but it's as if we do not exist. They ignore us." Participants in focus group discussions noted that while there was "zero tolerance" within the Army for racial discrimination, the same standard was not applied to sex discrimination. One woman soldier remarked, "You can't get away with saying blacks shouldn't be in the Army, but you can say women shouldn't be in the Army. How can men get away with that?"

Many of the women the Review Panel contacted said they felt devalued as soldiers just because they were women. A woman field-grade officer reported, "I always have to fight the male mind-set about what a woman can and cannot do." When I read her bitter comment, I thought back twenty-five years to the Military Intelligence officer at Fort Huachuca who told me women had no future in the Army. Certainly there had been progress in the years since then; women now comprised 15 percent of the total Army force and higher percentages in critical MOSs. In short, the Army could not run without women, as the senior leadership had made abundantly clear. But down at the company level, where the rubber sole of the combat boot met the road, women soldiers were still fighting the battle to be accepted. One junior enlisted woman reported of her male peers when she joined a new unit, "The automatic perception they have of me is that I don't know my job. If you're a female, you're always tested."

But women soldiers were not the only ones who perceived unfair treatment and inequality. There was a feeling among some of the men soldiers that the Army held women to less demanding standards. One of the most emotional issues was the Army Physical Fitness Test (APFT). In establishing the different standards that men and women soldiers had to achieve on the APFT, the Army considered gender as well as age. The test was designed to measure the fitness of the individual soldier, not to be a competitive exercise or race.

The different performance standards reflected physiological differences between men and women, and between younger and older soldiers. For example, a fit young man soldier could do more push-ups than his fit woman counterpart, and she could do more sit-ups. Equally, the average older man soldier would not be able to meet the Army standard set for a younger man. Some men soldiers, however, complained that the APFT standards for women were "too low," and that the test was "biased in favor of female soldiers." One soldier who apparently was firmly against serving with women commented that "The lower standards reflect a woman will never be in as good physical shape as a man."

I knew this to be preposterous, having often done better than my men peers in cross-country runs and in performing sit-ups on the APFT. I also knew that a twenty-year-old corporal would probably never say that a command sergeant major—a man in his late forties who achieved a passing score on the APFT based on age-adjusted standards—should not be in the Army. But that was exactly the implication of different gender standards for many of the men soldiers the Review Panel interviewed.

Pregnancy was an even more contentious issue. Some Army men reported that serving with pregnant soldiers negatively and unfairly impacted the unit. This was because Department of Defense policy required a pregnant woman to modify her physical training and the type and duration of duty she performed. For example, men pilots in a focus group complained that one of their women peers had to be removed from flight status, rendering her nondeployable, when her pregnancy advanced. The remaining pilots, both men and women, had to fly her missions and "pick up the other slack" caused by her absence. These sentiments were echoed by fuel handlers in a battalion where a pregnant woman had to be temporarily excused from her duties because the hazardous chemicals in the fuel might harm her developing fetus.

There was pervasive indignation that pregnancy gave women an unfair advantage and allowed them to shirk their duty. This per-

ception caused many women to risk their own and their developing fetus's health by continuing to work long hours and take part
in unit physical training simply to avoid loss of professional status.

But no matter how hard women struggled to be treated fairly
and equitably, almost one half of the men surveyed said the
women in their units were treated more favorably. While 77 percent of the women said that they "pull their load" in the company, only 50 percent of the men agreed with this assessment.
Again, however, some women soldiers complained that their
units effectively precluded them from working within the MOS
for which they were trained and assigned them instead to duties
seen as "more appropriate work for a woman."

In examining the effects of sexual harassment, the Review
Panel found a troubling erosion of trust among the soldiers in
units in which the problem was the most severe. None of the
women soldiers wanted to come to work in one unit suffering significant levels of sexual harassment. A qualified woman junior
NCO was leaving the Army after six years because men had "hit"
on her throughout those six years. And even when she reported
the incidents to her chain of command, no action was taken.

Some men said they were afraid of being falsely accused of
sexual harassment so they avoided any interaction or contact
with the women in their unit. Women soldiers confirmed this
trend and said they were concerned about becoming isolated and
shunned by men soldiers who would no longer even speak with
them.

Despite these widespread and troubling revelations, however,
both men and women soldiers assured the panel that "the mission is still being accomplished." There were, however, clear
signs that all-important cohesion—the bond of trust and loyalty—among soldiers was affected by problems in the Army's
human relations environment. The panel concluded that sexual
harassment and sex discrimination did have a negative impact
on the Army's effectiveness. We found a degree of tension and
uneasiness grounded in the perception of many soldiers that the
Army's leaders had overreacted to the media fallout from the

highly publicized incidents of sexual harassment and sexual misconduct at Aberdeen and in the McKinney case.

That view might have had some validity, but the fact remained that the Review Panel did unearth pervasive sexual harassment and sex discrimination, which erodes Army effectiveness.

I don't mean to imply, however, that there hasn't been considerable progress on the issue of Army men's behavior toward women soldiers since World War II. Most men soldiers never engage in improper behavior. But any degree of impropriety had less of an impact on Army readiness when women made up a much less significant percentage of the force. For example, when I entered the Army, less than 2 percent of the Army were women. Today the percentage is 15 percent and women fill a wide variety of jobs critical to operational success in combat. The readiness of the Army, therefore, will improve as the distraction of sexual harassment is eliminated from the lives of both men and women soldiers.

*   *   *

Secretary Togo West had ordered all of us on the Review Panel to examine "how Army leaders throughout the chain of command view and exercise their responsibility to address sexual harassment." We had all held positions of leadership. We knew that an organization's leader was responsible for every aspect of its mission performance and human environment. But in carrying out the Secretary's mandate, we discovered some aspects of leadership and human relations we had not anticipated.

First, we found strong confirmation for the basic tenet that good leadership is crucial to the creation and maintenance of positive human relations in an organization. The data we collected revealed a direct correlation between strong, concerned leadership (NCOs, junior officers, and commanders) and a reduction in inappropriate sexual behaviors. This was just common sense. An effective Army leader knew his or her soldiers and the conditions in which they lived and worked. The leader knew what was on their minds, what they felt good about, and what was bothering them.

These powers of perception were not innate mystical abilities; they came with experience and with making the conscious effort to know soldiers on a human level. We found that mutual respect among soldiers and their leaders, as well as increased acceptance of soldiers of diverse backgrounds—different races, ethnicity, and gender—as equally valuable team members was also connected with successful leadership.

The worst thing a leader could do was to ignore subordinates, to consider them just so many human cogs in the machine. Soldiers immediately detected their leaders' indifference and the lines of communication necessary for a healthy human environment broke down.

Second, we observed that the Army was not just a nine-to-five job, but a demanding profession that required shared values, beliefs, and assumptions that the Army held true—all based on the core values of honor, integrity, selfless service, courage, loyalty, duty, and respect. It was Army leaders who defined and reinforced those values for their soldiers. When they did so effectively, the units had relatively few sexual harassment or sex discrimination problems. However, when leaders were less directly connected to their soldiers and not committed to fostering a successful human relations environment every day of the year, the situation often deteriorated.

Yet we found good leaders could build positive human relations among their soldiers even in the most challenging situations. In one unit deployed in Kuwait, the chain of command refused to allow the harsh pace of operations and the unpleasant physical environment to detract from either the mission or from its commitment to take care of soldiers and ensure that the soldiers took care of each other. The leaders repeatedly emphasized that each soldier, man and woman, was important, both as a member of the unit team and as an individual. The leaders also encouraged soldiers to voice complaints and suggest solutions, without fear of retaliation. Although the unit was performing a difficult mission under great physical stress and isolation, the soldiers showed both personal discipline and a positive attitude.

From this and other effective units the panel visited, four characteristics necessary for the exercise of good leadership emerged:

- Good leaders set standards for the members of their organizations.
- Good leaders exemplified through their personal conduct adherence to those standards.
- Good leaders enforced and maintained those standards for the other members of the organization.
- Good leaders demonstrated genuine care and concern for their soldiers, no matter their rank, race, or gender.

Although these leadership characteristics could be applied beyond the human relations environment to building and sustaining military skills, we became convinced that, should a leader lack any one of these characteristics, both the unit's military readiness and human relations environment would be adversely affected.

For example, when asked whether their units' leaders set and enforced standards, significantly fewer women than men agreed. The proportion of women reporting this paralleled the perceived levels of sexual harassment and sex discrimination.

When it came to exemplifying standards, the adage that "actions speak louder than words" obviously applied. Official policies, Army regulations, or decrees alone did not create or enforce a positive human relations environment. One soldier in a focus group stated, "The more you hear leaders speak it, and then watch them maintain standards, you know that it is important." As with all the Army values, when it came to respect and consideration among soldiers, the chain of command had to lead by example, maintaining high standards of personal conduct.

But the Review Panel found that soldiers sometimes felt their leaders did not hold themselves to the same standards they set for soldiers. When asked if the leaders in their company set good examples for soldiers by behaving the way they expect soldiers to behave, 54 percent of the men surveyed agreed, while only 41 percent of the women agreed. Focus groups of most units found that leaders tried to set a good example. But there were a number of cases where commanders exemplified a "do as I say and not what I do" attitude. This applied to leaders who saw Temporary Duty assignments abroad as an opportunity for adulterous relationships.

In units where this situation prevailed, soldiers distrusted their leaders, perceiving them as not interested in soldiers' welfare.

When the Review Panel asked officers and NCOs what they found most satisfying about their Army experience, most cited the opportunity to work with and develop young soldiers. But the survey data revealed that most of these young soldiers did not feel their leaders' care and concern. For example, fewer than half of the Army men and women surveyed answered affirmatively to the question "My officers are interested in what I think and how I feel about things." This response was similar for the question "My officers are interested in my personal welfare." But the positive responses increased significantly when those questions were applied to the units' NCOs, who were in much closer contact with the soldiers surveyed. Overall, however, fewer than 40 percent of the soldiers responded affirmatively to the statement, "I am impressed with the quality of leadership in this company." And that level of negative response was almost as bad among both men and women to the statement, "I would go for help with a personal problem to people in the company chain of command."

This perceived lack of interest on the part of leadership no doubt contributed to weakening the critical bond of trust between leaders and their soldiers. One soldier in a focus group summarized this widespread feeling with the statement, "I would never trust my chain of command to deal with sexual harassment." And many leaders also recognized this breakdown in trust. One senior officer conceded, "I don't think we know what goes on with the junior enlisted," the soldiers who formed the vast majority of the Army.

The bonds linking a junior to a senior soldier are based on mutual trust and respect, which require that each know the other. The junior soldier counts on being able to confide sensitive information to the leader without fear of the leader's overreaction and in full confidence that there will be an appropriate level of reaction. But too often an inexperienced leader reacts to information on sexual harassment in a rigid, formulaic manner. The problem is compounded when leaders are uncertain about the issue and too focused on avoiding accountability for an unconventional response.

Equally troubling, many leaders, because they had not experienced sexual harassment, tended to deny it even existed. But the panel found that a leader must be sensitive to the possibility that enlisted soldiers' experiences may be outside the realm of the leader's personal experience.

Distrust of leaders was particularly evident in the survey responses from women soldiers. Only one third would go for help with personal problems to their chain of command. Army women in focus groups repeatedly asserted that they needed a system through which they could report inappropriate behavior and other complaints without fear of reprisal. They felt that existing agencies, such as the Equal Opportunity Advisor, the Inspector General, or the chaplain, worked more for the chain of command than for the soldiers.

The Review Panel was disturbed by the perception of many soldiers that their officers were more concerned with their own careers than with caring for their soldiers' welfare. This perception was shared by 37 percent of men and 40 percent of women. In the junior enlisted ranks, the perception was especially prevalent.

As we examined these problems, a pattern became evident: Army leaders from junior NCOs to senior officers were feeling the stress of expanding missions and diminishing resources. Further, downsizing increased competition for advancement. One leader complained in a focus group that "there is simply not enough time, money, equipment, or people to get the mission done and to concentrate on maintaining a positive human relations environment." But other leaders *did* find the time to work on human relations problems with their junior officers and NCOs. Creating a more positive human relations environment was certainly more a matter of attitude and consistency than of increasing the number of regulations or trying to find money to throw at the problem.

* * *

Among the more troubling issues emerging from the Review Panel's work was the concern that many leaders and soldiers said that the Army was becoming more like a civilian job than a profession. This attitude apparently stemmed from the mistaken belief that heightened concerns for soldiers' privacy prevented their leaders from any involvement in their private lives. But experienced leaders recognized that the Army certainly was not a nine-to-five job. A large number of the units we surveyed were deployable worldwide; they were in effect mobile communities that were never truly off duty. Soldiers depended on mutual trust and respect, and ideally this bond included their leaders.

When I was commanding soldiers at the company and battalion level, I made it a point to visit their barracks and homes, to understand their living conditions. And the most effective leaders the panel interviewed had never relinquished this concern and responsibility.

Another serious and widespread problem the Review Panel encountered was that many women perceived that the Army was not committed to accepting them as equal members of the force. Although the Army as an institution had officially accepted women as an essential element, it had not taken the practical steps necessary to inculcate this commitment into its culture. (Training the Army for the integration of women in the 1970s did not take place as it had earlier for racial integration.) Many women soldiers told the Review Panel that they routinely heard that their selections for promotion, schooling, command, or other highly visible assignments had "taken slots and opportunities" away from their men peers. Further, women said they were often excluded from competing for positions for which men soldiers of the same rank and qualifications were considered. And some women were still fighting the same struggle for operational or line assignments as opposed to the administrative and staff positions which were deemed "more appropriate for a woman" that I had known as a young lieutenant at Fort Devens.

* * *

At the end of its exhaustive work, the Review Panel concluded that the human relations environment in the Army did not engender dignity and respect among soldiers. We found that leadership was the fundamental issue, noting, "Passive leadership has allowed sexual harassment to persist; active leadership can bring about change to eradicate it."

We made a number of specific recommendations, which can be found in *The Secretary of the Army's Senior Review Panel Report on Sexual Harassment, Volume One, July 1997*. Among the key recommendations was to intensify human relations training during all soldiers' critical initial months in the Army, so that a relationship of mutual respect and dignity would be fostered from the onset of service. Also, we recommended a top-to-bottom reengineering of the Equal Opportunity program to make it more responsive to leaders and soldiers, to protect those who used it, and to ensure that those working in it were not stigmatized. Further, we recommended establishing a mechanism to hold commanders accountable for their unit's command climate.

One of the criticisms of the Review Panel's recommendations was that they would result in the "feminization" of the Army. The implication of this charge is that the Army's identity as a masculine organization is diluted by the presence of women. But the Army is neither masculine nor feminine; it is gender-neutral. And those who are so anxious about this matter ignore the record of the last two decades during which the Army has demonstrated both remarkable operational success and unprecedented diversity.

But all of us on the Review Panel recognized that the Army had cultural problems that needed fixing. Our summary statement epitomized this view:

The Panel very strongly believes that we must ensure that we maintain a positive human relations environment in the Army. Personnel readiness relies on a positive human relations environment. It is the vital base upon which we build our army, and the combat effectiveness of our most important weapon system—the soldier.

*   *   *

In May 1997, I was confirmed for appointment to the grade of lieutenant general and for assignment as Deputy Chief of Staff for Intelligence, United States Army.

This was the pinnacle of my career. My responsibilities, which involved overseeing policy and resources for scores of units and installations and 45,000 Military Intelligence soldiers and civilians serving worldwide, were engrossing. With the assignment and appointment to three-star rank, I also assumed a significantly higher level of official social obligations, sometimes attending more than one function a night. And there was the inevitable official travel, which took me from the Far East to the Balkans.

People outside the Army have often commented how much "fun" it must have been to serve as a three-star general in the Pentagon. In reality, I derived the most fulfillment and day-to-day satisfaction working with soldiers as a battalion and brigade commander. But I was proud to be the DCSINT, in part because serving in that position showed that the Army's glass ceiling was beginning to crack. This was no small consideration, given the troubling public perception of the role of Army women after the recent scandals.

Later in 1997 Larry Smith, now a major general, became the commander of the U.S. Army Security Assistance Command with its headquarters in nearby Alexandria. There were a lot of generals in the Pentagon, and we did not move on the same official or social circuit. So he was not present to remind me of the unfortunate encounter in October 1996.

But coming back from a break during a large conference in September 1999, I happened to overhear one general say to another that Smith was being nominated as the Deputy Inspector General, United States Army. I was surprised and made a note to myself to check whether this information was accurate.

Among other responsibilities, the Deputy IG investigates allegations of sexual misconduct by general officers. Further, the position involves evaluation of programs designed to eliminate sexual harassment.

It concerned me that the Army would nominate Larry Smith for this assignment and that he might assume the same position that former Major General David Hale had filled. Hale had retired in 1998 after serving a short stint as Deputy Inspector General. But when allegations that Hale had had a series of improper relationships with the wives of subordinates during assignments in Turkey, Hawaii, and Washington, D.C., he was recalled to active duty and court-martialed. He pled guilty to seven counts of conduct unbecoming an officer and one count of making a false official statement. Hale was reprimanded and fined. The new Secretary of the Army, Louis Caldera, convened a board to review whether Hale should continue to receive pay as a major general. It was determined his retirement rank should be reduced to brigadier general, the last grade he held when there was no evidence of impropriety against him. Clearly, the Army had made a mistake in appointing an officer like David Hale to be Deputy IG.

Now it seemed to me they were about to make a similar mistake in nominating Larry Smith for the job. I doubted that Smith's actions in the 1996 incident had been an isolated event. If he had done that to me, there might have been other women he had assaulted and who also had not come forward. Certainly Smith had made no effort to apologize to me or to excuse his behavior as an aberration. And, in view of all the disturbing revelations of sexual misconduct I had seen while on the Review Panel, I knew the integrity of the Inspector General's office was especially important. If a person like Smith held the number two position in that office, the Army would be in trouble.

For a short time, I tried to put the matter out of my mind. Then, early one morning as I prepared to leave for my office, I decided to face this situation and discover whether what I had heard at the conference was correct. After a few unofficial inquiries, I learned that Smith was indeed slated to be the new Deputy IG. I continued to weigh my options for several more days, retaining the fading hope that his assignment would be changed when some other woman presented negative information about him. However, there appeared to be no sign of anyone coming forward with an objection.

Finally, I decided that it would be up to me to present the information I had about Larry Smith. Although I have been praised for courage in this matter, I had a very strong wish not to be in this position. On one level, I felt the same apprehension I had experienced at Command and General Staff College when I had decided to report the officer who had broken the honor code. Again I would be stepping out of line, putting into play unpredictable dynamics. I couldn't dictate the Army's reaction. The leaders would handle the matter as they saw fit, and I couldn't control the outcome.

This situation, however, was far more serious than a question of a plagiarized research paper involving myself and another obscure young officer at a service school. I would be making my revelation in the Pentagon, notorious for leaks to the news media within the politically charged Washington atmosphere. I knew that whatever the outcome, once I presented my information, privacy would disappear. The case would inevitably become public, regardless of any assurances I would receive about anonymity.

But I also wanted to do all that I could to protect the Army from further embarrassment. I considered a number of options: I could contact Larry Smith directly and advise him to withdraw his name from consideration for the Deputy IG job; I could make an anonymous report, but that did not seem a fair way to present negative information about a fellow officer; or I could report the Smith incident to the Inspector General or to the Vice Chief of Staff.

I needed advice, so I consulted a senior civilian lawyer in the

Department of the Army, describing to him what had happened in my office in October 1996.

"That's sexual assault and battery," he said without hesitation. His further response was supportive. "Claudia, I sure am sorry this happened to you. You don't deserve this, and you should not have had to experience that sort of thing."

I was enormously relieved that he believed me and had first responded to the legal substance of the event before addressing the emotional issues involved. He treated me as a professional officer first and a woman second. Then we turned to how to deal with the problem.

When he asked me exactly what I planned to do, I said, "I had thought I could call Larry Smith and tell him he needed to withdraw his name from the Deputy IG assignment or I was prepared to go to the Army leadership with my account of the incident."

The lawyer frowned and shook his head. "No, Claudia, that would be extortion, even if you were to leave out the threat about going to the leadership."

"Well," I said, "it would be terrible for the Army if Smith gets that job, so I think I'll go to the Vice Chief and tell him what happened."

The next day, the lawyer called me at my quarters. "I've been thinking about this matter. Rather than reporting the incident to the Vice Chief, you should go to the IG himself." The lawyer had two reasons for this suggestion: One, the Inspector General was the correct channel for reporting general officer misconduct, and two, the matter ought to be investigated officially, not just dealt with informally without giving Smith the chance to clear his name.

This made sense. One lesson I had learned in an earlier case involving another officer was that making an official report might not result in a finding on one's own incident, but might bring forward evidence about more serious incidents that were disclosed as a result of that investigation, as it had during the earlier Fort McPherson Article 15 investigation.

So I understood the value of having the Smith matter investigated. And since I knew it would be hard to have my complaint substantiated due to lack of witnesses, I thought it was worth the exposure of a public investigation to pursue the question of Smith treating other women in a similar way.

The last week of September 1999, I spoke to the Inspector General, Lieutenant General Michael W. Ackerman, in a closed-door meeting. I described what had happened with Smith in my Pentagon office three years earlier. General Ackerman's demeanor was serious, his voice grave as he asked questions. It was clear from his manner that he understood why I had come: I felt that Major General Larry Smith was the wrong man to become Ackerman's deputy.

After describing the events, I added, "This is something you needed to know. But I'd just hate for it to become a public matter."

"I don't know exactly what I'm going to do about this right now," Ackerman said. "Are you willing to put it in writing?"

"Yes, I am."

He thanked me and I left the office. I wrote a memo by hand, a single paragraph describing the Smith incident. After dating and signing the memo, I made myself a copy and delivered the original to General Ackerman.

In the following days, people from the IG's office asked, "What exactly is it that you want?" My reply was consistent: I wanted them to believe me and I did not want Larry Smith to become the Deputy Inspector General.

Because of the pending investigation, Smith did not assume duties as the Deputy Inspector General. Instead, he took a temporary assignment at the Army Materiel Command.

I, of course, was not privy to any aspects of the investigation other than the two sworn statements I gave to a lieutenant colonel from the Inspector General's office. She took extensive notes and tape-recorded my statement. Her questions were probing, and she doubled back frequently, revealing she was a well-trained investigator. Several of her questions concerned my motives in making the complaint. Had I harbored any animosity toward Smith prior to the incident? No. Had we ever been in competition for the same assignment? No. Had I in any way encouraged Smith's alleged sexual misconduct? No.

After two interviews with the investigators in October and November, I heard nothing more from the IG's office. I had to assume they were proceeding with their investigation, what was known in Army culture as "murder boarding" the problem. I also had to assume Larry Smith had denied my complaint. This was a classic "she says, he says" situation. So my credibility and motives were of paramount importance.

Christmas and New Year passed and I heard nothing more from the IG's office. In February 2000, I publicly announced my plans to retire that summer. By then, I would have already served an extra year as DCSINT beyond the normal two-year tour and would be ready to take up civilian life. I had accepted the possibility that the Smith investigation would end inconclusively. From what I knew of IG investigations, women who had previously worked with Smith would have been interviewed about his conduct. I had heard no reports that they had lodged complaints against him. So it looked as if the matter might just be dropped.

It was better to let the case die without publicity. The previous fall, another senior officer, Major General John J. Maher III, had received nonjudicial punishment when the Army found that Maher had engaged in conduct unbecoming an officer by having improper sexual relationships with the wives of two subordinate officers and attempting an improper relationship with an enlisted soldier. Secretary of the Army Louis Caldera ordered that Maher be reduced two grades and retired as a colonel. Predictably, the Maher case received widespread media coverage. The Army did not need another scandal involving a major general.

So with Larry Smith removed from consideration for the Deputy Inspector General assignment, I would have been happy had the whole business escaped public scrutiny.

Having thought these matters through, I felt at peace. The investigators would recognize that I had nothing to gain by making the accusation. Smith would not get the assignment. And the Army could react toward him as it saw fit. That was out of my hands, although I knew an IG investigation was an extremely thorough process that would probe every angle before it was over.

* * *

By the evening of March 29, 2000, I had heard nothing more about the Inspector General investigation. I was rushing to dress for the annual USO benefit dinner when I got a call from Major General Gil Meyer, the Army's chief Public Affairs Officer.

"Claudia, this afternoon I received three questions from Rowan Scarborough of the *Washington Times* about a reported complaint of sexual harassment of you by another general officer that has resulted in an IG investigation."

Well, I thought, *the story has leaked.* "Tell him 'no comment,'" I told Gil.

"We've got to give him something," Gil persisted.

I could sympathize with his position. But I did not have to deal with the news media. And also, I didn't respect the *Washington Times,* which had taken a consistently antagonistic position toward women in the military. I did not trust them to give the story fair treatment. Besides, there was an Inspector General investigation underway, and it would be inappropriate for me to comment. "Tell him I'm not interested in speaking with him."

Gil Meyer was unhappy, but I advised him to ask the new Chief of Staff, General Eric K. Shinseki, how he wanted to handle the situation. At the USO dinner that night, a photographer from the *Washington Times* came up and took several pictures of me. *Great,* I thought, *now it begins.*

The next morning, the *Washington Times* story ran on the front page under the headline "Female General Accuses Peer of Harassment." Other than the fact that I had indeed told Gil Meyer to say, "Lt. Gen. Kennedy has no comment," the story contained many misstatements.

Obviously, somebody had leaked information to the paper. What had not been leaked, however, was Larry Smith's name. I was the only general named. This meant I was now the sole media lightning rod, especially as Scarborough noted that my complaint "apparently represents the military's first case of purported general-on-general sexual harassment."

The story then diverged widely from the facts, speculating that I was "said to be First Lady Hillary Rodham Clinton's favorite general." The *Washington Times* cited a 1997 interview I had given to *USA Weekend* in which I'd noted instances of sexual harassment during my career. One case concerned telling the man involved that if he ever did this to me again, I would report him "pretty high up" in our chain of command.

The *Washington Times* also linked me to the Army's Consideration of Others (COO) program, apparently trying to imply that I was obsessed with the subject. It did not note that the COO program had been originated by Major General Robert Foley, that General Foley was a Medal of Honor recipient, one of the most respected leaders in the Army. Nor did the paper reveal that Army Chief of Staff General Dennis Reimer had instructed *all* general officers to mention the COO program in their public appearances. But they did find space in the article to mention that the nonpartisan White House Project had listed me in 1998 among twenty potential female presidential candidates.

While thin on substance, the story was heavy on innuendo, implying that I was a politically motivated and politically correct officer who ruthlessly wielded charges of sexual harassment as a tool to gain individual power.

But the article was a model of restraint compared to the vituperation that the reporter's boss, editor-in-chief Wesley Pruden, launched against me in a column the next day. He accused me and my fellow Army leaders of being "Petticoat Generals." According to Pruden's snide account, I ("a helpless little thing") had suffered a "grope wound" unworthy of complaint, but for which I would probably receive a Purple Heart. Pruden further tried to associate my name with the Consideration of Others program, apparently implying that it, rather than my responsibilities as DCSINT, had become my focus. He also insinuated that "COOing" had become a dominant feature of a "woman's Army."

Once the *Washington Times* story was published, the media firestorm I had feared ignited. The Washington press corps badgered Secretary of Defense William S. Cohen and former Army Chief of Staff General Dennis Reimer. Both officials stated they had not been aware of my putative complaint three years earlier. That week the first of what would be repeated errors about the case began to accumulate. Media accounts incorrectly stated that I had complained "informally" to my superiors following the 1996 incident. That left the impression that the Army had either ignored my grievance or actively suppressed it.

This was simply wrong, but I didn't want to discuss the matter publicly at that time.

Meanwhile, television producers for all the leading news anchors and correspondents were tying up my office telephones and lobbing e-mails at me. Each TV personality wanted an exclusive interview; each presented compelling, apparently sincere reasons why I should cooperate to tell my side of the story. I told my staff to decline their persistent requests. All this took place during the Elián González situation, and my fervent hope that week as I switched on the television set in the morning was that the little Cuban boy's father would arrive in Washington to deflect the media glare from me.

A veteran media consultant in Washington whom I knew gave me some of the best advice I received during this unpleasant time: "Don't give *any* interviews," she said. "If you start talking now, you'll never have any peace."

But remaining silent was not easy. As the press accounts and television segments on my situation snowballed, the number of errors grew apace. Thomas Ricks's front-page story in the *Washington Post* on April 1, 2000, for example, reiterated the false impression that I had complained "quietly" to the Army leadership after the 1996 incident, and had only "recently" brought charges after the unnamed general had been promoted. Ricks cited one unnamed "Army official" as saying I had made a formal allegation because I felt the Army had not kept its implicit promise to not further advance the career of the other general. This was rumormongering. It was inaccurate. And it was splashed across the front page of the *Washington Post.*

Ricks continued that the high-profile confrontation "appears likely to bring a sour note to the end of the 31-year career of Kennedy."

He added that there was "widespread irritation within the Army" toward me, supposedly because I had raised "an old charge," but also because my work as the DCSINT "has won few admirers."

The article brought up further negative innuendo by stating "Pentagon insiders also speculated" that I was acting now out of spite, having lost in the competition to command the Training and Doctrine Command (TRADOC), an assignment that would have brought promotion to four-star rank. This was also not true. I had never anticipated being offered the assignment, as historically the commanding general of TRADOC has always been a combat arms officer. Further, I had known since 1992 that serving as DCSINT would be my last Army assignment.

Yet, Ricks and the *Washington Post* saw fit to tarnish my reputation by making it appear that my going to the Inspector General with an "old charge" had been an act of malice.

Most of the news accounts continued with the basic error that I had filed a formal sexual harassment complaint in 1999, more than three years after first complaining informally to my superiors. Usually the sources cited were unnamed "Army officials" or "officials familiar with the case."

Then, a week after the story broke, the news media learned through another Pentagon leak that Larry Smith was the general officer against whom I had lodged my complaint to the IG. Like me, Smith refused to discuss the case with the press.

The only positive aspect of this leak was that the media made the connection between my complaint to the IG the previous fall and Smith's nomination to the post of Deputy Inspector General.

News leaks continued, some purporting to contain evidence that the IG's investigators had gathered. Each time there was a new leak, another flurry of press and television stories appeared.

After the story became public, I gathered my senior Army and civilian staff and discussed what had happened with Larry Smith in my office. I did this so they would understand why I had gone to the IG after Smith was nominated to become the Deputy Inspector General.

"I want to talk to you about this situation," I told them. "You're affected by it almost as much as I am. You deserve to know what occurred, but I want you to keep it close hold."

They assured me they would do so.

It was important for me as a leader to keep my own team informed so that their uncertainty was reduced to a minimum.

"Any questions?" I asked my staff.

They had none.

They were supportive, especially as the volume of vindictive and wacky messages I received increased following each fresh news leak.

For example, an attorney in Massapequa, New York, scrawled a memo to Secretary of Defense William Cohen, subject: "Lieut. General Kennedy (her very rank is stupid; where are you Lt. General Patton!)" The memo went on to say that the Kennedy-Smith "saga" only demonstrated the "ridiculous" concept of the gender-neutral military. He referred to me as "the poor girl" who was sexually harassed by "that bad bad General Smith!" Concluding, "How stupid, how lame, how feminine the once mighty U.S. Army has become, shame!", the lawyer signed as a proud former enlisted man. On the face of the envelope containing his memo, he had printed, "(Poor Sexually Harassed Girl . . . a Lt. General, yet!)."

It looked as if I had lost a potential friend among the legal fraternity of Massapequa, New York.

Another writer, describing himself as a "WW II vet," didn't waste words. "The sooner you leave the Army, the better we will all be!" He suggested that I would have never "risen above corporal" if I weren't a female and that my entire Army career had been "mediocre." "Military women," he said, wanted the "best of both worlds." Women wanted to "prance around in your tight skirts and heels, makeup and false eyelashes, you think things are great and you have your pick of the litter." But if a man "makes a pass at you, a normal male preoccupation, you shout foul." He concluded that "we made a huge mistake when we allowed women into the ranks and your recent complaint is merely additional proof."

It seemed probable that this writer was among those in World War II who heartily backed the slander against women in uniform. Nothing in the intervening fifty years had changed his mind. I asked my executive officer to draft a polite reply in which I noted, "It is clear that you have a strong sense of loyalty to our nation and to our beloved Army." And I cited my gratitude to the sacrifices his generation had made during World War II. But I also noted that I was proud to have had the opportunity to serve my country in uniform for more than thirty years.

On April 8, 2000, I received a letter postmarked Colorado Springs with a return address "Highly Pissed Veterans." Whether that referred to their emotional state or their state of inebriation was not immediately clear. There were some obvious illogical elements to the letter, which was addressed to me by rank followed by "(Ms Gutless)." The writer had typed "Eyes only" on the envelope, but then proceeded just below with the message "Woman: you are a disgrace to all good American women. We are ashame [sic] of you. You are a man hater. You should volunteer for hanging at once . . ." The message on the envelope face continued in that vein for several lines, ending with, "Get lost!" The letter inside was equally enlightening. "Dear Trouble Maker: Good thing the women were not permitted to serve with men in WW II. The war would have been lost on their account. Did you ever have sex before? Go after that man. The military is no place for virgins."

This writer (writers?) apparently had never heard of the WAC or the several thousand military nurses who had helped save countless lives of wounded during World War II. But I didn't bother to reply to the letter.

A card from St. Louis, addressed to "Claudia 'He Groped Me' Kennedy, U.S. Homosexual Army, Pentagon," got right to the point: "Kennedy: By your idiotic accusations, you prove that women should *not* be allowed in the armed services. Perhaps male homosexuals, female lesbians and women could form one division to be used *in combat* not just high paid paper shufflers!"

He did not receive a reply.

Several men wrote, inviting me out for dinner, sending photographs and biographical information.

Every day, the staff would deliver similar letters to be sorted in my outer office. One called me a "Generalette," another the "Princess of COO." (The fallacy that I had created the program would not die. Conservative columnist Mona Charen wrote, "Gen. Kennedy introduced an innovation in military training with the acronym COO, 'Consideration of Others' training.")

With the Inspector General investigation moving slowly ahead, there was no way I could publicly reply to any of this criticism. Instead, I discovered the true value of having a thick skin. People I knew and cared about were wonderfully supportive. These detractors were strangers. That said it all to me.

In addition to the personal support my friends provided, a few became surrogates, taking it upon themselves to privately contact the media as inaccuracies about the case surfaced.

And the tone of media coverage began to moderate when it became evident that the reason I had not raised the Smith incident in 1996 was because it was not necessary to do so and that I had only come forward in 1999 after Smith was in line to become the Deputy Inspector General.

I also had a solid base of public and private support during this period. In a letter to the editor, retired Brigadier General Evelyn "Pat" Foote wrote a stinging rebuff to the original Thomas Ricks *Washington Post* article. She cited Ricks's "less-than-heroic and nameless sources of information" at the Pentagon who had attacked my personal and professional credentials. General Foote added that "Kennedy had the audacity to place her convictions on the line, knowing the price she would have to pay. Perhaps if more generals in the armed forces held all of their peers to the same standards they demand of the troops, fewer scandals of personal or professional dereliction would be played out in the press. Bless Kennedy. She truly has the 'right stuff.'"

Representative Carolyn B. Maloney, a Democrat from New York, told the *New York Times* that I "broke the glass ceiling but still was not immune from sexual harassment." She added that "It took courage to come forward and file a complaint, knowing her own reputation would be first on the line."

I was surprised that the *Washington Post,* apparently stung by readers' criticism, withdrew support for their original story on the incident. On April 23, 2000, *Post* ombudsman E. R. Shipp acknowledged that Thomas Ricks's April 1 story had "misfired," and noted that Ricks now said, if he were doing the first article again, he would "reconsider the tone of the story."

Even the *Washington Times* began to moderate its tone somewhat. That might have had something to do with the fact that politically savvy Washington attorney Chuck Ruff represented me. He didn't tell me what approach he was taking, but it's reasonable to assume he made a few phone calls on my behalf. Additionally, Kathy Bonk, executive director of Communications Consortium Media Center, provided wise counsel on the increasingly complex relations with the news media.

Throughout this period, Steve Meyer of the *New York Times* had the best track record for accuracy and balance.

At the private level, messages of support came rolling in. For example, a decorated Infantry colonel and colleague from a previous assignment e-mailed a brief message: "Just sending a very respectful 'hang in there.'" An Army chaplain sent an e-mail: "I continue to keep you in my thoughts and prayers." A member of the DCSINT staff sent a message with an uplifting quote from President Theodore Roosevelt praising those who stood by their beliefs. His message ended, "Again, you have our unequivocal support." Retired Major General Mary Clarke, who had been a colonel commanding the WAC Center and School at Fort McClellan when I'd been a young captain commanding a company, wrote a touching note citing my decision to file a complaint with the Inspector General as epitomizing the "special trust, confidence and fidelity" found in an officer's commission. These qualities, she said, came at a time when they needed reinforcement to show that the senior leadership of the Army really cared about their soldiers and was willing to "stand up and be counted."

And the support I received was often direct and personal. One evening as I was walking to my car in the South Parking Lot of the Pentagon, a Navy lieutenant commander ran up behind me and saluted. "Ma'am," he said, "you don't know me." *Okay,* I thought, *this could be good or it could be bad.* What he said was good. "I don't mean to impose, but I just want to tell you how sorry I am this thing happened to you and how grateful I am that you reported it. Guys like that general have no place in the service. Men are as outraged about this as women."

Later, after I had attended a promotion ceremony, a senior NCO approached. The man came to attention. "Ma'am, I just want to salute you."

All this support was a source of great strength. In the days following the first press stories, I had felt like avoiding the Pentagon corridors. But I knew I had to keep my head up and look people right in the eye. They smiled, indicating their strong support. "Hello, ma'am," I heard from strangers whenever I walked the corridors. There were as many men as women voicing this tacit support.

Among my close circle of personal colleagues and friends, everyone believed me and no one ever pressed for additional details on the October 1996 incident.

On May 8, 2000, the U.S. Army Inspector General Agency completed its investigation of my complaint against Larry Smith. Although the IG report was labeled "FOR OFFICIAL USE ONLY," parts of it were leaked to the press within two days. The press references to the report still contained errors, but the major conclusions were accurate: The Inspector General had substantiated my complaint against Smith.

But senior Pentagon leadership was reviewing the IG report, so that I received no official notification of the investigation results.

Later, I obtained a redacted version of the report under the

Freedom of Information Act. The report revealed no evidence that Smith had committed acts of sexual misconduct earlier in his career. In summarizing the reasons for substantiating my complaint, the Inspector General noted that evaluating the allegations "came down to a question of credibility. There appeared to be no motive for LTG Kennedy to jeopardize her career and reputation by making false allegations. . . . She was senior to him. They were not in competition for assignments. She did not arrange the office call. There was no apparent incentive for her to ruin his unblemished career and destroy their friendship with false allegations." I had acted "out of loyalty to the Army" to prevent similar incidents from recurring. "Thus, when one weighed all the testimony and considered all the evidence, coupled with the lack of motive to lie, the preponderance or greater weight of the evidence was sufficient to substantiate LTG Kennedy's allegations."

The report also substantiated that Smith had committed an "assault consummated by a battery," but that this "lesser included offense" would be combined into one allegation of improper sexual harassment. The Inspector General also substantiated that Smith was guilty of conduct unbecoming an officer and a gentleman.

It was not until July 7, 2000, however, five weeks after my retirement ceremony in the Pentagon central courtyard, that the Army officially announced that the Inspector General had "substantiated charges of sexual harassment made by Lt. Gen. Claudia Kennedy against Maj. Gen. Larry Smith." After briefly describing Smith's October 1996 behavior, the official statement noted that I "did not report the incident to any Army official until Maj. Gen. Smith was identified in 1999 to be the Deputy Inspector General of the Army," a position that involved overseeing investigations of sexual harassment.

The statement continued that Smith had received an administrative memorandum of reprimand from General John M. Keane, Vice Chief of Staff of the Army. Such a reprimand effectively ended Smith's career.

The Army had upheld my credibility, even though Smith

stated publicly, "I have always and continue to maintain that I did not commit these allegations and I am deeply disappointed with the decision to substantiate them. However, for the good of my family and the Army, we have elected to put it behind us and move on with our lives." The Army accepted Smith's request to retire on September 1, 2000.

I released a brief public statement through Army public affairs: "I am satisfied with the Army's action in this case. As far as I am concerned, this matter is closed."

                          *   *   *

That statement ended a troubling time for me. But the closing of the Smith incident certainly did not end the chapter on sexual harassment and misconduct in the Army. As the work of the Review Panel demonstrated, an unacceptably large proportion of women and men soldiers experience sexual harassment, sexual misconduct, and sex discrimination, but many of their colleagues and leaders did not share this perception or attach much significance to it.

Others, however, including the most successful commissioned officers and NCO leaders the panel contacted, were very aware that the human relations environment in their units was a key factor in achieving their missions. In this regard, these successful leaders held the same attitudes as their civilian counterparts. It is widely assumed among many women activists that men "just don't get it" when it comes to sexual harassment. But what I learned in my own case and from membership on the panel is that many men *do* get it. They feel bad about sexual harassment. And they work consistently to eliminate it from their organizations.

Here is the lesson to take from this: Sometimes women do not give these men enough support in discussions of sexual harassment when the issue of gender is raised as if it were an unbreachable barrier dividing men and women. From my own experience, it has become quite clear that it is not gender that divides us any more than it defines us. *Behavior* defines and divides us. If we act appropriately, and more importantly, if our leaders from the most junior NCO to the most senior general exemplify high standards of behavior and require all of us to follow them, the issues of fairness and equality would soon be resolved.

For me, recent troubling incidents have brought home some important lessons. It used to be entirely up to the individual soldier, not the Army, to deal with cases of sexual misconduct. But the shameful crimes at Aberdeen put an end to that. Now the Army has to respond to an individual soldier's complaints.

In my own case, some displeased senior generals have said that I should have dealt with Smith privately and not officially involved the institution of the Army. But they miss the point. I did deal with the Smith incident privately at the time. Only when he was assigned to become the Deputy Inspector General, a position for which he was not qualified given his behavior toward me, did the matter become an institutional responsibility.

Do I wish none of this had happened? On a personal level, absolutely. My last few months on active duty were a time of distraction and unwanted publicity. Until then I valued my privacy. And I also knew my decision to come forward with a complaint would definitely affect my professional future. There were positions outside the Army for which I am qualified, but which would never be open to me after the notoriety of the Smith case.

That is just a fact of life. It's human nature (not only in the Army) for people to react negatively to injured parties. They get cut from the herd. Call it the whistleblower syndrome. It is an important question for both civilian and military leaders to address as they try to resolve problems of fairness and equality in their organizations.

* * *

Given the nature of the highly publicized Smith incident, my guess is that a lot of readers will have turned to this chapter first. I hope they don't stop here, but go back to the beginning of the book. I think they'll find an interesting story.

8

Fitness

PHYSICAL, MENTAL, AND SPIRITUAL

*F*or most people today the image that comes to mind when they hear the word "soldier" is of a robust young man or woman in camouflage Battle Dress Uniform, the epitome of physical fitness and mental alertness. Indeed, the Army has been developing programs for decades to make that image a reality for all soldiers, no matter their rank or age.

And it has been my own experience that fitness is an essential attribute of effective leadership, that physical and mental fitness are intertwined, and that what I call spiritual fitness provides successful leaders an added dimension of character from which they can draw strength at times of stress and crisis.

* * *

Physical fitness is probably the best known of these three attributes. Some of the first newsreels of soldiers taken at training bases during World War I showed them doing calisthenics on the parade ground, an aspect of military training that has not changed much since the days of Sparta. Millennia later when the

United States sent its soldiers into combat during the Persian Gulf War, they were probably the fittest troops ever engaged on the battlefield.

When I was a company commander at Fort McClellan, our post commander, Major General Joseph Kingston, who believed strongly in the value of physical fitness to restore discipline among the soldiers of the "hollow Army" of the mid-1970s, re-flected one day as we stood in my company area on the connec-tion between physical fitness and morale. Units running together in formation—headed by their platoon leaders or com-pany commanders—enhanced that intangible but essential psy-chological factor known as esprit de corps.

"Captain," he said, "you need to make sure your soldiers have a physical training program."

"Yes, sir," I replied.

But when I later discussed the issue with First Sergeant Ben-son, she raised some pragmatic concerns. "When would we do this, ma'am? Will the Training Center release our people for PT? And where will we get the equipment and the trainers?"

In short, she correctly indicated that the Army then placed little emphasis on physical fitness. But for the last twenty-five years, physical training and fitness have become an Army priority.

Recent Army programs have included the Fit to Win and Fit to Fight campaigns, under which individual soldiers and units train for and maintain their fitness. The two main aspects of the effort are weight control and physical conditioning achieved through physical training. Soldiers must now maintain their weight within a certain range based on gender, height, and age. For example, a thirty-five-year-old woman soldier who is five feet five inches must weigh less than 146 pounds, while a man the same age who is five feet eleven inches must weigh less than 195 pounds. Soldiers who exceed these limits are put on remedial programs to learn about diet and to exercise more frequently. The Army takes this effort seriously: Soldiers' height and weight appear on their Efficiency Reports, and those who are unable to meet their weight standards within a certain period of time are discharged.

This was not always the case, especially for so-called garrison troops, the kind of soldiers General Kingston was concerned about. The mess halls of the past were not the place for a soldier trying to lose weight. The typical chow line at breakfast included creamed beef on toast, sausage patties, and grits dripping in butter. The main course at lunch was often pot roast and mashed potatoes swimming in gravy. Fresh vegetables were hard to find. Salad bars were unknown.

In the past, the problem of being fat and being in poor physical condition became serious when soldiers were no longer either in demanding training or assigned to units with a physically active mission. That was the main reason the Army revamped its nutritional program and modernized its mess halls, which are now called "dining facilities." Today the Army feeds its soldiers wisely, always providing lower-fat alternatives to traditional high-calorie meals. Fruits, vegetables, and whole grains are plentiful. And every year, the Army holds competitions among its cooks to recognize those who can provide the most nutritious and appealing dishes. The old saw about the mess sergeant having his taste buds shot off in the last war simply no longer applies.

* * *

In 1982, when I was a major on the staff of the Military Intelligence brigade at Field Station Augsburg, I became involved in competitive running almost by chance. I had enjoyed running individually about twice a week since arriving in Germany. My apartment in downtown Augsburg overlooked Jakobertor, one of the five standing Romanesque gates of the ancient walled city. I was lucky to have a two-bedroom flat in a new building with a grocery on the ground floor and a basement garage. By German standards, I lived well.

Most weekends, I ran along the inside perimeter of the wall, alternating from path to sidewalk. This kept me safely out of the warren of narrow streets, through which the local burghers careered in their Mercedes and Audis like so many Panzer-grenadiers at the battle of Kursk. (According to GI lore, Augsburg was one-hour driving time west of Munich, unless the driver was German, in which case the trip took twenty minutes.)

The weather was cool; the dirt paths were soft from the frequent Bavarian rain. But I didn't consider myself a serious competitor. Running was just an avocation that kept me fit and cleared my head after a busy day at the office. I began that tour at Field Station Augsburg as assistant operations officer and later became the station operations officer. The assignment perfectly matched the intensive specialized training I had undergone during the three-year Junior Officer Cryptologic Career Program at NSA. My work kept me in a huge windowless building all day. Soldiers doing shift work—"on trick"—came and went in large groups every eight hours. If there were a crisis, and the need to meet a "surge" requirement, everyone was so absorbed with their mission that they wanted to remain on the operations floor to observe and help out. The NCOs had to send soldiers home to get their rest to be prepared for their next shift.

For at least six months of the year, I would arrive at the immense gray building before the cold dawn and leave after the sunset. For many of us, skiing in the Alps on holidays and weekends gave us the one occasion to climb above the clouds and see the sun. But just getting outdoors and running provided a physical outlet I could tap into whenever I wanted.

Many soldiers, however, considered running just an irksome requirement on the semiannual PT test. Most still ran in their combat boots, and only changed to running shoes in the early 1980s. When one warrant officer went to the PX to buy his running shoes, the clerk asked him how often he ran. "Maybe twice a year," he replied, "if I can't get out of it."

"These will last you a lifetime," she said, handing him a pair of Nikes over the counter.

Then one day a captain named Dodson came into my office to announce he was forming a cross-country team to participate in the VII Corps championship. The competition would take place near Munich in a few weeks. The five-kilometer run required each team to field both men and women of a variety of ages.

"We can't do it without a senior woman runner," he said. "And we don't have one. Can you help us out?"

I was hesitant, having never run cross-country competitively before. What if my slow speed hurt the team's performance? But I had been successfully accomplishing the two-mile run on the Army Physical Fitness Test well within my age and gender standards. And the 5-K run was not that much longer. Besides, I tended to perform better on runs requiring more endurance than speed. This might prove interesting.

"Yes," I told him. "I'll run."

The day of the run was cold and misty after recent heavy rains. I ran in a field of women soldiers, most of them younger than me, including an enlisted woman who was considered the favorite based on her past record of unchallenged victories. After the start, I fell into a steady, dogged pace. The ground was so soaked and chewed up by earlier competitors that the backs of my legs and my shirt were soon slick with liquid mud thrown up from the soles of my shoes. The young woman soldier ahead was obviously concerned about being beaten by a runner she could hear gasping close behind her. But I didn't have the breath to reassure her that I was in the older, masters category and thus not a competitive threat to her.

To my great amazement, I became the VII Corps women's masters champion for 1983. To my even greater amazement, I discovered there was a follow-on competition in a few weeks in which I also had to run. I won that event as well, and became that year's U.S. Army Europe (USAREUR) women's masters champion.

A year later, I was assigned as an action officer in the Training Directorate of the Office of the Deputy Chief of Staff for Operations and Plans (ODCSOPS) in the Pentagon. When I reported for duty, my boss, Colonel Dennis Malcor (who retired as a major general), called me into his office for a brief introductory meeting.

At the conclusion of the serious discussion, he leaned back in his chair to point at a picture on the wall showing only a muscular forearm and hand. "Major," he said with mock severity, "I wouldn't expect you to know this since you're so new here, but you are talking to the world's foremost handball player."

"Sir," I replied in the same tone, "you have no way of knowing it, but *you* are talking to USAREUR's women's master running champion."

He grinned. "Good," he said, his tone growing more serious. "In this directorate you will do physical training three times a week during duty hours. That is mandatory, two hours of PT, three times a week. You will work the rest of your schedule around that requirement."

"Yes, sir."

The other action officers, all of whom loved and respected Colonel Malcor, confirmed his prowess on the handball and racquetball courts. "But don't worry about him beating you on the PT test," another major told me. "For the run, you'll need a calendar to time him, not a stopwatch."

Colonel Malcor's edict was rooted in concern for his officers' well-being and for the success of the organization he led. In the previous eighteen months, four people in the ODCSOPS had died of heart attacks, one right at his desk. This was just the beginning of the Army's antismoking campaign and the emphasis on better nutrition. It was also the early days of the effort to clean up traditionally heavy drinking and to encourage running as a social event rather than the nearly obligatory happy hour at the officers club.

However, the conversion of the Army from hard drinking to hard running was not without resistance from a few traditional soldiers. I'll always remember a particular sergeant in the MI brigade I later commanded in Hawaii. He had been injured in an accident and a "line of duty" investigation was conducted. The investigating officer summarized the accident this way:

"This NCO was bowling off duty. In the process of throwing the ball, he states that his ankle gave out, and he hit himself in the head with the bowling ball and also fell against the ball return, knocking himself out. He had a blood alcohol content of .31, which I believe contributed significantly to the accident, which I find is therefore not in the line of duty."

★ ★ ★

As Colonel Malcor saw it, mandatory physical training three days a week during duty hours would accomplish several goals. It would by definition improve his officers' physical fitness, thus give them some protection against cardiovascular disease, and the required break from the office would relieve some of the inevitable stress inherent to work in the Pentagon.

And no one could deny there was plenty of stress. The Training Directorate of DCSOPS had to "build" detailed resource packages to justify funding for the Army's widespread and extremely varied training programs. These packages covered the coming five fiscal years with projections for Basic Training, Advanced Individual Training, Intelligence Training, and other programs. All of these packages—which included computer printouts dense with budget numbers—had to pass through multiple levels of review as they made their way up through the Army bureaucracy.

The work was very demanding. Mistakes at my level might jeopardize the future of an important program. For example, I might be given the package for a proposed multimillion-dollar field exercise area expansion at Fort Leonard Wood, Missouri, designed to increase the effectiveness of Combat Engineer Training. But every aspect of the package had to be thoroughly justified.

And we were always required to complete this work under brutal time pressure. In bureaucratese, the deadline for a requirement was known as a "suspense." In other words, a red-tabbed file might be marked with a suspense of 1415 Hours 25

January, meaning the work had to be turned over to the Staff Action Control Office (SACO) by 2:15 P.M. on that date.

Often, I'd arrive at my desk at 6:15 A.M. to find at least one red-tabbed file some gnome had left the previous night marked with early morning suspenses clearly impossible to meet. My first task would be to pick up the phone and call SACO to get them to change the deadlines.

But during January and February, the period of most intense activity for Army action officers—due to the programming cycle in which the armed services sought to justify their funding requests—normal workplace stress grew fierce. People became short-tempered; patience among previously amicable colleagues became hard to find as we made our way from office to office in search of the precious "chops" indicating concurrence on a policy or resource change. Often this involved a lengthy discussion to provide information or persuade our counterparts on the finer points of complex policy.

Late one afternoon, I rushed a resource package to a lieutenant colonel's cubicle, only to stand in line almost to the point of my deadline. As he left the room before I could get him to initial my paper, I thrust the document forward.

"Colonel," I said, "could you please give me a quick chop on this?"

"You can just wait, Major," he snarled, his jaw rigid with tension. "This is the first damn break I've had all day, and I'm going to take it."

I dashed off to collect some more chops, then returned to get his.

Sometimes phone calls would begin normally and quickly escalate to sharp debates. That was the way a lot of days went during those months. Hence Colonel Malcor's emphasis on the need to relieve stress. He did not want people dying at their desks from cardiac arrest.

I was the only woman officer among my peers and seniors in the office. Army officers and enlisted soldiers then wore either the Class B uniform consisting of a black cardigan and green slacks (or skirt) or the Class A uniform with the skirt or slacks and jacket with name tag and insignia indicating branch and rank, as well as decorations. Men officers had a wide black stripe on the outer seam of their trousers; enlisted men did not. Women's skirts had no black stripe to distinguish officers from enlisted; a woman wearing the cardigan and skirt might be any rank from private through general officer. I therefore made a practice of always wearing my jacket outside the office so that my peers immediately saw I was one of them.

I had adopted this habit after years of men soldiers and women civilians misunderstanding that I actually was an Army officer. As a lieutenant, I might telephone a person, saying, "This is Lieutenant Kennedy." "*Louise* Kennedy?" "No, *Lieutenant* Kennedy." Or, "This is Captain Kennedy." "*Kathleen* Kennedy?" They just didn't expect to be talking to a woman Army officer. I had learned early that the symbols of authority are important in a hierarchical culture like the Army.

Most of the men I worked with had never worked with a woman as a colleague. I believed that my credibility in their eyes would be best built on some objective measure of competence. And since Military Intelligence was not appreciated by those outside the discipline, I had an added hurdle to cross before bonding with my colleagues, most of whom came from the Combat Arms. Physical fitness would be one such easily observable measure of competence.

I decided the best way to meet Colonel Malcor's PT requirement was to reach the office, work until lunch, then head over to the Pentagon Officers Athletic Club (POAC), a grungy facility located near the North Parking Lot. After PT, I'd return to the office and work straight through until 6:30 or 7:00 P.M.

I became quite familiar with the POAC. In the locker room, you could smell decades of stale sweat that had seeped into the splayed wood of the benches and chipped concrete floor. One day after performing sets of push-ups and sit-ups in the gym, I went outside to the wall to stretch before taking off on a two-mile run. Glancing down, I saw a dead rat. Two days later, the rat was still there. And the next time I returned, some wag had placed a shoe box over the rodent's corpse with the epitaph "RIP" emblazoned in black Magic Marker.

To me, the practical advantage of these workouts was that I got to practice three days each week for the semiannual Army Physical Fitness Test. The payoff came the first time the action officers in the directorate assembled near the POAC to take the test. I knew the men in my office were watching to see how well I'd do. The officers put a high premium on physical performance. So I was determined to do my best.

The test was comprised of three components: push-ups, sit-ups, and the two-mile run. When I joined the Army in 1968, no one over the age of forty was required to take the PT test. By 1982, however, every soldier in the Army had to pass it, but the minimum requirements were adjusted for age and gender. Even so, I wanted to show that I was not merely scraping by in meeting the standards adjusted for women's physiology.

It was a crisp northern Virginia fall morning when we all assembled in our T-shirts and shorts. In the push-up component, each officer took his turn on the gym floor and competed against a stopwatch. I came close to my maximum number of push-ups in the two minutes allowed and caught my breath for the sit-ups.

We all had partners to hold our ankles as we went to work, trying to complete the maximum number of sit-ups in a two-minute period. But if your form was bad, the graders standing above you would keep repeating the number you were stuck at until you got the form right.

I heard somebody chanting ". . . sixteen, sixteen, sixteen . . ." to some poor soul who was flagging.

This only increased my resolve. Over the years, critics have complained that women have it easier when taking the Army Physical Fitness Test, that they are held to lower standards than their men peers. This is an argument based on a lack of understanding of what the test measures. The test measures levels of effort and scientifically reflects the physiological differences between men and women and between old and young. A man's weight is high on his frame, in the chest and shoulders. And his upper body muscles are more adapted to push-ups. But women have an advantage over men in sit-ups. A woman's center of gravity is lower, in her hips, and her abdominal muscles are better suited to sit-ups. The Army PT test is normative, not comparative.

Nevertheless, I wanted to show my new colleagues I was not content to meet minimum standards. As I knocked out my sit-ups in quick succession, one of my fellow action officers teased, "You're just hotdogging." But I didn't let him distract me. At the end of my allotted two minutes, I had racked up over eighty sit-ups, the best score of anyone in our group.

We all went outside the gym and assembled beside the North Parking Lot for the two-mile run. When I crossed the finish line back at the parking lot, I was pleased that my training had paid off, that I'd kept up my optimal pace, and proud to note that I had run faster than many others.

From that day on, I noticed a perceptible change in my colleagues' attitude toward me. I had proven that I could "hack it" in an arena they considered their own. The numbers in the PT test gave them a concrete means to measure my competence in an important part of our profession.

That was when I realized that physical fitness offers a real benefit to women working in a man's world, including civilian workplaces. There is an unfortunate double standard between men and women when it comes to appearance and fitness. In civilian life, a man in power might be obviously overweight and out of shape, but be considered a vital executive in his organization or a respected leader. Women, however, are denigrated as being "dumpy" if their weight and perceived level of fitness do not meet certain expectations. Coupled with that disdain comes the perception that such women are not capable of leadership. Conversely, if a woman in a largely male group is seen as physically fit, she will be perceived to be more competent in other areas as well. That was an important consideration for me in the early 1980s when many of my men peers still saw the women soldiers around them as being in the Army only by fiat, not serving based on their own qualifications.

Armed with that awareness, I made it a point to work hard on my physical fitness while I was on active duty, and I encouraged my women colleagues to do the same. And when I commanded a recruiting battalion and spoke about the Army to young women, I tried to allay their concerns that they would not be up to the rigorous demands of Army physical training.

That self-doubt is unnecessary, since the Army trains soldiers from the most inexperienced stage of physical fitness. Our leadership has carefully studied the fitness level of the young Americans who enter Basic Training. The Army challenges those who arrive in good condition and shapes up the couch potatoes. Eventually the teenage Nintendo wizard might make an excellent operator in a Patriot missile battery, but he will have to become a physically fit soldier first. This process starts with diagnostic tests that measure strength and stamina. Soldiers are then assigned to PT groups according to their ability. The Army believes in progressive and sequential training: As young soldiers improve, the training is geared to keep them working hard. Further improvement is followed by setting higher standards in strength, endurance, and dexterity.

I remember visiting Fort Leonard Wood, Missouri, one summer a few years ago and being amazed to see the transformation the young soldiers had undergone after only eight weeks of Basic Training. They had developed from rather soft, often clumsy high school graduates to strong, lean, fit adults. Both men and women looked terrific after less than sixty days of instruction from drill sergeants who had trained them at a speed appropriate to their individual ability and fitness level. Young people who would have had trouble briskly walking a couple miles before entering the Army were running that distance carrying M-16 rifles and wearing Kevlar helmets and web gear on their way to the Infiltration Course. There, they deftly low-crawled under barbed wire while machine guns blasted overhead and dynamite artillery simulators thundered around them. Past that obstacle, the trainees vaulted wooden walls and climbed ropes before running on to their next training site.

People who had never seen this kind of metamorphosis often can't believe their eyes. A civilian friend of mine, despairing of losing weight on his own, once asked me, "Does the Army have spas for weight loss?"

"Yes," I told him. "We call them drill sergeants."

* * *

While at the Pentagon in 1984, I began to enjoy athletic competition. And it was culturally acceptable for me to compete hard because I was seen as nonthreatening since I started from what was widely believed to be a physically disadvantaged position, i.e., women were "weak." Yet I had stamina, discipline, and the determination to come from the back of the pack when running a race.

I entered a number of races at that time, many competing with runners from whom I learned a great deal about the sport. One of the most important lessons I acquired was the art of passing. When I began running, I had been conflicted about passing a man on the trail. In one ten-kilometer cross-country race on a Saturday morning soon after arriving at the Pentagon, I overtook a group of young Marines. They were in bad shape, no doubt having hit the Georgetown bars the night before, and I suspected they were hardly volunteers for this event. Although they had sprinted across the starting line with great determination, they were clearly fading only four kilometers into the race. One husky young man with a white sidewall haircut stumbled onto his knees in the grass and vomited spectacularly. Some of his buddies looked just as sick, but they were blocking the trail, and I needed to get around them.

"Come on, guys," I called, gasping as I spoke, "you can do it. We're almost halfway through."

They glanced back, stricken to see an older woman closing the gap to edge past them on the narrow trail. I slowed for a moment, as if to demonstrate empathy, but there was another factor involved. I came from a generation that had been taught not to compete with men. In the Virginia school I had attended in seventh through ninth grades, boys went to the gym and climbed ropes or ran on the track. The girls assembled in the auditorium and were taught the rules of games, but were given little chance to actually play them. With a final word of encouragement, I passed the faltering young Marines and moved on ahead.

But the experience taught me a lesson; by breaking my pace and slowing to speak to them, I had lost my concentration and speed for the rest of the race. As I finished the event, I realized that we were all equal competitors, men and women, and it was better to let the chips fall where they may. That was the last time I gave in to the urge to encourage a competitor.

After that race, I came to view passing opponents as a good thing. I have to admit, I took a great deal of private joy in stealthily running up to the lead runner, matching his stride for a while, marshaling my oxygen and strength, and then choosing the moment for a definitive pass, which I would execute in a "blow-by" sprint, continuing for a sustained distance until he was too far behind to catch me. Of course, there were times when he did catch me, but he always had to work hard at it, and that provided equal entertainment for me. None of these guys wanted to be beaten by a woman. It was as if the natural order of the universe had been upset.

But I was enjoying myself. One of my regular runs led from the POAC, across the Potomac on the Memorial Bridge, around either the Reflecting Pool or the Washington Monument and back, the longer route being just over five miles. Near the Pentagon on the return, there was a choice in approaches, one that offered the hypotenuse (shorter route) of the triangular course, the other the two sides of the triangle (slightly longer route). Some afternoons, I would watch the runners around me approaching the shorter, hypotenuse route at the point of the triangle. Then I would head down the two other sides, pumping hard to beat them. Often they would look across the field and notice what I was up to, then redouble their efforts to stay ahead of me. Sometimes they won, sometimes I won. Of course, when we arrived sweaty and winded back at the POAC, nobody ever acknowledged that a race had been run.

The joy of completing these arduous runs complemented a day in which most of the conflict and friction arose over abstract issues. I was also resolving the personal conflicts my generation had in competing with men. These unofficial races helped me overcome another barrier by which women are excluded. Winning an amateur competition was not very important to me. But discovering my own strength gave me the enduring confidence that I could compete and win on the playing field, whether athletic or professional.

*　*　*

The Army's emphasis on physical fitness might seem draconian to some civilians. After all, soldiers could be removed from the service in mid-career if they did not meet the weight standards established for their age and gender or pass the Army Physical Fitness Test. But this is not merely an arbitrarily demanding requirement.

The Army has a different mission than civilian organizations. Units in most Army branches are deployable, ready to move to distant sites overseas on minimum notice. If you visit the barracks or offices of Army units from the Rangers to a Signal Corps battalion to a Medical Corps evacuation hospital, you will find TA-50 web gear hanging in lockers or on coat hooks—canteens filled, batteries in the flashlights—ready to pull on when the deployment alert is issued. And, as we've seen, America has asked its soldiers to "move out" briskly on a variety of dangerous or demanding missions that took them to East and Central Africa, the Balkans, and the Caribbean in the last ten years.

Once deployed, soldiers in the combat arms must be prepared to fight, those in the combat support arms ready to back them up. Soldiers in combat service support units must also often operate in harsh environments, working long hours for weeks on end in jobs where physical endurance is an important factor. Physical fitness is a minimum requirement for all these members of the Army team, from the most junior enlisted rank to the most senior leader.

Without question, being a soldier is a younger person's profession. One of the reasons the Army retires its top leaders in their early fifties—usually after a little over thirty years of service—is that soldiers need to maintain high levels of physical fitness and be ready to deploy to serve in the field. Army leaders must be at the top of their game, both physically and mentally.

In this regard, the service requirements under which we see three- and four-star generals retire in their early fifties—the equivalent of a huge corporation losing its most successful company presidents each year—is not really a waste of talent. This attrition opens the lower ranks to advancement, providing an incentive to those potential top leaders on their way up. The turnover of new leadership also permits younger officers to bring new ideas with them as they reach the top. Thus, even though the Army was shrinking in size in the 1990s, it could correctly claim to be a "growing organization" due to the new ideas it was welcoming.

To meet the challenges of the rapidly changing military threat our country must now face—terrorists and minor powers such as Serbia have replaced the Moscow-led Warsaw Pact—the Army's senior leadership needs to be at the peak of their mental fitness, but not yet past the top of their performance. This is one of the reasons our senior leaders do not retain their positions as long as their counterparts in the corporate world.

* * *

Certainly the Army's use of physical fitness as a tool for stress management has proved effective. This effort, begun in the 1980s, coincided with similar corporate programs emphasizing the mind-body connection, and the need for executives working under great stress to unwind on a regular basis before their mainsprings broke and the clock stopped. Since the 1980s, a variety of stress-busting relaxation techniques—ranging all the way from yoga to aromatherapy—have flourished. Basically, they all have the same goal: the creation of harmony and the elimination of inner turmoil.

I have to confess that I once took a twenty-minute yoga lesson, which proved to be the longest twenty minutes of my life. "Om" did not come naturally to my lips. Dynamic conflict is part of being a soldier. Like most Army officers, I thrive on action; it's part of our profession. We are trained to take on multiple tasks, to seek out and solve problems, not to avoid them. Army officers with a potential for senior leadership learn to harness the energy that can be unleashed from confronting stress. They embrace it because high-level jobs are inherently stressful. There's no such thing as a tranquil leadership position. If you seek senior leadership responsibility, accepting major accountability defines your authority and power. Every morning is going to bring new problems. We have to remain engaged in our missions and productive, not withdrawn, sheltered from the daily *Sturm und Drang*.

Much of the popular stress-amelioration movement of the last few decades is based on unreasonable expectations about modern life. We often nostalgically wish to return to an ostensibly simpler and less stressful past, the good old days that never truly existed. In reality, the past was fraught with uncertainty and turmoil. Before antibiotics, fatal disease was rampant. Starvation and malnutrition were widespread. Wars lasted for decades, slavery for centuries.

Leaders should assess the source of stress in the workplace and determine what they can do to confine stress on their subordinates to a manageable level. One way to do this is to view the workplace as a system. Often sources of stress that are apparently unresolvable are actually linked to a part of the system that can be changed.

For example, when I took command of the recruiting battalion in San Antonio, one of the first things I noticed was how stressed the recruiters were. This was due to demanding missions that included deadline pressure and long hours six or seven days a week, for eight or nine months with no break at all. I could not do much to reduce my battalion's mission to more manageable levels. But I could add leave time—days off—to their work schedule. This gave the overworked recruiters the certainty that they could count on their vacation.

* * *

Part of any successful stress management effort should involve connecting physical and mental fitness. Anyone who has ever practiced an aerobic exercise such as running can attest that the activity clears the mind. Researchers have confirmed that this description is valid. Exercise triggers the release of endorphins in the brain, the "runner's high" that athletes experience during sustained effort. But this change in brain chemistry involves more than pleasure. Running, swimming, or a brisk workout on exercise equipment helps purge a person's mind of anxiety and negative repetitive thoughts. In short, staying physically fit through regular exercise allows a leader to keep her mind focused on the larger task at hand.

As recent research has also confirmed, people with stressful lives are at greater risk of physical illness if they do not develop means of relieving what Pamela Peeke, M.D., of the University of Maryland, has called "toxic stress." In her recent book *Fight Fat Over Forty,* Dr. Peeke shows that women are especially prone to linked emotional and physical afflictions triggered by overproduction of stress hormones, particularly cortisol. This often leads to overeating and buildup of lower-body fat, which in turn disrupts the body's complex hormonal balance. This might account for the recent surge in diabetes and cardiovascular disease among women.

Harold G. Koenig, M.D., a noted Duke University researcher on the mind-body connection, has also shown that "the stresses of hectic daily life" can produce an unhealthy cascade of stress hormones that weaken the immune system and increase risk of cardiovascular disease.

Significantly, regular physical exercise is one of the few proven techniques that can break the connection between the inevitable stress we all face each day and the emotionally crippling and physically debilitating effect that stress has on too many people.

For me, running also provided a connection to nature, shifting into a meditative state, as I moved steadily along trails beneath trees and across fields. I literally felt the burden of negative thoughts fall away. There have been times when I've been especially caught up in my work or gnawing on a problem that I have found myself running for long periods, my mind absorbed in the beauty of the river and the sky above. At the end of these runs, the problems always seemed much less significant.

For soldiers, formation runs take on another dimension. The vital element of unit cohesion is strengthened through running in formation, whether the unit is a basic training platoon, or part of an elite intelligence brigade. For this reason, formation runs have become almost universal in the Army.

Competitive sports offer another means of combining physical fitness and organizational cohesion. The Army War College in Carlisle, Pennsylvania, follows the old service tradition of making team sports mandatory for the seminars into which the field-grade officers are divided.

When I entered the War College in August 1990, there was a sense of missing "the Big One" among my colleagues because the Gulf War was underway, and here we were idling in classrooms in the hilly Pennsylvania countryside. The battalions that many of my seminar colleagues had trained to peak fighting efficiency had gone off to war without them. It wasn't so much that these officers wanted to taste combat—many already had as lieutenants in Vietnam—but they felt a deep loyalty to the people they had just commanded who were now in harm's way.

As the academic year got underway, the distraction of Desert Shield grew. But the commandant of the War College, Major

General Paul Cerjan, told us in one of our weekly meetings that we might as well stop calling our assignment officers. We would not be released for assignment to the Persian Gulf. At Christmas, in a personal trip to London, I sought out my Navy intelligence friends and encouraged them to ask for me by name in preparation for the ground war. The ground war ended in just one hundred hours, and I remained at Carlisle.

The first mandatory sport, softball, seemed frivolous. I was physically exhausted from the last four years of battalion command. I certainly knew nothing about the game, and the last thing I wanted to do was show up each week at the ball field to make a fool of myself among a bunch of competitive ballplayers. But in our first team-planning session, the sixteen members of my seminar took the team's organizational problems quite seriously.

First we had to give the team a name, which would symbolize our "tactical" approach. Some favored the gutsy old World War II favorite "Go for Broke!", by which only the best players would compete while the rest of us warmed the bench, cheering them on as they tried to trounce the other seminars. The other tactic would be to name the team after the Army recruiting slogan, "Be All You Can Be," which would allow everyone (even me, the seminar's only woman) the chance to play regularly.

We opted for the bona fide team endeavor. When Seminar 8's Be All You Can Be softball team trotted onto the diamond, I played right field. One day when we didn't have enough players, the coach acted in true desperation and gave me second base. It seemed only logical that the person in this position should stand on the base bag. But in a stage whisper, Lieutenant Colonel Dick Crampton said, "Claudia, I know you realize this. The second baseman usually stands over there." He pointed between first and second base. "Sure," I responded, following his direction.

In a different game, Colonel Mark Walsh, one of the faculty advisors, coached me. "If you can't catch the ball," he advised, "just throw your body in front of it."

I never became a real softball player. But the games became

one of the high points of the week. We got to know one another in a way that would have been impossible in any other form of activity. I discovered that I needed this kind of mindless fun after so many years of intense work. But I never would have availed myself of a team sport had it not been mandatory. Although I couldn't throw very far, I was fast and could run well if I ever got a hit. And it was exciting to watch our teammate Colonel Shami Mehta of the Indian Army at bat. He was a veteran cricket player, and the relatively huge ball made this game child's play for him.

All in all, Be All You Can Be didn't do badly and we developed a camaraderie that transcended our divergent backgrounds.

Even though the War College is considered by many the military equivalent of a Ph.D. program, it also has aspects of a sabbatical. Most of us had come from command responsibility and many would probably return to the greater challenge of brigade command. Our year at Carlisle gave us a chance to step back from the unending daily demands of being a commander and to broaden our intellectual horizons. This was a great luxury. The standing joke at the War College was, "The reading is only hard if you do it."

Although we weren't always the most diligent students at Carlisle, we all acquired new perspectives that helped sharpen our mental fitness, a key attribute of senior Army leaders. For the first time, many of us were reading in disciplines outside our own demanding specialties. Our class studied strategic leadership, economic philosophy, international security policy, and joint operations. Much of our initial classroom discussion noted that this was a transitional year for us as leaders. In the past, our problems had been concrete. In the future our work would be in an environment described as "volatile, uncertain, complex, and ambiguous." This formed so much of the intellectual dialogue that we started calling the War College "VUCA U."

Part of our Carlisle experience was regaining balance in our lives. General Paul Cerjan spoke to us about restoring family relationships and the need to create and meet fitness goals on all three fronts: physical, mental, and spiritual.

Teaching us to transcend our own practical nature—deeply ingrained by years of Army service—was one of the primary goals of the War College faculty. They wanted us to be more thoughtful and reflective. I could see their reasoning, but, again, I did not concede that a stress-free existence would be my best preparation for future command. In trying to teach us strategic leadership and vision, the faculty put us through a health risk assessment to examine our physical and mental fitness to cope with stress. As expected, they nailed me as a classic Type A personality, someone who finished other people's sentences and couldn't abide standing in line.

One of the fitness counselors found me at soda machine, getting a caffeine fix, and wanted to discuss this issue. He wanted me to take a Type A class to modify my attitude and behavior.

But I would have none of it. "I don't like Type Bs," I told him flatly. "I don't want to be a Type B. And I don't have time for the class. I've just got way too much to do."

The officer looked grave, unaware that I was spoofing the Type A diagnosis, but too determined to demonstrate the benefits of Type B behavior to interrupt his pitch.

". . . and besides," I continued, "I've already had a Type A class at the Pentagon. It didn't do any good."

I had my own relaxation program. When I had read enough weighty strategic study material each night, I'd plop the book on my bedside table and turn to my perennial favorites, Agatha Christie or Jane Austen (currently Mary Wesley fills this important role).

I also expanded my reading to more challenging periodicals such as *The Economist* and *Foreign Affairs*. The Army wants senior leaders with broad international perspectives, conversant in global problems. The Army expects its leaders who advance to the highest ranks to understand complex foreign cultures, to have lived abroad for years at a time, and to take a much wider

view than their often less-traveled civilian corporate counterparts.

Mental fitness is a dynamic process. I fully accepted the
Army's challenge that leaders should never become intellectually
complacent, but rather should exercise their minds, just as they
were required to stay in good condition to meet physical fitness
standards.

Commanding the 703rd Military Intelligence Brigade in
Kunia, Hawaii, I wanted to improve the officer development program. We had a very high level of physical activity, judging by
their deep North Shore suntans. What we needed to enhance was
their mental acuity. For a Military Intelligence officer, knowledge
of a foreign language would help make them competitive in a
rapidly downsizing Army.

From now on everyone would study a foreign language under
the Defense Language Institute program until they achieved a
minimum level of proficiency.

"Everyone, ma'am?" a major asked.

Obviously, the officers wanted to know if I intended to follow
my own edict.

"Everyone."

Since I already had received considerable training in French
and German, I knew there would be no challenge in reaching
minimum proficiency in either of those two languages. So I
opted for Mandarin Chinese, widely considered to be among the
most challenging languages for Westerners to learn. This difficulty lay in the tonal quality of spoken Chinese—level, rising,
falling, and high rising—and also in the bewildering nature of its
traditional ideographs, which did not reveal these tones through
markers. The student had to infer the tone by the position of the
syllable or word within a phrase or sentence. This was indeed a
hard language. However, I have always considered Chinese a
beautiful language. And I recognized that China was emerging
as a potentially important global strategic power.

I went to work diligently, studying one-on-one with a soldier
linguist. Our lessons were based on a study book that included

the English translation of phrases, their Chinese characters, and the pinyin phonetic representation of those characters. Each of these lessons was accompanied by a tape recording of the words and phrases, which I had to repeat by rote. This sounds much simpler than it actually was.

Despite my other duties, I made time to take my Chinese lessons several times a week. My progress was glacial.

But I stuck to it, even though I had to admit I would never become proficient in the language. At the end of four months of the hardest mental work I have ever performed, my instructor and I agreed that I had given Mandarin Chinese my all. I had completed Lesson One. She did not recommend I continue.

I told my officers that they were released from their language study obligation. But to my great pride, many continued their lessons. (Somehow, many still found time to work on their tans.)

* * *

In recent years, the Army has worked to provide soldiers with spiritual guidance, because the spiritual dimension is terribly important to soldiers as they perform their duties, often deployed away from their homes on confusing and tense peacekeeping assignments. Army chaplains years ago could simply provide generic character guidance based on Judeo-Christian traditions. Today, however, the Army is a much more diverse organization. The chaplain corps includes Buddhists, Muslims, and clergy from a variety of nonmainstream Christian denominations. Given this diversity, the interventional role of chaplains in shaping soldiers' lives has become more subtle than it was in years past.

In addition, the Army has inculcated a set of seven core values: honor, integrity, selfless service, courage, loyalty, duty, and respect. To a certain degree, each of these values runs counter to the prevailing trends in the civilian society from which young soldiers enter the Army. For example, surveys have revealed widespread erosion of honor and integrity among high school and college students who regularly cheat on tests and plagiarize with research papers they buy through the Internet. And many high school teachers note that the traditional level of respect between the generations has also eroded.

Yet, as was revealed through the extensive work of the Review Panel, successful Army leaders have been able to instill these values in young soldiers, their NCOs, and their officers. Again, this is never an automatic process involving pep talks and platitudes. Rather, the successful leader personally embodies these values, which without question have a spiritual, not just a secular, dimension. In a word, Army leaders who succeed demonstrate character. And I believe the most important core value underpinning that character is selfless service. If soldiers understand that their leader is sincerely devoted to their well-being and to accomplishing the mission, they will trust and follow that leader and modify their own behavior accordingly.

I have personally taken considerable satisfaction and spiritual fulfillment through service to others, both inside the Army and out. And I have found serving those who need help provides a synergistic connection that somehow bolsters both my physical and mental fitness.

This connection became clear in 1984, when I returned from my staff assignment in Germany to go to work in the Pentagon. I had been overseas for two and a half years, largely isolated from multichannel American television and the daily print media. I was bombarded by new information and no longer even knew how to have a telephone installed in my house. And I was struck by the avalanche of troubling news stories. There was another famine in Ethiopia. Homeless activists in the District of Columbia were on a hunger strike. And there was alarming talk about the political ascendancy of the Christian Right, which could impact women's reproductive rights.

I knew I had to become involved in at least some of these issues. But should I try to give money or volunteer my time? Or both?

I didn't have a lot of money to spare, but I did sponsor a little girl in the Caribbean through the Save the Children Fund. That gave me some sense of spiritual satisfaction, but, frankly, the effort was a bit impersonal. I wanted a closer human connection.

In Germany, I had volunteered through Army Community Services to give temporary shelter to battered women. But this was no great sacrifice. I had a two-bedroom apartment, and I was working such long hours that there was hardly time to interact with the women who came to stay there for a few nights.

The problem of homelessness in the District of Columbia was one I could not ignore, however. Even though I was working very long hours, I found a way to effectively be of service to homeless women. I volunteered to be one of the weeknight leaders at a House of Ruth shelter for homeless women located in a row house on a chaotic street in a drug-infested neighborhood of northwest Washington. Given my long hours at the Pentagon, this was an ideal way to be a volunteer. The shelter needed a responsible woman for the night shift, and I could perform the duties while sleeping. The shelter rules were simple but strict. No one entered or left after 8:30 P.M. All the women had to be in contact with their social workers. They had to bathe daily and wear clean clothes. And they also had to perform housekeeping chores. Although many were emotionally disturbed and had difficult drug or alcohol problems, at least the shelter protected them from the street and gave them the chance to lead less dangerous and chaotic lives.

The experience taught me that, even if I was extraordinarily busy, I could find the time to volunteer. But I wasn't naive enough to believe my effort alone would achieve dramatic results. The poverty, abuse, and emotional instability that had driven these women to the streets in the first place were widespread. It was easier for most people simply to ignore these conditions.

One night, for example, I woke to hear a woman screaming at a man on the street outside the shelter. It sounded as if the argument might come to blows. I grabbed the phone and dialed 911 to report the situation.

"Okay," the bored dispatcher said, "we'll send somebody to check."

A few minutes later a police patrol car cruised down the street with its red lights flashing . . . right past the man and woman on the sidewalk. They moved off in the opposite direction. The show of force temporarily prevented the man from harming the woman. But she was still out there alone, at the man's mercy, after the patrol car had disappeared around the corner. I knew the reprieve would not last until morning.

It is scenes like this that conveniently convince so many of us that deep-seated social problems are impossible to solve. Nothing is impossible. But people must make an effort. And I do not want to be among those who will not even try. Everything a person does or does not do has an effect on our society. People have to ask themselves which side they want to be on—the side of change or the side of inaction.

Certainly, we don't have to attack the most intractable problems to make a difference. Former President Jimmy Carter has helped transform Habitat for Humanity into a nationwide volunteer program that builds decent inexpensive houses for low-income families. Christmas in April is a similar nonsectarian program that repairs and revamps homes, children's clubhouses, and shelters in both inner cities and blighted rural areas. Meals on Wheels provides nutritious hot food and companionship for isolated shut-ins across the country. These and literally hundreds of other volunteer efforts tap the wellspring of altruism that has always run deep in our country.

I've always found working with children rewarding. When I was in college at Southwestern at Memphis and later as a young lieutenant at Fort Devens, I took great pleasure as a Brownie Scout leader. Girls at that age are very enthusiastic, and the attention we give helps them know they are valued and respected. Beyond my work with battered women in Germany and homeless women in Washington, when I was stationed in San Antonio I joined a friend, a retired Army nurse, who fed homeless men living under a highway bridge. The Army War College at Carlisle hosted a Christmas tea for the residents of a local nursing home. Many of these elderly people did not have families in their final years and sincerely welcomed our kindness. But we officers reaching the pinnacle of our careers also gained priceless spiritual insights through these personal contacts. We saw what life could be like as it wound down. And this insight made us value even more the freedom and vitality we enjoyed in robust and successful middle age. Later, as a brigadier general at FORSCOM, I tutored a second-grade girl in reading at an inner-city school the Army sponsored. She was a shy child who had no concept of military rank, which only increased my personal connection to her. Whenever I would go on a trip, I'd show her my destination on the map, trying to widen her horizons beyond the confines of her world and awaken her imagination about other places.

* * *

During my last year in the Army and since I've left active duty, I have become involved with First Star, a nonprofit organization dedicated to improving the lives of abused and neglected children.

I began working with First Star as a volunteer when it became clear that the need for such a program was dramatic. For example, the framers of the Constitution excluded three main groups from representation: slaves, women, and children. The first two groups through emancipation and suffrage have been granted full civil rights. While their struggle for equality is still underway, the battle for children's rights has only begun.

Attitudes in the legal profession, the judiciary, and society at large are still rooted in the pre-Victorian belief that children are the property of adults, that children's civil rights should be withheld because they lack the maturity to advocate for themselves. Almost universally, the rights of adults have priority over children's.

For example, no court in the land would knowingly force an abused woman back into the control of her abuser. But this is

232 ★ ★ ★ Lieutenant General Claudia J. Kennedy (Ret.)

done to children every day in our courts nationwide. In late 2000, the shocking case of twenty-three-month-old Brianna Blackmond stunned the District of Columbia when a judge ordered her out of foster care and returned to a previously neglectful mother. Brianna died from blows to the head two weeks after being returned.

Abused adults who suffer injury in state protection have legal recourse to sue for damages. But children are barred from recourse.

On average nationwide, laws protecting animals from violence inflicted on them by their owners are substantially stronger than those protecting children from beatings by their parents.

This is the situation First Star addresses. Begun in 2000 by Hollywood producer Peter Samuelson, who founded the Starlight Children's Foundation in 1982 and the Starbright Foundation in 1990 (initiatives aimed at helping sick children), the mission of First Star is to build cooperation, trust, and common ground with child-focused groups to improve the basic civil rights of abused, maltreated, and neglected children.

First Star's mission is to create new initiatives to strengthen existing laws and policies that improve the safety, health, and family life of America's children. The nonprofit organization does so by trying to determine the best practices for local, state, and federal agencies and other organizations involved in at-risk children's welfare.

Other First Star missions include educating the public and specific groups involved with children about the challenges they face and how we can all help solve these problems. In addition, First Star advocates improved federal, state, and local laws and policies to enhance the lives of children.

First Star's programs include research on the vast and often confusing network of laws affecting the lives of children nationwide and is developing a continually updated database for professionals across the United States to keep themselves abreast of the latest issues and programs. The First Star Institute will be a center of excellence for the study and enhancement of laws affecting children and the psychology of children. The institute will provide continuing education for legal professionals in close collaboration with state bar associations.

First Star's legislative objective is to engender accountability for official action or inaction with a focus on the elimination of laws that deny a child the right to sue any state for malfeasance and which provide a shield of secrecy protecting institutions and officials from accountability.

Public awareness on the plight of millions of American children at risk for neglect and abuse is another First Star priority. Kathleen Reardon, Ph.D., a University of California professor and founding member of First Star's board, is currently writing a book intended as a wake-up call on the extent and degree of the problem so many of our children face. The book will be published in conjunction with a documentary film produced by award-winning filmmaker Mark Jonathan Harris.

I am now the chair of First Star, a position that gives me a great deal of personal satisfaction, a sense of spiritual fulfillment, which I know I would not find in any other endeavor. America's children are our future. Too often this nation, the most prosperous and democratic in history, seems to forget this fact. It is too early to tell whether First Star will succeed. But one thing I learned in my long Army career was that you never accomplish a difficult goal without hard work and dedication.

9

The Leader As Coach

I grew up well versed in the lore of coaching. My mother's father, "Smiling Jimmy" Haygood, was one of the most beloved football coaches in the South. Often compared to his better-known Northern contemporary and close friend Knute Rockne at Notre Dame, Jimmy Haygood deeply loved collegiate football, but saw the game as a metaphor of life, a means of character building, rather than strictly as a competitive sport in which the aim was defeating the opponent and amassing the most impressive record.

Jimmy Haygood coached football at a number of Southern colleges for almost thirty years before his untimely death from a sudden heart attack at age fifty-three in 1935. Although only a slender 150 pounds, Jimmy Haygood was a dedicated athlete who earned a position as Vanderbilt's quarterback in 1905 through his sheer perseverance—"I used to lie awake for hours at night calling signals aloud and rehearsing plays," he recalled decades later.

A soft-spoken man with a restrained temperament, he was absolutely dedicated to his players. In Jimmy Haygood's day, coaches had both classroom and athletic responsibility. He taught math and coached at Henderson-Brown College (now Henderson State University) in Arkadelphia, Arkansas, from 1908 to 1925. There he became known as one of the best defensive strategists in the South. But he also earned a reputation as a coach who considered character off the field as important as skill on the gridiron. After coaching at other small colleges, he took over the freshman football team at the University of Alabama for several years, and then became football coach and athletic director of Southwestern at Memphis in 1931, the school attended by my mother, aunts, and uncle, and from which I graduated in 1969. (In 1984, Southwestern became Rhodes College.)

At the time of Jimmy Haygood's death, sports reporter Walter Stewart wrote, "He lost games he could have won—by pushing an injured player into the heat of the scrimmage or by slipping an ineligible tackle into the breach. But Jimmy Haygood didn't play football games that way. He believed that a boy's future was more important than a touchdown." Even though Jimmy Haygood's teams held their own against powerhouse competitors such as Alabama's Crimson Tide and scored an amazing 20–20 tie against the South's juggernaut Ole Miss, the University of Mississippi, Jimmy Haygood always retained the perspective that their glory years of college football would end, and the young men he coached would have to move into adult life. He molded them as team players and discouraged play that we would recognize as the showy superstar ambition of today's college athletes.

In those days, the college football field was not merely an antechamber to the National Football League. Jimmy Haygood took great interest in the young men he coached and kept in contact with them after graduation. Whenever he could, he used his reputation and contacts to help them land jobs in the depths of the Depression. But this generosity was not just limited to his players. Other students came to him, and Jimmy Haygood was always ready with guidance and advice. He carried a much folded sheaf of paper in the pocket of his worn gabardine trousers, a roster of his former players and students who were now working. At the start of the 1934 football season, Jimmy Haygood showed that list to a reporter. "Look at this," the coach said proudly, "practically every one of my boys has a job. Pretty good jobs, they are, too."

The Arkansas Sports Hall of Fame inducted him into its ranks in 1960, five years before it installed the much more renowned native Arkansan Paul "Bear" Bryant.

Years later, as a professional Army officer, I recalled hearing the stories of my grandfather from my family. And I believed that being an Army leader and coaching, as Jimmy Haygood had practiced the profession, might actually be closer than was generally assumed. Both involve gaining the confidence of a team, passing on specific skills to its members, inspiring them to practice strenuously (train to meet the mission), and not become discouraged when inevitable setbacks occur.

In many ways, coaching was an extended form of mentoring. While one mentors an individual, the coach guides a group striving toward a common goal. Both coaching and mentoring are relationships that involve mutual trust and confidence.

Ideally, a commander—at least up to the battalion level—should personally know as many of her soldiers as practically possible. The commander, an officer, will never know the soldiers as well as the NCOs because soldiers and NCOs work closely together every day. But to be an effective leader who achieves the trust and respect of those led, either a commander or a private sector executive should try to develop the personal connection with the people in her organization.

I'm not suggesting a leader-coach become personal friends with those on the team. That type of familiar connection is actually counterproductive. People within most structured organizations—certainly in a hierarchical body such as the Army—prefer traditional formality separating those in the chain of command. That's one reason we exchange salutes and other forms of military courtesy as well as address each other by rank. One practices these courtesies in deference to the position, not the person.

Deference to one's seniors is a reminder of the importance we place on discipline and obedience to proper authority.

But this formality does not interfere with the commander knowing as much as possible about her soldiers. Like my grandfather's football players, soldiers are people, and can never be viewed as so many interchangeable parts. Soldiers want personal contact with their seniors, especially the commander, not to seek favoritism, but because they want to put a human face on those who exert so much authority over them in the form of duty hours and Efficiency Reports and for whom they are asked to sacrifice so much. Even as generals today discuss rapidly evolving strategic and tactical networks that depend on high-speed data links or e-mail, there is still the need for personal contact between leader and led. As former TRADOC commander retired General William Hartzog noted in the April 2001 issue of *Army* magazine, there will be an ongoing need for "force of personality" on tomorrow's battlefield, "when a subordinate commander will need to hear the tone of the senior commander's voice and see the nonverbal cues that only presence brings. I suspect that no tactical commander will ever value a digital attack order scrolling across a computer screen." Rather, tactical command will want to hear the "energy and sense of urgency" when such an order is issued. This can be achieved by imbedding an audio-video teleconferencing channel in the digital communications links. But even teleconferencing will not sustain these important bonds of understanding without a background of previous personal contact.

To form this bond, an Army leader must understand the entire lives of the soldiers in her command, just as a successful coach must be familiar with the lives of her team members off the playing field. Both successful coaches and commanders draw upon the resources of the total person on their team. Coaches take their teams on the road and live with them through the tensions, joys, and disappointments of athletic competition. Because commanders deploy with their soldiers, often on short notice, they must understand these soldiers' characters as well as their individual job skills. What is a soldier's level of maturity? How stable is an NCO during times of crisis? Will the younger men and women follow him? So it is essential for the successful commander to learn as much as possible about the lives of the soldiers she leads.

Over the course of my career, I learned a very valuable lesson: Listen to your soldiers' private concerns when they choose to raise them. Many times soldiers will bring up seemingly trivial matters when they are sounding you out to see if they can trust you, to learn if you really care about them.

For example, I recall a young woman announcing in a casual manner, "My daughter is a real handful." I responded and led this soldier into conversation, during which I learned that her civilian husband, who had not found a job in Germany, was unhappy; their child care arrangements and personal finances were in disarray; and from what she said, I suspected possible domestic violence. It was completely appropriate that a specialist-4 with a young family should raise this issue with her supervisor. She needed help without blame and support in solving her family's problems. We expect soldiers to be on call twenty-four hours a day, seven days a week. The Army can order them to any corner of the world on virtually a moment's notice. The lines of trust and respect have to flow both ways.

Years later, when General Dennis Reimer became Army Chief of Staff and I served on his transition team at the Pentagon, he told us to study the leadership ideas of the great college football coach Lou Holtz, who believed that there are three critical questions any two people ask in a relationship, whether it is between parent and child, man and woman, or between a leader and the people led.

Can I trust you?

Do you care about me?

Are you committed to excellence?

With an effective leader or coach, the answer was demonstrably "yes." In considering the Lou Holtz leadership principles, I often thought of my grandfather Jimmy Haygood, who epitomized them.

Certainly, however, after the experience of the devious NCO in our battalion in Germany, the soldiers had every reason to answer "no" to each question. But when they dealt with Command Sergeant Major Gant and benefited from his invaluable counsel, we regained the trust and respect of the soldiers the Army had assigned us to lead.

Command Sergeant Major Gant and I tried to build normal military standards throughout the battalion, including formal duty rosters and training and promotion boards. At the enlisted level, the soldiers knew where they stood. We operated on a spectrum of discipline intervention ranging from occasional advice to company punishment, to court-martial on the very rare occasions when it was required. Sergeant Major Gant insisted that his company first sergeants maintain good order in their barracks, including clean arms rooms where the weapons were stored and perfectly maintained chemical protective gear for all our people. Even though we were nearing the end of the Cold War, the threat of attack with weapons of mass destruction was real to us, and our unit in Augsburg was ready.

I relied on the mentoring network that Sergeant Major Gant put in place among his subordinate NCOs. It worked beautifully. Again, leadership is a partnership. There was never any doubt that I was the battalion commander. But I was not a micromanager; nor was Sergeant Major Gant. He too delegated authority and responsibility to the company first sergeants, who in turn worked with their platoon sergeants. On the officer level, the battalion staff coordinated all support my company commanders needed to accomplish their missions.

I also tried to spend as much time as possible on the operations floor, where most of the soldiers worked in rotating shifts. We were a Signals Intelligence battalion, whose soldiers carried out their demanding duties in a huge windowless building. Even though we all had name tags on our uniforms and security badges, I made it a point to learn as much as I could about each soldier and his or her family. For most of the younger ones, this assignment was their first extended absence from home. They were in a foreign country for the first time, still adjusting to military life. The mid-grade and senior NCOs had multiple assignments behind them; they knew the Army well. But most were also struggling to raise their families on inadequate pay and in cramped housing.

I did my best to meet the wives and children, and encouraged my company commanders to discuss the issues their soldiers faced. This served three purposes: It permitted company commanders to share solutions; it gave me the opportunity to provide them additional resources; and it helped synchronize battalion staff work in support of the company commanders. I liked to think of myself as less authoritarian than a more traditional commander. But I realized I had room to grow in this regard when one of my company commanders, Captain John McDougall, walked into my office one day with a notepad in his left hand, pen in his right, and white towel neatly draped over his left forearm.

"What are you doing, Captain?"

"I'm just here to take your order, ma'am."

We then discussed his feeling that I had been too specific in "tasking" him (to use Army parlance), instead of giving him mission-type orders. This frank discussion helped me realize the unintended effect I had had on him. I adjusted accordingly.

As a young company commander at Fort McClellan, embroiled in the struggle to restore discipline, I also acquired another lesson that I've retained over all these years. A commander, no matter how overworked and harassed by pressing duty, should seek the advice of a mental health expert when dealing with a troubled soldier.

A young basic trainee, diagnosed with clinical depression including the wish to commit suicide, was sent to my company to spend her last week in the Army, pending discharge. I always met with every new soldier reporting for duty. Before she came to my office, my senior officers had told me to keep her from killing herself and to provide a room for her to live in during her few remaining days in the Army, which is not equipped to deal with serious psychological problems. The approach is to identify and discharge such emotionally disturbed soldiers.

Without formal training in this field, I thought my best course of action was to interrupt her path toward self-destruction, to provide her time to reconsider her options.

As she sat quietly before my desk, I looked up to catch her eye. "I understand that you are considering killing yourself," I said in an even tone.

"Yes, ma'am."

"Well, don't do it here." I swept my hand to indicate the surrounding company area. "We have other people with lots of problems who need help. Don't kill yourself here in the company, on this post, or while you're in the Army. It will cause no end of paperwork."

"Yes, ma'am."

I thought that, if she could put off suicide for the week remaining in the Army, she could find new reasons to delay this irrevocable step later.

I was wrong.

A few days after the young soldier had been discharged, the first sergeant came in to tell me that the police had called the MPs with the information that the trainee had been found in a hotel room dead, a victim of suicide.

By the time I commanded again, I understood more about the nature of suicide and the meaning of gestures and threats.

* * *

There are many incentives for taking care of soldiers. During holidays, single soldiers worked shifts on Christmas, while married soldiers worked New Year's. Jews, Christians, and those of other faiths worked out exchanges of work shifts. But with the young PFCs and SP-4s who worked Christmas, I made it a point to visit the operations floor to discuss the mission and to chat with them about their homes and families in America. It was amazing how many had not heard from the folks at home and couldn't afford the then expensive international commercial telephone rates.

As battalion commander, I had more than simply the feelings of some homesick young soldiers to consider. I took command in 1986, just as the AIDS crisis became a matter of public discussion. Two decades into the epidemic, it is sometimes hard to remember the degree of ignorance about AIDS that prevailed at that time. Soldiers, young and old alike, needed more information. Then, the Army's emphasis was on the HIV testing and notification process, not on prevention.

For most soldiers, AIDS seemed to be purely associated with homosexuals, one more reason for them to be unconcerned. AIDS was a problem "out in San Francisco."

But when it became clear that HIV and AIDS could afflict both men and women, straight and gay alike, some people verged on panic. For the first time in the twentieth century, sexual relations could be equated with death.

One of the company first sergeants told me, "Why would I talk to the soldiers about AIDS? If they get it, there's no hope and they're just going to die."

"First Sergeant," I said, "the people who think it's hopeless are the ones who'll end up infected with HIV. You just can't sit back passively and pretend it's not happening. There may *be* a cure one day. You can also manage your own behavior and be careful who your partners are."

Seeing I had not been persuasive, I decided to be proactive. Once every quarter, battalion commanders held Commander's Call in which we directly addressed the soldiers on important issues, including health and safety. I held my Commander's Calls in the conference room on the fifth floor of the old Wehrmacht barracks that was our headquarters. Since we were a four-shift battalion, and wanted to provide three makeup training sessions, I gave my presentation seven times.

"The subject of today's safety discussion is sex," I announced. When I said the last word, I saw the drowsy eyes pop open throughout the conference room. Many of these soldiers were hardly out of adolescence, and sex was either an embarrassing or forbidden topic. So I continued, "What I'm going to talk about is very sensitive. I'm not trying to present a religious or moral viewpoint. The reason I am raising this issue is that your lives are at risk and you need practical information. These are the facts you need to know to protect yourself."

I had considered asking one of the chaplains or Medical Corps doctors to help me in this task. My soldiers could seek pastoral or medical advice if they wished. But I was their leader, so a practical general discussion to cut through the confusion was my responsibility.

Mutual trust is an equally strong bond between commander and soldier (coach and player). In the Army we take young people, most straight out of high school, and train them in a relatively few months to function as adults in a demanding, often dangerous, and always serious profession. We hope to instill in them a level of stable maturity and self-discipline far beyond that of their peers who have remained in the civilian world. This is why the Army's Basic and Advanced Individual Training process is so critical. After only six or seven months, young soldiers join their units anywhere in the world. A soldier who was dancing in his high school prom in May could be driving a Humvee through the snowy hills on the Kosovo-Macedonia border on Christmas Eve, mindful of the land mines that might lie in the frozen mud ahead.

Soldiering demands self-discipline, and that is what we try to develop through our training. This is one of the reasons the Army reacted so vigorously to the sexual harassment scandal centered at Aberdeen Proving Ground. If those drill instructors assigned there to serve as role models to the young trainees could not maintain even a modicum of self-discipline, what kind of lesson did that teach the trainees themselves? I'm pleased to report that, during my membership on Secretary West's Review Panel on Sexual Harassment, I personally found the great majority of Army drill instructors to be soldiers of great integrity, sincerely concerned with training the soldiers assigned to them, and worthy of the respect and trust of those young soldiers.

* * *

Maintaining the trust and respect of those who serve with you is a dynamic and often difficult process. Some people actually believe becoming a leader entitles you to work less and instead draw upon the energy and production of the people assigned to your organization. In fact, the reverse is true. A position of leadership is a responsibility, not an occasion for privilege. Truly effective leadership in the Army at either the senior noncommissioned or commissioned officer level entails even harder work for longer hours than other duty assignments.

The popular image of goldbricking NCOs and officers fostered over the decades in such classic television programs as *The Phil Silvers Show* (Sergeant Bilko) and *M*A*S*H* is misleading. In these fantasies, all the NCOs ran some scam, while the officers' responsibilities seemed to diminish and their degree of flagrant luxury increased as they advanced in rank. I can tell you from personal experience, it just doesn't work that way. Even in *M*A*S*H,* Colonel Potter portrays a multidimensional character who is more true to Army life than the other colonels and the occasional general who parade through the series.

In reality, command in the Army involves selfless service. A good commander spends more rather than less time on the job. In my battalion in Germany, my days began early and usually ended around 6:30 or 7:00 P.M. Although social events were not a frequent requirement, I did attend battalion parties during the holidays and soldiers' athletic events.

Because I concentrated on running the best Military Intelligence battalion I could while looking out for my soldiers' welfare, I had very little time for housekeeping and personal activity. I lived in a rented farmhouse owned by one Herr Knöpfle in the ancient dairy farming hamlet of Kuhbach (Cow Glade) about thirty-five miles west of Augsburg. This was a quiet corner of German countryside. The Knöpfle house dated from 1607. It had gleaming hardwood floors, marble windowsills, and carved doors. My adjacent little house was postwar, very comfortable.

There was no television so I enjoyed reading. And whenever I got back early enough in the summer, I changed into old work clothes and helped Herr Knöpfle and his two adult children with the chores in the dairy barn. Pitching grass to the lowing cows or sweeping their stalls was a good way to unwind. In return for my work, they invariably invited me to a traditional German farm dinner.

At dawn every morning, I was on the road in my BMW, headed back to the "real" world of Intelligence operations and leadership issues. If I chose the autobahn route, I usually came to full wakefulness by roaring past the green fields in light mist at about ninety-five miles an hour.

The Army had adopted the camouflage Battle Dress Uniform (BDU) for all ranks. They replaced the green fatigues I had worn in Korea. I had a large number of BDUs with the machine-embroidered name tag, rank, and branch insignia sewn on each set, and kept the uniforms rotating through the post laundry weekly. This saved time getting ready each day. For me there was a bonus to the BDU: I never had been very adept at keeping a shine on brass insignia. The dull green and black cloth appliqué lieutenant colonel's oak leaf and Military Intelligence insignia did not require cleaning with Brasso.

Throughout my life in the Army, keeping track of my uniform hat had been a problem, an issue that my civilian women friends never need to consider. But I would have been out of uniform with no hat. So I stashed extra hats in my briefcase, my office, and my car, as well as in my quarters. It cost me a few extra dollars to buy these hats, but the expense was justified by increased peace of mind. As a lieutenant general, I had at least fifteen hats of four different types, ranging in level of formality from BDU to Army Blue.

I was lucky when it came to eating. The battalion had a good mess hall that served four meals every twenty-four hours to meet the requirements of our soldiers working shifts. So I could always buy a good, cheap meal (officers paid, and the soldiers living in the barracks ate free) and could spend time talking to soldiers while we ate. But when I missed dinner in the mess hall, I returned late to my farmhouse, hungry. There my highly refined culinary skills came into play: chunks of German brown bread torn from the loaf, wedges of cheese sliced on the kitchen counter, and hunks of salami with the rind peeled back. Not very *gemütlich*, but some nights food had simply become fuel. So much for a luxurious European assignment, finally freed from the drudgery of Pentagon staff work.

The popular conception of Army officers followed by a retinue of aides and personal assistants catering to their whims is also false. Only general officers in certain positions are entitled to enlisted aides who clean the public entertainment rooms of their quarters and prepare their uniforms. This is not a wasteful perk meant simply to make life easier for a particular general. Rather, having an enlisted aide frees that officer to spend more time on professional duties and official social obligations.

When I became the Deputy Chief of Staff for Intelligence, I was assigned Master Sergeant Wayne Smith as my enlisted aide. He transformed my life from chaos to order. I lived in quarters on the second and third floors of a beautiful brick house built in 1838 on Fort McNair, a small, shady enclave nestled on the Washington, D.C., waterfront. My position entailed long days at the Pentagon, inevitably followed by mandatory social events. Some days would start at 4:00 A.M. and not end until nearly midnight. My normal workday schedule was a minimum of twelve hours.

But Master Sergeant Smith was there to support me, making sure my uniforms were clean and pressed, the downstairs of my quarters were spotless, and my refrigerator stocked with appetizing food. I now had a full homemade meal to microwave when I got home late. The days of spaghetti or eating vegetables straight from the can were over. When I entertained, which I often did as DCSINT, Master Sergeant Smith handled each occasion with military precision, freeing me to spend time with guests, often from some interesting foreign country.

★　★　★

From the time I was a girl hearing stories of my grandfather Jimmy Haygood, I knew that good coaches inspired their teams to high performance. In that famous 20–20 tie against Ole Miss in 1931, Coach Haygood took his Southwestern team into the locker room at halftime trailing 20–0. There's no record of what he said to his players. But he was renowned for inspiring rather than bullying. Whatever message he delivered, his players held Ole Miss to their twenty points, scored twenty of their own, and only missed winning when an extra point kick went wide. Clearly, my grandfather was a positive leader.

Years later, I read Dr. Henriette Anne Klauser's provocative book *Write It Down, Make It Happen,* and I thought of my grandfather. Dr. Klauser believes one important responsibility of the leader is to be inspirational. By this she means the leader seeing things in the most promising light, envisioning a great future, inspiring hope in the team, and most essentially, sustaining group energy toward meeting their common goal. To me this is a great definition of an effective leader, whether in the Army or in civilian life.

Sometimes, however, mid-level, younger leaders think the senior leader is being overly optimistic due to ego or self-aggrandizement. But the leader who expresses doubt about achieving a goal will be much less likely to succeed at the level originally intended. If the leader doesn't think the mission is possible, neither will those on her team.

This does not mean that a commander or successful executive is a cheerleader, but rather a practical guide who bridges the gap between the purely inspirational and the concrete, between today's reality and tomorrow's dream. In short, like a winning coach, the leader must be able to convince the team members to continue struggling against difficult odds to achieve an unlikely goal. If the leader (commander, coach, or executive) becomes discouraged and loses energy, team morale suffers, and with it, the mission.

After I had taken command of the battalion in Augsburg, I discovered that finding good, affordable child care was a real problem for many of my soldiers. Some were dual-career married couples, others, single parents. Almost all worked on rotating shifts, which meant the soldiers could not use the local German day care centers or U.S. Army facilities, which were almost always full to capacity. In any event, the Army child care center did not open early enough in the morning for our day shift or stay open late enough at night for my soldiers working the 11:00 P.M. to 7:00 A.M. "Mids" shift.

And many had to be on the physical training field by 6:00 A.M. Those families who hadn't been able to make other arrangements brought their sleeping children to the field in their cars, locked them in while performing PT, then drove the kids to a baby-sitter. Still, those on rotating shifts faced the problem of finding in-home care. There were very few baby-sitters, either American or German, willing to take children at 10:30 P.M. from parents about to begin the Mids shift.

I began to investigate the battalion establishing its own around-the-clock child care center that would be open seven days a week. Our brigade commander, Colonel Ed Tivol, identified a nearby pre–World War II Luftwaffe building that might be suitable. But then our battalion ran into an absolute wall of Army and Department of Defense regulations governing the structure and facilities of child care centers. And the Army engineers we'd consulted on the project said they couldn't bring the building up to standard.

By the time I left Augsburg, the only progress I'd been able to make was to slightly increase the number of American homes certified to provide care. And my sole satisfaction was knowing that we had explored a new possibility and had furthered the body of knowledge surrounding requirements for child care in anticipation of some future innovation. And this helped soldiers understand that lack of adequate child care was not their fault, but was due to deficiencies in support to working families.

We cannot say, "Serve in the Army for minimal pay. Have families. Be good parents. Work long hours," and then expect that there will not be friction and stress borne by both the soldier and the institution.

For me, the failure taught two lessons: It's better to have tried than not, and I would try again at the next opportunity.

* * *

In the spring of 1990, I was sitting in my sunny office in the recruiting battalion headquarters in San Antonio when I got a phone call from Brigadier General Larry Runyon. He had been the deputy commander of Field Station Korea, who, with Colonel Charles Black ("the Prince of Darkness"), had been so influential in shaping my future in Military Intelligence.

"Claudia," he said, "you've been selected to command a brigade."

I felt like shouting in triumph. This meant I would not have to retire, as I had thought a year earlier in Germany. As a result of seeking additional command time with the recruiting battalion, my record as a leader was more competitive. I had been selected for promotion to full colonel, to attend the War College, and, with this telephone call, I learned, I was to command a brigade.

I smiled as I realized I would now have to take the Army's mandatory Pre-Command Course for the third time. But the minor irritation at having to repeat the course yet again was far outweighed by the joy of knowing I'd been selected for brigade command—one of twenty such assignments in Military Intelligence—after twenty-one years as an officer. I suddenly recalled late one afternoon in Colonel Black's car driving back from Seoul to Pyongtaek during a long day of meetings and impromptu inspections at the field station during which he had asked a series of questions that immediately helped the junior officers make sense of what needed to be done to accomplish the mission.

"Sir," I'd asked, "how do you know how to *do* all this?"

"The first twenty-six years are the hardest."

Now it looked as if my own Army service would probably extend that long.

* * *

In July 1991, I took command of the 703rd Military Intelligence Brigade at Kunia on the Hawaiian island of Oahu. Kunia was adjacent to Schofield Barracks and Wheeler Army Air Field of Pearl Harbor fame. Beyond my brigade of three battalions totaling about 1,200 soldiers, the station had joint facilities for U.S. Air Force, U.S. Navy, and Department of Defense civilian strategic intelligence functions.

Built soon after the 1941 Japanese attack on Pearl Harbor, the main facility, "the tunnel," was a 300,000-square-foot concrete building between two low hills that had been bulldozed over with earth and planted with pineapples as camouflage. Originally intended as an underground aircraft factory, the tunnel was now a high-security intelligence center at which my brigade was the host organization. I was now a full colonel, the senior officer at the station.

Although our work was so sensitive that we did not openly acknowledge the mission of the facility, everyone knew about us. Among some, the Kunia station was called "the used-car lot" due to the huge asphalt parking area next to the green hillside, which was filled with parked vehicles around the clock.

When I arrived at Kunia, I held a series of meetings with my brigade staff officers, the battalion commanders, company commanders, the brigade command sergeant major, and the brigade NCOs down to the sergeants leading squads. As I had in Augsburg on a smaller scale, I posed the basic question about the organization, "What's good, what's bad, and what shouldn't I touch because I'll just screw it up?"

I also told them I believed loyalty flowed in both directions. "If you've got a problem with the way I command the brigade, let me know. Don't just bad-mouth me behind my back. That doesn't accomplish anything."

I also believed in candor as an aspect of loyalty. "Tell me your real view. I'm not interested in yes-men or -women. But try to keep the bad news within the brigade until we've had a chance to address the issues. Grumbling and spreading rumors works for misfits, not for soldiers pulling their weight."

I asked them to have the courage to trust me and their leaders, to serve selflessly. "Remember you're not alone. You are working for your company, battalion, brigade, INSCOM, the Army, and your country. We will support you.

"I'm going to walk the operations floor during all the shifts," I continued. "Don't get worked up. I'm not looking over your shoulder, but I have to get a firsthand sense of how we're meeting our mission."

In these staff orientation briefings, we discussed ways to protect soldiers' break time to the degree possible, even during stressful operational surges when the tendency was to remain on duty. SIGINT required a soldier's concentration; a stressed-out zombie could not do the job properly. Additionally, we decided to conduct awards and promotions ceremonies on the 11:00 P.M.–7:00 A.M. Mids shift so that soldiers permanently assigned to that duty would feel more personally connected to the brigade and also to avoid interrupting their daytime sleep period.

When these purely military matters were introduced, I met with the civilian wives, husbands, and older children of my soldiers in order to get some sense of their morale. It was futile to improve conditions for soldiers on the station if they faced insurmountable difficulties in their off-duty lives.

As at Augsburg, most of the soldiers worked rotating shifts. And I had an even higher proportion of dual-career military couples. With the incredibly high cost of living in Hawaii (30 percent above the Mainland), private child care was beyond the reach of most of my soldiers. This led to even greater personal disruption in their lives. Depending on their shift schedules, couples with small children often ran dangerously short on sleep, as one of the parents had to remain awake to mind the children while the other was on duty. The situation was simply not acceptable.

They should not have had to make that choice. I was determined to establish an Army child care facility on the station itself so that these soldiers could be relieved of the cost and anxiety of this pressing problem and devote their full attention to their duties.

I discussed my intention with Brigadier General Michael M. Schneider, Deputy Commanding General, INSCOM, at Fort Belvoir, Virginia, and with Lieutenant General Johnny Corns, Commander, U.S. Army, Pacific. From my very first meeting on this matter with General Corns, a concerned, decisive leader, I could see he intended to help.

"Colonel," he said, "I'll put my staff to work on this."

The general's staff quickly discovered that they had an un-filled but funded civilian child care "slot." By shaking the bu-reaucratic woodwork, the staff also found funding for another child care slot. They filled these positions with Helen Stine and Debbie Hewitt, two women who had long experience in the De-partment of Defense child care system.

They energetically approached the problem of providing af-fordable, around-the-clock child care for my brigade. One of the first things Helen and Debbie learned by rereading the complex Department of Defense regulations was that a child care facility need not meet all the expensive building standards if the parents worked within ten minutes of the center itself. Also, since the re-quirement was for a custodial, not a developmental, program, the proposed center would not require expensive staffing.

This information was a real breakthrough. Chief Warrant Of-ficer Hope Bean and Lieutenant Colonel David Pagano identi-fied an unused cinder block building near the tunnel entrance as the ideal candidate for our proposed child care center. With con-tinuing staff support from U.S. Army, Pacific, the brigade launched into the detailed planning to move from concept to re-ality, never an easy matter in any large bureaucratic organization.

One unintended but beneficial consequence of this was that the soldiers recognized their leaders were working hard to solve the problem. So, at every Friday brigade staff meeting in our headquarters auditorium, we discussed the progress (or lack thereof) on the child care center after purely operational matters had been dealt with. Soon, groups of off-duty soldiers were attending these meetings, listening to key staff members, Lieutenant Colonels Gary Royster, the Operations officer and later a battalion commander, David Pagano, the Logistics officer, and Kay D'Enbeau, the Resource Management officer. The soldiers, I knew, would carry the word back to their peers that the brigade leaders were addressing this difficult issue.

At one weekly meeting I recall asking the staff, "What's the latest thing they say we *can't* do?"

Another week we fought the battle of electric wall outlets. Then the campaign continued on the height of bathroom partitions, followed by the famous Battle of the Toy Sanitizing Facility.

One difficult roadblock we had to meet head-on concerned the outside play area, which the Department of Defense insisted had to be rubber-padded rather than grass or asphalt. "I'm just trying to remember," someone asked, hoping to lighten the moment, "did we have rubber padding in the backyard when we grew up?"

As these frustrating questions arose and we addressed them one by one, the number of platoon and company first sergeants attending the weekly staff meetings increased. Clearly they were passing the word back to their soldiers: The brigade leadership considers this an important issue.

And we kept "working the problem," as Army parlance has it, for a full eight months. Beyond building standards, there was the vexing issue of funding. The brigade did not want to charge parents for child care, so we struggled to develop a barter system through which soldiers would trade time working at the center for hours of care.

But there was concern about fair equivalency: Was an hour spent during the day when there were forty children ranging from babies to preschoolers equal to a late-night hour when twenty babies and toddlers slept in cribs? Further, soldiers paying back the time they owed the center had to work around their duty schedules, but everyone needed to sleep eight hours, and we all had PT and other training. Many soldiers also moonlighted off-duty to survive financially. One afternoon I saw a soldier from the brigade working at the PX garage.

"Is this your second job?" I asked.

"No, ma'am," he said. "It's my third."

Those were the days when military pay was so low that many of the married couples with children among the junior enlisted ranks qualified for food stamps.

Throughout the effort to create the child care center, I projected the doggedly optimistic assurance that we would succeed. Again, one of the responsibilities of the leader or coach is to inspire the team. Had I voiced the pessimism I sometimes felt, the junior officers might have given in to their own doubts. But I never indicated in any way that we might fail. And I knew from experience that no younger officer would tell the colonel commanding the brigade, "This can't be done."

Finally, our stubborn effort paid off. In June 1992, the brigade child care center opened with an official ribbon-cutting ceremony attended by our staff, soldier parents, and staff officers from U.S. Army, Pacific, and Schofield Barracks. The center was the first free military around-the-clock facility open seven days a week. As I visited the center with Brigadier General Ray Roe, Commander of the Army's Community and Family Support Center, we noted the bright, freshly painted walls—the effort of volunteer parents—and the "surplus" furniture some of the more inventive senior NCOs had delivered.

"The actual larceny involved," I assured another officer, "was very minor."

In fact, the parents had sewn curtains, held car washes to raise money, and donated baby bottles, car seats, toys, and disposable diapers. Creating the center was a true community effort.

And it functioned almost flawlessly for over a year. It would be nice to report that the center continued in operation, but it was a very high maintenance effort that would never run on automatic. Unfortunately, after my very energetic and innovative brigade staff and the equally energetic senior NCOs in the battalions and I moved on to other assignments, the child care center could not be sustained. The work of juggling volunteer schedules was just too demanding. But the soldiers knew that their children were a brigade priority.

My motives were not purely altruistic. The availability of quality child care directly related to the problem of retaining trained soldiers in the Army. In the 1990s, the civilian economy was booming, and most of my soldiers, who had high-technology or other marketable skills, did not have to put up with the long hours, low pay, and the dislocation of moving their families every two years. Military Intelligence soldiers were very well trained: Some linguists received over a year of intense special training. And the required clearance process for each soldier could cost tens of thousands of dollars. It was essential that the Army not suffer an unnecessary continual hemorrhage of these valuable soldiers due to circumstances such as poor child care, which we could make an effort to improve.

Military Intelligence has one of the highest percentages of women of any Army branch. But although we often think of child care as solely related to women, the issue concerns the majority of our men soldiers as well because a higher percentage of soldiers are married than ever before, and most men soldiers' wives work. So addressing child care problems is a priority for any commander, not for just me. But in the early 1990s, the Army as a whole was completely preoccupied with post–Cold War downsizing and would only later make a concerted effort to improve the quality-of-life issues of child care and housing that we all now recognize play such a critical role in the retention of trained soldiers.

Another issue we dealt with in the brigade concerned our mess halls. Originally, there had been a mess hall in the facility, serving four meals within a twenty-four-hour period to the soldiers on shift work. But in 1990, during one of the post–Cold War cost-cutting efforts, a decision was made to eliminate one of our two mess halls, which were located in the tunnel and at Schofield Barracks.

This had been an ill-advised decision. Most of the soldiers

working in the tunnel only got a twenty-minute lunch break. When there had been a mess hall, that was adequate time to go through the serving line, and sit down to a meal. But once the mess hall was removed, the only options were packing a bag lunch, buying a cold sandwich or junk food from a vending machine, or facing the unappetizing prospect of the greasy fare offered at a small, rather unsanitary on-site snack bar run by a private concessionaire.

When I took command of the brigade, I found this situation unacceptable. The Army had removed the mess hall at the height of the effort to keep soldiers fit and healthy. So vending machine Twinkies or greasy snack bar hot dogs were hardly the answer. And the single soldiers living in barracks did not have kitchens in which to prepare a bag lunch. The mess hall at Schofield Barracks—across the post from the quaint old *From Here to Eternity* buildings—was modern and offered appetizing food. But it was just too far away for the shift workers to reach on their short lunch breaks.

It was obvious to me that putting an Army mess hall back in the tunnel was the best solution to the problem. But this remedy would have to come in the 1992 budget year, which saw the greatest drawdown in Army history. The Cold War was over; we won the Gulf War. Entire divisions were rolling up their flags and being deactivated. Cost-cutting was the live-or-die byword. A mess hall open twenty-four hours a day was an expensive proposition, requiring three shifts of civilian cooks.

I knew that this effort might be viewed by some as tilting at windmills, but it was my job as a commander to support my soldiers as energetically as possible. However, the first reply to my request to reopen the mess hall was predictable: "You've got the snack bar."

This called for a "tactical" response. As commander of the entire facility, I was able to influence the frequency and thoroughness of the health inspections to which the snack bar was subjected. To no one's surprise, the health inspectors found rotten spaghetti sauce, tainted hamburgers, and unacceptable quantities of grease, which supported a thriving population of roaches and rats. The snack bar regularly failed health inspections, went through halfhearted efforts to improve, and failed again. Whenever the 2,000 annual visitors passed through Kunia—Hawaii just happening to be a "required" stop for many official travelers—I raised the issue of reopening the mess hall.

Eventually we prevailed. The mess hall in the tunnel was renovated and reopened. The young soldiers on shift work received three free nutritious, well-balanced meals a day.

* * *

Treating team members with respect and dignity, and helping make their lives easier, extends far beyond the purview of the Army. Many of the most forward-thinking and successful private sector companies invest heavily in their employees' morale and welfare.

The innovative software corporation SAS, with its headquarters in Cary, North Carolina, is one of the most eminent in this area. Having grown from a small entrepreneurial venture in 1976 to one of the world's ten largest independent software vendors and the largest privately held software company today, SAS has over 3 million users worldwide. SAS has consistently ranked among the very best employers in surveys taken by *Working Mother* magazine, *Fortune,* and *Business Week.* The company provides inexpensive on-site child care that begins early in the day and extends late into the evening for those employees working long hours on a deadline project. Other SAS perks include a company pool, gym, and athletic fields on the headquarters campus.

This attention to employees' needs has paid invaluable dividends to the company. For example, software programmer Doug Teasly brings his preschool son, Philip, with him to work most days and leaves him in the nearby child care center. This perk costs him $250 a month, but he is happy to pay in order to have the chance to visit his son during the day. Teasly is so satisfied with his conditions at SAS that he has declined job offers for more than $30,000 a year more than he is currently making.

To me, such examples clearly indicate that mutual respect and loyalty within an organization—what has often been called the cohesiveness of an effective team—is a goal to which we should all aspire.

* * *

In September 1992, I was on Temporary Duty in Washington when I received yet another unexpected phone call. It was from Major General Chuck Scanlon, commander of INSCOM, with whom I had briefly discussed my controversial slating in 1985, when my assignment to command an MI battalion in Korea had been inappropriately handled.

"Claudia, how are you doing?"

"Fine, sir."

"I'm calling you with some good news."

Was he calling about some professional issue we'd discussed at Kunia?

"You have been selected for promotion to brigadier general. Congratulations."

I felt almost numb. What a great honor.

As soon as I hung up the phone, I called my father. "Daddy, guess what?"

"What?"

"I've been selected to be promoted to brigadier general."

There was a slight pause, then he whooped with exuberance.

He had pinned on my second lieutenant's bars twenty-three years earlier.

10

Pentagon Hardball

As my Army assignments increased in responsibility, I found myself confronted with challenges more complex than any I had faced as a younger officer. Staff positions and previous battalion command had prepared me for brigade command, which in turn honed the leadership and management skills I would later call upon as a general in the Pentagon. But the test I faced as commander of the 703rd Military Intelligence Brigade was unique by any standard. In what became known in Intelligence circles as the "Kunia Mutiny," I had to confront defiance of good order and discipline while simultaneously conducting a demanding organizational transformation.

The situation began in 1992 when the National Security Agency decided to reduce the number of strategic Military Intelligence facilities worldwide to just three major joint stations, each under the command of a separate armed service. Shifting to joint command at each station would streamline staff and provide more centralized operational control—a move that was made possible by advances in technology and changes in philosophy about service roles and operational styles. This became a priority during the belt-tightening after the Cold War and would allow the services at the stations to combine their staffs and share the responsibility for a single, integrated operation.

Kunia was scheduled to be one of these three joint stations, the other two being at the Air Force Intelligence Center near San Antonio, Texas, and the INSCOM facility at Fort Gordon, Georgia.

Eventually, a Navy captain would command the joint operation at Kunia. But since the 703rd Military Intelligence Brigade was host organization in 1992 and the other armed services' units were "tenants," the NSA and its military leaders decided that the Army would retain command of Kunia for a few more years after joint operations began on January 1, 1993.

None of us liked this change ordered from Washington, especially because we preferred service autonomy. For years, the Army, Navy, and Air Force had existed in "co-located" status, working side by side in the vast subterranean building but retaining their separate chains of command. The task of ironing out the complex details of the transformation had to be completed within a year. Now, struggling against our own cultural resistance, we had to mesh those operations into a single joint station, of which I, an Army colonel, would be the senior officer and commander. Getting the armed services to move beyond the ingrained aspects of operational control is never easy. In fact, "going joint" invariably involves considerable angst and negotiation over the details. But my colleagues and I were professional officers; we didn't choose our orders, we obeyed them. At least that was what I thought in 1992.

As our preparations for the details of the shift to a joint station progressed over a six-month period, however, my Navy colleague Captain Hugh Doherty and I noticed a distinctly unusual pattern of behavior on the part of the commander of the Air Force contingent at Kunia, Lieutenant Colonel Larry Strang. At first, he had appeared cooperative, attending meetings with Captain Doherty and me to work on the bureaucratic nuts and bolts of the transformation. Then, after many of the details had been hammered out, Larry Strang became harder to contact, just when his cooperation was most needed. Ostensibly, he was still cooperative and would even call Captain Doherty and me to schedule planning sessions. But Strang would then either find some excuse to cancel the meeting, send a junior officer, or even an NCO as his representative to discussions where a commander's decision was required. Once, when I asked Strang's representative what his instructions were, the man replied, "I'm only here to take notes, ma'am."

Then Larry Strang would go through the charade of scheduling a makeup meeting, which Captain Doherty and I would fit into our calendars, and no one from the Air Force would appear.

I called Strang to ask for an explanation.

"Why didn't you show up at the meeting, Colonel?"

"I was too busy, ma'am," he said.

"Please check your calendar and let me know when you are free."

"Yes, ma'am. I'll do that today."

He failed to do so. But what I found most unusual were official memoranda that Lieutenant Colonel Strang had signed and distributed to his staff, which they passed on to mine, declaring unequivocally that the pending station operations at Kunia would be a "consolidated," not a joint, command. In the military, there is a world of difference between the two. A joint operation has a single commander under whom the separate service contingents coordinate their efforts. This is what the NSA and the three strategic intelligence commands had ordered us to accomplish. But Strang seemed to have either misunderstood or decided to defy those orders.

Just to make sure *I* wasn't the officer misinterpreting the Major Commands' intentions, I had my staff consult closely with INSCOM headquarters to verify that our proposed plan was consistent with the U.S. Air Force Intelligence Center interpretation of the new directives. Word came back from INSCOM: There were no "crossed wires." Still, I had to be certain that Strang's resistance represented foot-dragging at the local level and not quasi-official United States Air Force policy. Among Army officers, the Air Force had a reputation for publicly proclaiming one policy at the higher command level and allowing more junior local commanders latitude to defy that policy when it suited their service's purpose.

So I called the Air Force Intelligence Center directly. They verified what INSCOM had told me: The Kunia facility would be integrated into a joint command in the first quarter of 1993.

During this time, Captain Doherty and I managed to discuss this issue directly with Lieutenant Colonel Strang. His first argument was that the proposed shift to joint operations was not yet official policy. We presented ample documentary evidence to the contrary. Then Strang persisted that even if a joint command were in the offing, the change did not have to be implemented as quickly as we proposed. Again, we produced directives to prove him wrong. But Strang remained uncooperative.

When Strang had left that meeting, I told Captain Doherty, "We need to think through exactly what steps he has to comply with after January first. I just can't imagine him remaining openly defiant beyond that date. But we must have some observable benchmarks."

Captain Doherty agreed and our two staffs examined the integration plan for the most important elements of Air Force cooperation. If Strang and his people decided to disobey NSA and Major Command orders, I wanted to know what the legal tripwires were in the event this situation escalated. By now, I was aware that I might have unexpectedly entered an interservice turf battle in which the Air Force, for reasons of its own, had decided to use Kunia as a test case to push its claim for a different definition of the new joint centers. This was murky stuff. I was a colonel who had just been selected for promotion to brigadier general, still a relatively junior officer by the standards of Pentagon Hardball this looming confrontation might represent. One thing was clear, however: I would have to plan my actions very carefully in my dealings with Lieutenant Colonel Strang and the Air Force.

And those dealings had become openly strained. My action officers dreaded discussing the transformation with Strang because he had become so verbally abusive. Although he was polite with me, all of my attempts to have him face reality and change his approach to the transformation failed. When I tried to elicit Strang's specific concerns about the process we were undergoing, he avoided discussing either the substance of the transition or his objections to it.

Just before the January 1 deadline, Strang's immediate senior, Colonel Cassidy, entered the picture. He called me at my quarters and requested that the negotiations begin all over again. I considered his suggestion to be just another stalling tactic. Obviously, there were real differences in the three services' commitment to this change. Here at Kunia, the Army and the Navy had worked diligently to hammer out the many details, some complex, some mundane, while the Air Force had first dragged its feet and now was more openly attempting to derail the entire process.

I clarified that Cassidy had been kept up to date throughout the preceding months and that he had never presented any objection (or support) during that time. He agreed that was the case.

"Well, Colonel," I told him, "we've gone well beyond the time for discussion. You have not participated in that discussion for months. Why would anything be different now?"

Still, he persisted that deadlines were arbitrary and all parties involved should negotiate in good faith.

"Colonel," I reminded him, "the timeline for the transition was *given* to us, not created *by* us. We are proceeding with the transition."

New Year's Day 1993, the deadline to begin joint operations, fell at the start of a long weekend. The situation with the Air Force was still vague, although the Army and the Navy were implementing all of the administrative and technical procedures we had previously agreed on. The Air Force, however, continued to back and fill, on the one hand saying they wanted to cooperate but had no authority to go joint until directed to do so by their headquarters, and, on the other hand, protesting they did not agree with various aspects of the new organization's design.

Even more troubling, throughout January and much of February, Lieutenant Colonel Strang issued orders to the Air Force contingent contradictory to mine. Finally, I told Strang's operations officer that the situation was unacceptable. There was no change. Then I met with Lieutenant Colonel Strang and informed him in a direct manner, "There can only be one commander at this station."

He chose not to respond openly. But his actions spoke for themselves.

The Kunia station was a Special Compartmented Intelligence Facility (SCIF) that held some of our country's most highly classified secrets. Everyone inside the facility had to have a high security clearance badge or be escorted. All persons leaving the building had to present their briefcase, knapsack, or gym bag to the Military Police for inspection. This followed the old security adage, "In God we trust. All others we verify." The security regulation had been enforced in Kunia and other similar installations for decades. We all took it for granted and kept the amount of gear we toted in and out of the tunnel to a minimum in order to speed up the line at the MP gate.

Then one day in February, while the Air Force stalling tactics were still dragging on, Lieutenant Colonel Strang refused to have his briefcase opened for inspection at the MP checkpoint on leaving the facility. I received word from a major on the Operations staff that Strang had been very rude and arrogant to the junior NCO on duty at the gate and had basically bullied his way through.

Now the situation had reached a serious new level. None of us could pick which security regulations we chose to obey on a particular day. All of us submitted to inspection on leaving the facility. I was always happy to do so because it set an example to the younger soldiers just beginning their Army careers: *If the colonel can line up to have her briefcase inspected, I can stand in line at the end of the shift and open my gym bag for the MPs.* But Strang was defying this practice.

I called him early the next morning. "I understand you left the building without opening your briefcase. Why?"

Strang was sullen, but not abrasive. "I'm a separate commander, Colonel. I don't have to follow that procedure."

This was a test of wills. I suddenly realized that he had mistaken the patience I had employed since New Year's for weakness. I intended to correct that misunderstanding.

"Of course you do, Colonel," I said in a flat, cool tone. "You have a badge that permits your entrance to this facility, and that badge is contingent on your complying with security regulations. From now on, you will either follow standard security procedures and have your briefcase inspected, or you will turn in your badge."

I wasn't sure if he believed that I intended to follow through on this. Its implications were serious: Without a security badge, he could not enter the building. What had begun as possibly local bureaucratic infighting at the level of colonels might quickly escalate to much higher echelons.

That afternoon, I carefully reviewed all the issues surrounding the transition process to make sure that this current crisis was not just the explosive conclusion of a simmering personality clash. Clearly it was not—because Captain Doherty had been just as stymied and frustrated by Strang's actions as I had been. The next day, I asked Strang to my office. "Are you prepared to comply with station security regulations concerning inspection of your briefcase?"

"No, ma'am. I can't do that. I'm not going to comply because I'm a separate commander."

I gave him a deadline of an additional week after which he was to either comply or turn in his badge. A week later he came to my office to tell me his decision. He was not going to comply.

"Please give me your badge," I said, reaching out for it. "I'll have the MPs walk you out of the facility." If Strang felt any emotion over this unprecedented incident, his face did not betray it. A rather grim MP staff sergeant appeared in my office doorway to escort this Air Force lieutenant colonel from the building.

Next, my Operations officer, Lieutenant Colonel George Gramer, reported that about a dozen of Strang's Air Force NCOs planned to stage a protest by putting down their own badges and refusing to comply with security regulations.

"Colonel," I said, considering this latest development, "if they do that, it's very serious."

I immediately called the Staff Judge Advocate General at Schofield Barracks to explain the situation. "The issue is not ambiguous, Colonel," he told me. "You are the installation commander. You set and enforce the security rules. Your responsibility is to establish good order and discipline."

This was obvious. Discipline was the glue that bound all the military to our national civilian leadership. Without order and discipline, we would be a banana republic.

I attended a previously scheduled meeting in our small auditorium where the Air Force NCOs planned to stage their walkout. I got straight to the point. "You're sitting in this room with security badges that indicate your willingness to comply with the security rules of this station. You'll have to live up to those rules. But I understand that some of you intend to put down your badges. Do it now if you're going to do it at all."

I stared at the faces of the men and women seated before me. This was a Showdown at the O.K. Corral. Many of them were senior Air Force NCOs with years of service. About fifteen NCOs rose and walked down to the table to turn in their badges. The MPs collected them and escorted the NCOs from the building.

I had not believed that Lieutenant Colonel Strang would carry the issue this far.

Captain Doherty immediately called the Naval Security Command in Washington. And I telephoned INSCOM commander Major General Chuck Scanlon, who was on Temporary Duty in England, where it was the middle of the night.

He agreed that the situation was serious and said he would immediately confer with his counterpart at the Air Force Intelligence Command, Major General Gary W. O'Shaughnessy.

Meanwhile, I contacted the Staff JAG again, who reconfirmed that my actions had been legal and appropriate.

Within two days, General Scanlon called me. "Okay, Claudia," he said. "I've worked things out with the Air Force. Give Strang back his badge. He'll comply with security regs. But he will not be back in the tunnel very much."

That was the outcome of the situation at Kunia. We returned

the security badges. When Strang did enter the facility, he usually had an enlisted airman carry his briefcase for him to be inspected by the MPs. The rest of the Air Force contingent complied with the security regulations as they always had. We got on with the business of integrating the command.

But the dust that the "mutiny" had kicked up took a long time to settle. I received a hand-delivered official letter from Major General O'Shaughnessy in which he took me to task over the incident. He was "disappointed" with the events, which had received "such widespread (and negative) publicity." The general added that "The seniors in the Pentagon and NSA are not used to seeing this type of emotional reaction to a disagreement or even a confrontation." He was "mystified" by my "overreaction to what most of us deal with daily." He suggested that "this cloud from Kunia will linger with you" as a sign of the time "when your emotions overshadowed good judgment." He implied that I had irrevocably damaged my reputation with the NSA, the organization with which I would have to work in one capacity or another as a senior Army strategic intelligence officer.

The general then proceeded to question my management ability and ended with the wish that I would "turn this unfortunate episode into a learning experience."

It was clear from General O'Shaughnessy's tone that he was engaging in damage control by disguising the Air Force responsibility for the crisis through dismissing my actions as those of an incompetent and emotional woman.

I chose not to let this defensive maneuver go unanswered. In my reply (which I discussed with Major General Scanlon), I provided General O'Shaughnessy detail about the lack of cooperation and active obstruction that Lieutenant Colonel Strang had exhibited throughout the transition process. I also indicated that the Navy and the Army had worked well together in integrating the command, but both Colonel Cassidy and Lieutenant Colonel Strang had resisted this integration in various ways. "My relationship and reputation with NSA remain solid," I concluded. "It is based on an association of eighteen years of mutual respect."

Several months later, following a meeting at NSA, an Air Force brigadier general tried to admonish me over the way I had handled the crisis at Kunia. The senior Navy admiral present was Vice Admiral Mike McConnell, Director of NSA. He interrupted the Air Force officer and addressed me. "General Kennedy," the admiral said, "you did the right thing. When you're in command, you have to act accordingly. You cannot allow others to dispute your authority."

But even today, I hear occasional reports that Air Force officers are pleased that I was forced to take such drastic action with Strang and his NCOs. "That lets us treat Army people the same way" has become their refrain. This is absurd, a terrible and inappropriate interpretation of the events. Strang had always complied with security procedures until the endgame of the Air Force resistance to the change in operational structure. Then he had chosen to precipitate the crisis.

I am still not sure what lay behind this incident. Very possibly, the local Air Force commanders were giving their headquarters a completely distorted version of the situation. Or the Air Force had used them as pawns in some larger power struggle invisible to people at our level.

But none of that speculation really matters. The lesson I took from the crisis was not to ask questions about hidden agendas, but to only consider external behavior. Lieutenant Colonel Strang chose to act in a manner contrary to good order and discipline. In so doing, he forced me to react. I did so decisively, and the crisis was finally resolved. Contrary to General O'Shaughnessy's opinion, my professional reputation did not suffer.

* * *

In August 1995, I was a major general, serving in the Pentagon as Assistant Deputy Chief of Staff for Intelligence. The assignment was both demanding and fulfilling, and left little free time for watching television.

One morning, the phone began to light up and people

stopped me in the corridors to ask if I had seen CNN's latest coverage of the Shannon Faulkner story. I had not.

"Last night she held a news conference at the Citadel," a colleague said. "She's dropping out."

"You have got to be kidding," I said, stunned.

"I wish I were," my acquaintance replied.

Shannon Faulkner was a twenty-year-old South Carolina student who had fought an almost thirty-month legal battle for admission to the Citadel, the venerable state-funded, male-only military academy in Charleston. Her campaign began in March 1993 when she sued the school, charging that its all-male Corps of Cadets was unconstitutional under the Equal Protection Clause. She had earlier been accepted for admission based on her excellent high school academic transcript, but one on which no reference to gender had appeared. The Citadel rescinded its acceptance when it was revealed she was a woman.

After months of litigation, which reached all the way to the U.S. Supreme Court, Faulkner was accepted as a day student in January 1994. That summer, the U.S. District Court ordered the Citadel to admit Shannon Faulkner into the Corps of Cadets, which was the heart and soul of the institution's student life. Although officially named the Military College of South Carolina, most of the Citadel's graduates did not enter military careers. And the school, founded in 1842, had a long tradition of offering its graduates access to a lifelong network of influential alumni contacts. The Citadel was a state-funded institution, however, and received considerable indirect financial and personnel support through the armed services' ROTC programs, which provided instructors and educational material. These were factors that heavily influenced Shannon Faulkner's lawsuit.

After the July 1994 court order instructing the Citadel to admit her into the corps, the school appealed. The U.S. Circuit Court of Appeals rejected this appeal in April 1995. That summer dragged on in tense legal exchanges, during which Faulkner spent much of her time either in hearings, consulting with her attorneys, or trying to avoid the mounting level of acrimony directed toward her. Since 1993, when vandals had defaced her parents' small-town home with giant blood-red letters forming obscene epithets, Faulkner had been subjected to almost continual harassment. Morning rush-hour motorists in Charleston encountered a large transportable commercial sign reading "DIE SHANNON" that had allegedly been rented and wheeled out in the night by a group of Citadel cadets, following the U.S. District Court order that Faulkner be admitted to the corps.

Finally, in August 1995, the Citadel was running out of options to comply with the law. But resistance continued, with a school spokesman arguing that Shannon was too heavy and had an injured knee, and would thus be unable to meet the demanding physical requirements of a cadet life. Once more, the legal maneuvering reached the U.S. Supreme Court, where Justices William Rehnquist and Antonin Scalia refused to bar Faulkner's admission as a member of the Corps of Cadets. The next day, she arrived guarded by federal marshals and reported to the campus with other "knobs," as first-year cadets were called due to their extremely short haircuts.

On August 13, she and the other knobs began Hell Week, seven days of purgatory that combined obsolete military academy harassment by upperclassmen with an exhausting regimen of physical training. The weather in Charleston was terrible, with high humidity and temperatures exceeding 100 degrees. After only one day of training, Shannon Faulkner and several male cadets became ill and were taken to the infirmary. Four days later, Faulkner announced her intention to leave the school. At a brief press conference, she told reporters the stress of the long legal battle "came crashing down," making it impossible for her to continue as a cadet.

When the news of Shannon Faulkner's decision spread across the campus, groups of cadets unleashed rebel yells and abusive chants, deriding her. A notorious, widely circulated press photograph of the cadets' reaction showed young men in a variety of uniforms, arms raised, stomping in joy. One of the most prominent figures was a cadet officer dressed in green trousers with a wide black stripe similar to an Army officer's uniform. He was twirling in gape-mouthed, delirious ecstasy at the news that one isolated woman had failed.

I thought of the substantial Army ROTC program that we supported at the Citadel. Rejoicing in a young person's failure was absolutely counter to Army values. Although the Citadel and the Virginia Military Institute, the remaining all-male bastion among state-funded military academies, liked to compare themselves favorably to the armed services' academies, I knew that the cadets at West Point would never stoop to such a spectacle.

Soon after Shannon Faulkner's departure from the Citadel, Ken Bode, moderator of Public Television's *Washington Week in Review,* asked me to watch the taping of the show and have dinner with him and journalists Cokie and Steve Roberts. At dinner, Cokie Roberts, who was rushing to prepare for that Sunday's *This Week with David Brinkley* show on ABC, asked my opinion on the Shannon Faulkner matter. I told her that I believed the young woman had fought a good fight, but in the end, events had overpowered her.

Cokie Roberts did not agree. "Getting that far and washing out after one day simply isn't to Shannon Faulkner's credit," she insisted.

I raised the issue of the intense legal battle, the death threats, and the stress to which Faulkner had been subjected over the previous two years. "You can't put up with all that and prepare yourself physically for the challenge they were going to throw at her," I said.

Again, Cokie Roberts disagreed. Many people shared that viewpoint, feeling that Shannon Faulkner had set back the cause of women's rights by her "failure."

I saw things differently. One young woman, backed by a few able attorneys, had forced one of the most politically influential educational institutions in the South, where traditions of antebellum male gallantry still stubbornly persisted, to comply with the United States Constitution. Although she herself had not been able to continue at the school, the legal precedent had been set; other women soon enrolled at the Citadel.

But the case of Shannon Faulkner remained troubling for many of my friends and professional associates. Since I was the Army's senior woman officer, they came to me to voice their opinion. Why was the Army continuing to support through the ROTC program an institution such as the Citadel that obviously did not accept basic Army values? Why didn't the Army leadership "stand up and be counted" on this important matter? If Shannon Faulkner's battle had concerned race, some argued, the country's political and military leaders would have stepped forward immediately to go on the record supporting her. But because she had been one isolated woman, her struggle seemed to have not registered with the Army's senior leadership.

I found these questions compelling. After thinking about them, I went to see Sara Lister, Assistant Secretary of the Army for Manpower and Reserve Affairs. One of her responsibilities was the Army ROTC program at the Citadel. We discussed the Shannon Faulkner case, and she agreed that the young woman had not been treated fairly. I told her I thought the matter ought to be brought to the attention of Secretary of the Army, Togo West. She told me to go see him.

When I had reported to the Pentagon as ADCSINT, Secretary West had told me, "As senior woman in the Army, you should feel free to bring any gender issues to me." Now I took up his offer and made an appointment for a meeting in his office on the Pentagon E-Ring.

During our discussion, we could look out the window overlooking the Mall entrance toward the early autumn foliage.

"Mr. Secretary, women are very distressed about the Shannon Faulkner matter," I said. I listed the concerns that had been brought to me. "Sir, we want our Army leadership to speak out on this matter."

Secretary West was silent for a few moments. "This struggle is not being fought by the United States Army, General. Ms. Faulkner's case, and the other litigation involving VMI, is being dealt with in the federal court system." Togo West was an experienced attorney who understood legal matters far better than I. "It would simply not be appropriate for me or any of the Army's uniformed leaders to take a public stand on matters under active litigation."

I understood his argument. The people who had come to me were justifiably angry. They correctly saw Shannon Faulkner as a trailblazer who had been treated badly. But we did not have the broader perspective on the issue that someone serving at the strategic level of leadership such as Secretary West enjoyed.

At that level, a leader simply cannot speak freely on a controversial subject such as the Shannon Faulkner case, no matter what his personal feelings on the issue might be. Although people are often critical of leaders who seem to remain aloof on such matters, these leaders can lose authority if they overplay their hands.

I did not achieve the results I had sought entering Secretary West's office for that meeting. But I left having learned a valuable lesson about the exercise of power.

* * *

Secretary West was absolutely correct in trusting the legal system to resolve the acrimonious issue of gender integration at the Citadel and VMI.

As of April 2001, the Citadel had eighty-one women in the Corps of Cadets. Many have suffered inexcusable hazing, but they have persisted. And their numbers are increasing. The school had resisted complying with the law of the land for as long as it could, but ultimately, one brave young woman who never wore a formal cadet uniform had forced the Citadel and all its influential alumni to obey the provisions of the Constitution.

The struggle for gender integration at the Virginia Military Institute had been even longer. Begun in 1990 by Attorney General Richard Thornburgh in the administration of President George H. Bush, the suit against the school wound its way through the federal courts for six years. Finally, in July 1996, the Supreme Court ruled seven to one that VMI must accept women as cadets. Justice Ruth Bader Ginsburg wrote the majority opinion that an all-male admissions policy violated the Equal Protection Clause of the Constitution. The school would either have to admit women or forgo state funding. VMI could not find financial support for conversion to a private institution, as some diehards had urged. As at the Citadel, women cadets were soon admitted.

In February 2001, First Classman (senior) Erin Claunch was honored on the floor of the Virginia General Assembly for the academic, military, and athletic excellence she had shown during her four years at VMI. She was an academically distinguished physics major, commanded the 2nd Battalion in the VMI Corps of Cadets, and had won a letter in cross-country. As an Air Force ROTC scholarship cadet, she planned to become a career officer.

It will be years, if not decades, before the most tradition-bound alumni of the Citadel and VMI accept the fact that defying the United States Constitution was futile and that the admission of women as cadets has not ruined their cherished schools. But eventually, they *will* see the wisdom of this new policy.

I am confident of this because, eventually, rational people accept reality. Over a decade ago, the Commandant of Cadets at West Point was briefing elderly visiting alumni. He showed them data concerning the Physical Training performance of a group of cadets, comparing this data to the alumni's less impressive record from decades earlier. These contemporary cadets had done more push-ups and sit-ups in two minutes and run two miles faster than the alumni.

"That's impressive, General," an alumnus said to the commandant.

"And those are just the women," the general replied.

* * *

One of the responsibilities I assumed in 1997 as Deputy Chief of Staff for Intelligence was oversight of policy affecting a widespread, complex network of relationships with foreign military and civilian defense delegations involved in procuring American weapons systems developed by the Army. Over 200 Foreign Liaison Officers (FLNOs) were assigned to every Training and Doctrine

Command post in the U.S. Army where our advanced war-fighting doctrine was developed and technology was tested. This was a numerically lopsided relationship because the Army had only about thirty such officers at similar facilities overseas.

The situation sometimes reached ludicrous proportions. For example, the French LNO at Fort Rucker, Alabama, managed to get more training time on the latest U.S. aircraft than the American aviators assigned there. The problem of the "Flying Frenchman" became well known to elements of the Army staff and was emblematic of the strange new post–Cold War world in which we operated.

Arms sales drove this large foreign military presence at American installations. After the Cold War, U.S. defense contractors faced the prospect of either selling more weapons, selling fewer weapons at higher prices to the United States, or being forced to shut down their research and development facilities and production lines. With the downsizing of the U.S. military in the 1990s, the defense contractors saw foreign military sales as a means of continuing to sell their weapons systems. From the Army's perspective, foreign military sales helped reduce the per-unit development cost of these weapons. Further, selling advanced weapons to friends and allies around the world became an increasingly important part of our overall foreign policy. These countries were a diverse group, ranging from our traditional NATO partners, to Middle Eastern countries with which we wished to establish or retain close relationships, to small, prosperous nations such as Singapore. The sales bound those countries to us through shared military technology and doctrine.

This transfer of American military technology abroad involved billions of dollars each year. The process was closely observed and directed by senior officials in the Office of the Secretary of Defense (OSD). Because successful defense contractors enjoyed considerable influence on Capitol Hill—components of large weapons systems were subcontracted to companies in as many congressional districts as practicable—the mantra from OSD was "Sell, sell, sell." This inclination perfectly matched that of many foreign countries eager to obtain state-of-the-art American arms.

In order to both scout the prospects for emerging technology and to monitor the progress of weapons systems already under contract but not yet delivered, these foreign governments maintained their growing presence of LNOs and Cooperative Program Personnel at Army posts and other military bases. There were several programs governing these arms sales, all of which were subject to review by the Pentagon. Prosperous countries such as the United Kingdom often chose to purchase weapons as direct commercial sales that involved corporation-to-corporation partnerships to share the technology on a multinational basis. Less prosperous or less technically advanced countries such as Egypt usually obtained their American weapons under Foreign Military Sales programs, which included provisions for spare parts, training, manuals and computer support, and maintenance. There were also hybrids of these two basic types in which a country would pay the lower commercial price and negotiate for military training and the other provisions. These hybrid methods of procurement were preferred because they combined lower prices and less U.S. government control.

During the sometimes headlong rush to promote these exports in the 1990s, commercial and foreign military sales tended to snowball, often outpacing the detailed Memoranda of Understanding (MOU) required to protect sensitive American military technology secrets from transfer abroad. After I became DCSINT in 1997, I was involved in tense internecine Pentagon disputes concerning the question of how to handle technology transfer. As the Army's senior intelligence officer, my responsibility was to protect the security of the high-technology "crown jewels" embedded in our most advanced weapons. But that was exactly the technology that the foreign buyers wanted to obtain.

There was another essential element of my responsibility. By keeping our most sensitive advanced technology from foreign dissemination, we could extend the lifespan of that technology's competitive edge on the battlefield. This would reduce the costly research and development cycle and allow our soldiers equipped with these new weapons to retain their lethal war-fighting dominance at less cost. But this position ran counter to the prevailing trend in Congress, where members took a truly bipartisan and enthusiastic approach to foreign arms sales to "friends and allies."

The issue came to a head in the spring of 1999 in a heated dispute involving our closest ally, the United Kingdom, and one of our most advanced weapons systems, the AH-64D Apache attack helicopter equipped with the state-of-the-art Long Bow radar. The Long Bow Apache was a quantum improvement over other attack helicopters. Its ultrasensitive APG-64 radar mounted atop the main rotor mast was linked through integrated computer circuits to Stinger air-to-air missiles carried on the wingtips, which would allow the Apache Long Bow to seek out and destroy other helicopters day or night, in any weather. The electronics in the most sophisticated U.S. Army version of this system (as well as in the aircraft's ultramodern defensive countermeasure equipment) made the AH-64D truly one of our country's crown jewels.

Those were the jewels the British wanted to acquire when they decided to procure sixty-seven Apache Long Bow helicopters in 1996. The purchase was a direct commercial sale involving the British corporation GKN Westland in partnership with the American Apache contractors, McDonnell Helicopter Company (now part of Boeing), General Electric, and Martin-Marietta (now Lockheed Martin). Because the sale represented substantial sums to be spent in several critical congressional districts, high Pentagon officials involved with defense procurement supported the contract. But instead of hammering out a Memorandum of Understanding detailing exactly which technology the British would and would not have access to, these officials merely exchanged letters with their British counterparts that stated that the U.S. government supported the sale, which would include such data as required to field the system, in "accordance with our laws and regulations." However, the American letter did explain that there were certain categories of support that would require government-to-government arrangements, not purely commercial accommodations.

As the procurement moved forward, the contractors worked closely together and maintained contact with the Army Apache Long Bow project manager, an Aviation Branch colonel assigned to Redstone Arsenal, Alabama, the center for Long Bow R&D. But the British developed the perception that the U.S. Army was not supporting the commercial procurement in the spirit of the original exchange of letters at the Pentagon–Ministry of Defence level. Their displeasure was based on the fact that the Army did not grant British officers or technical representatives full access to the most advanced Apache Long Bow technology emerging from the labs at Redstone, which was by law reserved for the U.S. Army.

As DCSINT, I had been opposed to granting *any* foreign representatives access to such technology. This was not a personal decision, but rather one based on decisions made by the National Disclosure Policy Committee, under the Arms Export and Control Act. Without question, the British were our friends and close allies, but they were not the only country to which we were selling the Apache Long Bow. Israel and Singapore had also contracted to buy the attack helicopter. If we acceded to the British request and allowed their LNO virtually unlimited access to Redstone, in the absence of a negotiated, detailed Memorandum of Understanding, the Army position would be precariously outside the limits established by law.

But the British pressed their case in order, I believe, to determine how much technology they could obtain under the rather vague original procurement agreement. Security, legal, and other elements of the Army staff dug in, maintaining that the British should gain the access they wanted only after they had negotiated a Cooperative MOU that clearly delineated exactly what technology they were entitled to examine. Simultaneously, we did approve almost all their requests for on-site visits to Redstone. And we even shared with them new "First Article Test" data on ultra-advanced components of the Long Bow system concurrent with delivery of that information to our own Army. You couldn't get any more cooperative than that. However, the British requested even more access.

But every foreign representative at U.S. Army installations needed to operate under the provisions of an MOU that made clear the level of access to which he was entitled. Under many ad hoc arrangements, these foreign military officers were operating with vague ground rules. They might have access to the part of a system to which their own countries' laboratories contributed and then be denied access to a purely American, but closely related, component.

As foreign arms sales increased in the 1990s, the situation became more confused when the Pentagon created a new position, the Deputy Undersecretary of the Army—International Affairs, through whom all foreign liaison activities were to be coordinated. In theory, this relieved the DCSINT staff from much of the often frustrating negotiations over technology transfer. But we still had the responsibility of maintaining the security of our secret technology.

Because the lines of Pentagon authority were still unclear, I requested that the Inspector General conduct a very thorough review of the entire foreign disclosure procedure. As I expected, the IG's report concluded that most of our relationships with foreign liaison or exchange officers were too vague. And, from the DCSINT perspective of wanting to balance arms sales with protecting our most critical technology, the situation had not been settled. So, while we addressed and resolved the specific issues concerning the Apache Long Bow that the British had raised, we helped facilitate the negotiation of a detailed Cooperative MOU with them to augment the vague terms of the original commercial agreement.

But that was only one of a series of battles that I waged to moderate arms sales with security safeguards. I knew that this caused ripples of reaction in the staff of the Secretary of Defense. Word reached me that I had too often taken an "obstructionist" position on technology transfer and that I did not seem capable of striking the proper "balance" on these complex (i.e., politically charged) issues. Some in the OSD even referred to my stance on security as tantamount to wanting to give the DCSINT "veto" authority. This was more Pentagon Hardball, a game in which it helped to have sharp elbows and a thick skin. My sense was that the leadership did not need me to be "balanced"—that was *their* role. My role was to provide expert security advice.

Eventually, this was discussed with senior Army leaders. I believed the Army should separate the decisions on disclosing technology to foreign governments from the staff elements responsible for foreign military sales, for reducing the cost of new weapons, and for furthering the U.S. strategy of engagement and enlargement through such overseas arms sales. "We have a higher responsibility to protect our Army's lead in advance technology over and above the benefits we gain from closer association with foreign allies as well as U.S. businesses," I said. I noted that those in the OSD who suggested that the DC-SINT "doesn't get the point" of our arms sales program had themselves "failed to consider the broader responsibilities of the Army leadership in providing for the national defense and avoiding the perception by the public of an inappropriate bias toward foreign military sales."

I wanted to frame a course of action that protected my country's best interests. The Army eventually established a formal Memorandum of Understanding structure governing the access to our technology for all foreign liaison and exchange officers at our installations.

★　　★　　★

Ironically, as I was most deeply involved with Pentagon disputes about technology transfer, as well as fulfilling my other duties, I was also aware of sniping from detractors who were simply unable to accept the idea of a woman lieutenant general serving as DCSINT. In March 1999, I spoke to a conference of Military Intelligence Command (sergeants major and sergeants major) at Fort Huachuca, Arizona. It was a pleasure to be back at the post, where I had attended the MI Officer Advance Course as a young captain, and years later had been the deputy commander of the Military Intelligence Center and School. I addressed the senior Military Intelligence NCOs for about forty-five minutes, briefing them on a variety of issues, including shortfalls in the projected Army budget, and other updates that had been presented at a recent conference of Army four-star generals. I also presented a detailed analysis of Military Intelligence operations in the future, "Intelligence XXI." At the very end of my presentation and following the instructions Army Chief of Staff General Dennis Reimer had given all general officers, I made two points about the Consideration of Others program. My brief comments were that the program was more effective if discussions were held in small groups and that these groups should retain the same membership over the several discussion periods in the program.

But in mid-April, the Army's Office of Congressional Liaison received a letter from influential South Carolina Republican Congressman Floyd Spence concerning a complaint by one of his constituents, a retired Army colonel. In that retired officer's rather muddled letter, he referred to a speech I had purportedly made to the "Sergeant Majors Academy at Fort Bliss, Texas," that had "set the e-mail circuits alight." Allegedly the soldiers called this my "This Ain't Your Father's Army" speech. The officer admitted he had not seen my comments in their entirety, "but excerpts make me wonder if one of the Army's top intelligence officers does not have more to do right now than worry about 'Coos' [sic] training." In his final paragraph, the retired colonel's thread of thought seemed to unravel: "Concern [sic] of Others Training (Coos or Co2) AKA TF Touch-Feely training seems to be a major concern as we conduct combat operations in Serbia while being prepared to defend the rest of the world. Congressman, s you [sic] office COOS Qualified?"

Neither the Congressional Liaison people nor my staff could ignore Representative Spence's query. He was an important member of the House Armed Services Committee. So I replied explaining the true nature of my briefing to the senior NCOs at Fort Huachuca. Unfortunately, the intentionally distorted version was already out there on the Internet. Only recently, I understand, have retired officers made an effort to clarify the point that *I* did not create the Army's Consideration of Others program. Rather, as mentioned earlier, retired Major General Robert Foley, one of our most respected Medal of Honor recipients during the Vietnam War, conceived of this innovative program.

Sometimes during these months of Pentagon infighting over "program builds," operational and policy "defense," and a schedule that extended for sixteen hours a day, I would return home to Quarters 21 at Fort Lesley J. McNair with very little energy. But my enlisted aide, Master Sergeant Wayne Smith, had always prepared an appetizing, well-balanced meal for me to warm in the microwave, and I thoroughly enjoyed this luxury.

My quarters on the second and third floors of the stately tan brick house were of historic interest. The sixteen-foot ceilings with high windows (some still holding the wavy old glass of the nineteenth century) made it a unique residence. The post itself was a quiet refuge, with a view of the Anacostia–Washington Channel waterfronts, and a mall shaded by graceful old hardwoods. My living room and dining room had served as the courtroom for the trial of the conspirators in the assassination of Abraham Lincoln in 1865. After they were convicted, they were hanged that July in the area of the mall that was now the post tennis court. One of the conspirators was Mary Surratt (the first woman to be hanged by the U.S. government), and it was she who was reputed to be the particular ghost of Quarters 20, next door.

That was all part of the Army adventure.

11

The Future

*I*n my final year in the Pentagon, the DCSINT staff participated in one of the most revolutionary organizational changes in recent military history: the transformation of the United States Army to face the challenges of defending our country in the mid-twenty-first century.

When General Eric Shinseki became Army Chief of Staff after well over thirty years of service in June 1999, he decisively ended a long period of weighing options and experimentation about the shape of the post–Cold War Army. It had been obvious that the Army no longer needed—nor could depend on—all the "heavy" divisions centered on the M1 Abrams tank and the M2 Bradley fighting vehicle. These massive tracked armored vehicles had been designed to counter similarly equipped Soviet forces in Europe. Cold War doctrine did not require the Army to rapidly deploy the bulk of its heavy forces in the event of war: They were already on the ground in Germany or in South Korea, the other most likely flashpoint.

But just as the Cold War ended in 1990, the Army was called on to rapidly deploy its heavy divisions to the Middle East for the

Persian Gulf War. The logistics challenge of the buildup in Saudi Arabia had been formidable. This conflict was quickly followed by a series of unanticipated operations in the Balkans, Africa, and Haiti. It became clear that the lumbering, but lethal, Armor and Mechanized Infantry divisions that had held the line against the Warsaw Pact in West Germany for almost fifty years were not agile enough to fight the brushfire wars now flaring across the world in the wake of the long American–Soviet conflict.

But what kind of Army would be needed in the next five years, the next ten, or even the next thirty to forty when we might expect serious challenges to our status as the world's sole superpower? One lesson we had learned in Somalia and Kosovo was that the new Army had to be rapidly deployable, yet retain the unparalleled war-fighting "lethality" and survivability of the last few decades.

Leading the top Army uniformed team, General Shinseki helped develop a three-pronged plan to completely transform the Army by 2030, while retaining its ability to fight and win ground wars worldwide during this challenging process. The plan calls for a Legacy Force based on the existing traditional heavy divisions to be modernized while an Interim Force of Brigade Combat Teams equipped with new lighter air-deployable combat vehicles comes on line and assumes increasing responsibilities for the Army's core war-fighting mission. One possibility under consideration for the major equipment of the Interim Force is a basic wheeled (rather than a tracked) armored vehicle that can be carried directly to forward airstrips by the Air Force's rugged workhorse transport, the C-130. This wheeled vehicle could be fitted with a variety of missile or gun systems to make it almost as lethal as much heavier tanks.

Meanwhile, an Objective Force equipped with revolutionary new weapons (many remotely operated) and based on new fighting doctrine will pass through the science and technology, research and development, and procurement phases to become the Army of the future. What General Shinseki and his staff have set in motion is nothing less than a revolution from within. It is an example of a huge, complex organization reinventing itself while simultaneously retaining all of its global responsibilities and capabilities.

The DCSINT staff contributed to this effort by consulting with other elements of the U.S. intelligence community to project what kind of military threat our country would face in coming decades.

Our projection of events in the twenty-first century was that this period would prove very unstable, a continuation of the multiple and simultaneous revolutions of the previous century. These social and technological upheavals will include the Information, Socio-Biological, and Efficiency Revolutions, as well the projected transformation of the U.S. Army, which will be paralleled in the other armed services.

It seems inevitable that in 2025, the world will still be divided into three distinct populations: the advanced nations comprising less than 2 billion people; the next and largest group of less advanced nations (China, Brazil, much of Southwest Asia) with a population of about 5 billion people; and the third group, the unstable nations of Africa and South Asia struggling on the brink of disaster, whose population will number about 2 billion.

With the exception of North America, the expanded European Union, a few Latin American countries, Japan, and some isolated zones of stability in the Middle East and South Asia, much of the world will be ripe for an ongoing conflict. Based on America's experience in the 1990s, it is clear that the military forces of the United States will be called upon to operate at an exhausting pace through a series of peacemaking and peacekeeping operations, as well as to respond in combat operations to various crises in corners of the world far from our logistics bases.

As this analysis emerges, one thing has become obvious: Our military is going to have to function at those places in the world where societal and cultural success and failure collide, where optimism over a progressive future confronts a longing for the past, and where technologies such as global television and the Internet erode traditional cultural values, thus igniting atavistic, often violent, reactions. One only need examine the current situation in unstable states such as Indonesia, Afghanistan, and Somalia to understand this pattern.

But we cannot simply wish for a peaceful, stable world and hope to achieve it. If I have learned anything in more than thirty years as a soldier, it is that the price of stability is diligence and military readiness. This will become increasingly true as the major revolutions currently underway accelerate and political and military events play out in unexpected ways.

The Information Revolution has become so ubiquitous that many of us forget its recent advent. Today, there are just over 200 million computers in America. In four years, the number of computers in the world will be rising toward one billion. By the year 2025, computers will operate incalculably faster than they do today. Wireless, global satellite computer networking will become commonplace. This inexpensive universal interconnectivity will have many positive effects. But what technology empowers, it can also destabilize. For example, a religious zealot in a hopelessly poor corner of some wretched country might be motivated by the information he receives through this high-tech window to simultaneously reject "sinful" technology for his own followers, while using its communication channels to obtain weapons and conduct unconventional combat that destabilizes his already feeble national government.

While information technology continues to make national borders transparent, its presence might harden cultural barriers, especially in countries such as Iran, Libya, Sudan, and Afghanistan, which already feel assailed by outside influences. Equally, the intrusion of foreign values can foment conflict in parts of the world where systems of social organization are breaking down and people seek new equilibrium. While this is often an exciting process, it can also be chaotic, and occasionally violent. The current situation in Indonesia and social instability in parts of Latin America reflect this phenomenon.

Finally, as the United States continues to be the dominant force in the popular culture disseminated over the global information network, people of many nations will react negatively to the dazzling (albeit distorted) glimpses of our culture and lifestyle. The already serious problem of illegal migration might be exacerbated. And for those unable to migrate, a reaction of bitterness based on envy might engender widespread hatred of the United States that can easily be exploited by nationalistic leaders. There is the potential for this problem in vast areas of overpopulated Asia.

The Socio-Biological Revolution that began with the control of human fertility and the widespread entry of women into the workplace in the 1960s in America will continue to accelerate in the twenty-first century. This revolution will evolve with major changes in the nature of work. Manufacturing will be relentlessly displaced by Information Age occupations. By 2025, over 95 percent of work in America and other advanced nations will involve some use of information technology in direct or embedded forms. The silicon chip—or its photon successor—will become as ubiquitous as the nut and bolt of the nineteenth and twentieth centuries.

Workers in the advanced countries will be compelled to work in smarter ways; our workforces will include more women with children and more seniors, who will take advantage of the demographic shift of our aging population. But education, not manual strength, will be the key to workers' success.

This transformation will prove disquieting, however, to those nations that rely on muscle power and fail to educate their people for the new age. Again, the potential for resentment of the poor toward the rich will only increase.

The Efficiency Revolution is often overshadowed by the Information Revolution, to which it is linked. The fact is that not every society or culture can exploit the Information Age efficiently. American culture, in which men and women increasingly share responsibility, is particularly and peculiarly geared to efficiency. The Wall Street adage "What's the bottom line?" has become our twenty-first-century mantra. The Europeans and Japanese often see this as a cold-hearted, indeed ruthless, form of capitalism. But, while there are psychological costs, in general our focus on efficiency has enabled us to generate more wealth for more people in less time than ever before. Productivity is the most important factor resulting from efficiency. This productivity has been possible through fuller participation in education throughout virtually every sector of the workforce. We don't offer the false promise of lifelong work made to the Japanese after World War II, or ultralucrative automatic social benefits the European working class enjoys. But the American worker is educated to perform a variety of increasingly complex assignments that develop as the Information Age progresses.

The transformation of military forces is best known to the public through the employment of "precision" munitions, usually displayed in armed service–provided (and edited) video clips shown on the news media. Those exciting videos are only part of the story. The fact is that the transformation has made profound changes, not only in the technological realm, but also in the area of human behavior in our military. As in the Information and Efficiency Revolutions, sheer kinetic strength is no longer necessary for lethality. Without question, the U.S. Army and its sister services can dominate any battlefield both today and into the foreseeable future, thanks in large measure to this revolution.

But I am also concerned that this transformation could prove to be largely irrelevant. That was one of the most sobering lessons my analysts took from the projection of the Army's future challenges. Most analysts predicted that no "peer" competitors, such as Russia or China, would arise to challenge us on an equal footing for the next fifteen to twenty-five years, if then. And neither of those nations will have the same dynamic mix of conventional and strategic, ground, air, and sea forces that we will enjoy far into the future. So the United States is likely to remain the world's sole superpower with all the challenges and responsibilities that entails.

But what are we likely to do with this power? Unless Russia rebuilds its Air Force and China modernizes its own, large-scale aerial combat does not seem to be in the offing. Nor will there be large surface fleet battles. Instead the future threat the United States faces will most likely involve intertwined elements of the evolving revolutions acted out on unpredictable battlefields with nontraditional foes. This being the case, our undisputed superiority in technology might do us little good, and, indeed, might lure us into a false sense of invulnerability.

Who might these future threats be? DCSINT analysts predicted they would include warlords, tribal chiefs, drug traffickers, international criminal cartels, terrorists, and cyber-bandits. And, just to up the ante, we might have to engage many or all of these characters simultaneously, while also playing a major role in humanitarian emergencies. Conventional warfare involving our Legacy and Interim Forces might also be a possibility, especially in regional conflicts that could flare up again in the Balkans and the former republics of the Soviet Union. All of these contingencies might be exacerbated by the pressures of growing populations, the global spread of "mega-cities," and unprecedented diasporas of people fleeing conflict, economic chaos, and the breakdown of order in failed states. Significantly, the proportion of refugees and internally displaced persons has outpaced overall population growth since the 1960s.

With the ongoing transformation of the American armed forces, no conventional military could ever defeat us. But the primary challenges may well come from those who are ruthless in the "asymmetric" use of violence. For example, a single terrorist truck bomb inflicted terrible casualties on the Americans in the Khobar Towers barracks in Dhahran, Saudi Arabia, and drove the entire U.S. Air Force contingent from that base to an isolated airfield in the central Saudi desert. A few years later, the alleged mastermind of that attack, Saudi exile Osama bin Laden, purportedly ordered the attack on two U.S. embassies in East Africa, which killed 224 people, including twelve Americans. And last year, the Navy destroyer USS *Cole* was attacked in the Yemen port of Aden by suicide bombers, who killed seventeen American sailors. American and Yemeni officials have charged that bin Laden ordered this attack as well.

But the Saudi terrorist remains at large, reportedly guiding his organization, al Qaeda ("the Base"), from a sanctuary in Afghanistan. Although the Clinton administration attacked bin Laden's Afghan base with cruise missiles following the 1998 embassy bombings, his hideout was never raided by highly trained U.S. Special Operations Forces, in part due to international political considerations and concerns about sovereignty. Such concerns will extend indefinitely into the future as terrorists continue to test our resolve and inflict damage when and where they can.

As we have already seen in conflicts in countries such as Congo and Sierra Leone, tribal warriors go into battle with cell phones and target their rockets with GPS satellite receivers linked to laptop computers. This trend will only continue. The nearly universal Soviet Bloc Kalashnikov will give way to sophisticated sniper rifles with night-vision scopes and advanced shoulder-fired antiaircraft missiles. Warlords will trade commodities such as diamonds or drugs for such ordnance. Within decades, these people could face off in combat armed with virulent chemical and biological weapons of mass destruction. These are the grim realities for which the Army is now preparing today.

How might some of these conflicts evolve?

Suppose there is a sprawling mega-city in 2025, population 20 million and growing, the capital of a developing country where civil control has completely broken down. Although rich in resources, this nation is a failed state, and warring factions struggle for control over this shantytown metropolis. Already jammed beyond the capacity of its infrastructure, the city is flooded by millions of refugees fleeing battles in the countryside. Starvation and epidemic disease add to the collective misery.

The competing warlords are themselves astute and well protected, with easy access to human source intelligence on their rivals and on the small contingent of international peacekeepers trying vainly to stop the bloodshed. When forced to communicate electronically, the warlords use obscure tribal dialects unfamiliar to foreign intelligence interpreters listening to voice intercepts in orbiting aircraft. The warlords ruthlessly use the local population as human shields and rely for protection from air attack on the thousands of foreign hostages held in squalid hotels and warehouses throughout the city. Relatives of the hostages besiege their governments to save these innocent people. Meanwhile, media-savvy representatives of the warlords promote their causes through global television, while clandestine terrorist forces bomb and kidnap to further these same ends.

There is increasing pressure in the United States for the Pentagon to intervene and use our superpower status to restore order. But how does the U.S. military respond to such a situation?

Another future war scenario involves a small, relatively prosperous country that has had a history of alternating friendship and animosity toward the United States. For the first two decades of the twenty-first century, the country sends thousands of its brightest young men to study computer sciences in American universities. While obtaining their degrees, many of these students also absorb details of our complex economy and analyze its institutional and social vulnerabilities. In about 2025, relations between America and this country again become strained, but not before that country's private sector and government construct multiple channels of access to the most important information networks within the United States. Soon they are using this access to hack information on an unprecedented level. Once the intricate web of America's interconnected computer systems has been analyzed, government and corporate data begins to disappear, banking networks collapse in chaos, telecommunications fail, and then the transportation collapses. With trucking, corporate agriculture, and food and fuel distribution paralyzed, commerce ends. Inevitably, the economy grinds to a halt. Although hundreds of thousands of Americans (mainly the elderly and hospitalized) have died, a debate rages in Washington over whether or not this "nonlethal" information warfare attack warrants a nuclear response.

An additional future threat could involve a would-be regional "hegemon" who diverts considerable natural resource revenue into amassing a huge conventional arsenal, composed mainly of former Soviet weaponry. In 2025, the dictator invades a neighboring state and quickly occupies it.

The United States assembles an intervention force, incorporating ground, air, and naval components. But as the U.S. forces converge on the area, the enemy leadership responds asymmet-rically. Foreign hostages are held prisoner in and around impor-tant facilities and, before American forces can occupy ports and airfields in nearby friendly countries, the enemy launches ballis-tic missiles with warheads containing strains of long-lasting an-thrax that contaminate these facilities, rendering them unusable for the U.S. force. What is the American response?

In the final scenario the DCSINT staff developed, a major mil-itary competitor does indeed arise to challenge us by 2020. Al-though this nation cannot compete with us on all levels, it can field a certain number of ground divisions as a power projection force; its navy has excellent coastal defense capability; and its strategic missile systems can threaten the United States with nuclear attack. It also has some capability for information warfare to disrupt our computer systems. More importantly, this country has developed a working antiballistic missile system, which, although not perfect, could blunt many of our incoming ICBMs, thus providing some promise of protection to its missile silos.

As 2020 unfolds, this nation ignores American protests and runs roughshod over its perceived sphere of regional influence, seizing offshore islands and oil-rich sections of nearby international water without regard to its neighbors' sovereignty or protests. The United States is faced with a risky and potentially costly conven-tional war where its opponent will have significant advantages. Fur-ther, the United States cannot bully its way through the region under the cover of a nuclear umbrella, since this enemy has a bal-listic missile defense and can also strike the U.S. mainland with nu-clear missiles of its own. How does America proceed?

As these projections were developed, I did not take pleasure in their disturbing ramifications. Having spent most of my life in uniform during the tense years of the Cold War, I longed for peace, as did my fellow soldiers. But our job wasn't to thrust our heads in the sand. It was to protect our country. And, as the United States prepared its military forces for the future, we had to see the world as it was likely to be, not as we would want it to be.

Most importantly, we had to remember that warfare is first and foremost a human endeavor. Our technical advances have been truly impressive. But the Army and the other services have not reached the point of operating on automatic. The human mind is still the best judgment on the battlefield. The potential for both victory and defeat is present in each of these future war scenarios. Good judgment, courage, decisiveness, and discipline will mean the difference between success and failure. Obviously, weapons will play their part, hopefully the best weapons our soldiers and scientists can develop. But, for the foreseeable future, men and women will be the key factor in controlling those weapons.

Considering the shape of future conflict and the steps that our country must take to respond to it, we need to recognize that the advances in technology will inevitably cause a blurring or melding of the Army's existing branches and Military Occupational Specialties. Further, today's demarcation between the tactical and strategic level will become less sharply delineated. And, finally, the traditionally defined roles of women and men soldiers will change as qualification to accomplish the mission, not gender, becomes the most important criterion the Army considers.

Let's examine how these changes might play out on the future battlefield, as I have defined it in the conflict scenarios.

In the battle involving the ruthless warlords struggling for control of the squalid mega-city by using thousands of foreign hostages as pawns, advanced technology and nontraditional operations might play a critical role. Suppose the most brutal of the warlords, Commander X, decides to leverage his power by beginning the systematic (and globally televised) execution of hostages. But also imagine that the U.S. Army has a small stealth helicopter capable of silently penetrating the airspace Commander X controls in the city and electronically ferreting out his exact location through the use of his unique digital voiceprints forwarded by secure satellite link to a super-computer database on the other side of the world. The helicopter pilot can identify him, no matter what tribal dialect he chooses to employ. Now imagine that this low-flying aircraft is equipped with small "brilliant" munitions that can penetrate roofs or walls and hone in on Commander X's voice before exploding. Finally, let's imagine that the pilot who successfully targets Commander X is a young woman Army captain.

Is she a Military Intelligence officer? Part of the Aviation Branch? A member of our Special Operations Aviation Regiment? Is she operating on the tactical or strategic level? Answer: Her mission encompasses some of all these elements. The important aspect of her assignment is that she accomplishes her mission. Commander X's force is decapitated, the hostages are freed, and the other warlords must accept the fact that they too are equally vulnerable.

Now let's turn to the information warfare scenario. Imagine that America already has teams of highly trained military specialists whose mission is to detect and counter at the lowest level the hostile penetration of vulnerable information systems. When this penetration is detected, the team immediately erects firewalls to protect our country's critical computer networks. Women play vital roles on those teams. Girls and young women are as computer-literate as their male peers. And research indicates that women actually spend more time working or studying online. Women now play essential roles in guarding our country from cyber-attack, and this contribution will only increase. Again, will these soldiers operate at the tactical or strategic level? Will their MOSs be considered "combat" jobs? The distinction is irrelevant if they accomplish their mission.

Women soldiers serving in such revolutionary specialties and assignments would also make extremely valuable contributions to victory in the other two possible future conflict scenarios I have outlined.

Such a blurring of traditional military echelons and branches is already underway. The pattern will continue as the American military modernizes. And it is essential that we see this modernization through to its completion. Now, and in the foreseeable future, we will not have the largest military establishment in the world, but it is critical that we continue to have the best. It is also vital that this force be fully ready for complex, demanding combat operations virtually anywhere in the world.

But there are still those who wish to turn back the clock, to jeopardize our future readiness in order to further their own political agendas.

For example, the false issue of allegedly "rampant" pregnancy among women service members has been waved like a firebrand to inflame public opinion against the role of women in the military. But the facts do not support such uninformed and inflammatory claims. When the Army studied the cause of the "nondeployable" status of the approximately 10 percent of the total force unable to join their units sent to new locations overseas, it found that pregnancy accounted for only 6.1 percent of this already small group. By far the largest number (49.6 percent) were soldiers undergoing scheduled training that could not be interrupted for deployment. Soldiers with either permanent or temporary disabilities, pending legal cases, or who were on leave comprised the rest of the nondeployables. Yet the myth persists that women "choose" to become pregnant only when their units are about to be deployed. Since women comprise approximately 15 percent of the Army, the numbers simply do not support this claim; it's just malicious slander against women.

After the Aberdeen sexual abuse scandal, the entire issue of gender-integrated military training was revisited.

For the past two decades, the Army doctrine of "Train As You Fight" has proven eminently successful. During Operation Just Cause, the invasion of Panama, 770 women deployed. Three women helicopter pilots flying paratroopers of the 82nd Airborne Division performed well under heavy enemy fire. During the Persian Gulf War, the 41,000 women deployed made up 16 percent of the ground force. Women flew aerial refueling missions in the war zone, flew helicopters on combat air assault missions into Iraq, and performed a number of critical jobs close to the fighting front. Five women were killed in action, two were taken prisoner of war and served honorably in captivity.

In October 1997, I met one of those former POWs, Colonel

Rhonda Cornum, an Army flight surgeon. She is a wife, a mother, an accomplished military leader and public speaker. In early 2001, Colonel Cornum deployed to the Balkans to command an Army medical brigade.

Men and women who enlisted to serve in gender-integrated combat support, combat service support, and Special Branch MOSs trained together from their first day of Basic Training. Men who enlisted to serve in combat arms MOSs trained in gender-segregated One Station Unit Training posts.

There has been no "feminization" or softening of the Army as critics have charged. Instead, both young women and men enlistees have been toughened by increasing the length and rigor of Initial Entry Training (which includes Basic and Advanced Individual Training). Research has shown that the performance of women soldiers undergoing this training has improved, while the training of their male peers has maintained its high quality.

I spoke out on this issue when those critics of gender-integrated training used the Aberdeen sexual abuse scandal as a pretext to demand the renewed segregation of men and women trainees, a refrain that continues to this day. What had occurred at Aberdeen, I told a congressional commission in 1998, had been "falsely associated with gender-integrated training." I reminded the members that the Aberdeen incidents were abuses of power that had been distorted to appear as fraternization in order to further the accused abusers' legal defenses. "The basic issue at Aberdeen is that established Army leadership standards were not upheld," I told the commission. The goal of sexual harassment is power, control, and dominance, not affection and desire. I think I made some headway. But my frank views were not popular among the conservative members of Congress who hold the view that there is simply no place for women in the military (nor, I suppose, in law enforcement, fire departments, nor in medical school, nor on the bench) and who will seize any excuse to further their outmoded belief.

But it is essential to make policy based on current experiences in military training. It is also important for soldiers to train in integrated units when they will serve in integrated specialties because first impressions are lasting and strong. Basic Training provides soldiers' first impression of their place in the Army. It is their first experience of learning to be a soldier, a safe, intensely supervised experience, where they learn discipline, acquire a sense of duty, and develop mutual respect. It is vital that all soldiers who eventually will serve together start off learning how to work with each other, and to learn that they all have had the same preparation and meet the same standards. This training builds trust: trust in oneself, trust in one's buddies, and trust in the team. We cannot expect that young men and women who are trained separately by gender-segregated drill instructors can later serve well together as equal partners in gender-integrated units.

In thirty-two years of military service, I saw the Army undergo many changes. When I enlisted in the gender-segregated Women's Army Corps in 1968, the Army was made up mainly of draftees. WACs trained separately, were assigned separately, and we were promoted separately. But in the early 1970s, the Army made the transition to the All-Volunteer Force, women were integrated into the rest of the Army, and the WAC Branch was dissolved. At that time, there were those who predicted the downfall of the Army, just as there are those today who claim the Army is being softened and undercut by the incremental increase in the percentage of women, training side by side with men, within its ranks.

But I know better. I have been trained by women only. I have seen gender-segregated units trained by gender-integrated instructors, and I have seen integrated trainees trained by cadres of integrated instructors.

That final process has produced the Army of today, the Army that defeated Saddam Hussein's massed divisions in just one hundred hours of Operation Desert Storm. The soldiers of this Army have displayed incredible courage, maturity, and discipline during challenging peacekeeping and humanitarian operations, from Haiti, to the Balkans, to Africa and Central America. I am extremely proud to have served with them.

America is going to need its women soldiers in the future, particularly as soldiers' jobs evolve. In the coming decades, demographic pressures will add to that urgency. Our population is inexorably aging. By 2021, the first of the baby boom will turn seventy-five. The pool of young, able-bodied workers contributing to Social Security to support the great bulge of the elderly will shrink. There will be increased competition for skilled workers between the military and civilian marketplace. None of the armed forces will be able to preserve obsolete concepts of gender segregation and male dominance of the military.

Further, the Army will fill its traditional role of assimilating new waves of immigrants, for whom the attraction of a military career will be the transformation to full integration as citizens and the acquisition of technical and leadership skills. Again, I am proud that the Army has served that role so well in the past and will continue to do so.

Today, people often ask if I believe an Army woman will achieve the rank of four-star general and advance to the top leadership. "No question about it," I always reply. Sometime in the next twenty years, a woman who is today a major or lieutenant colonel will stand proudly as her fourth star is pinned to her epaulets. But that inevitability evades a broader issue. How many company first sergeants, battalion and brigade command sergeants major will be women in 2020? Will the percentage of women commanding battalions and brigades be proportional to their numbers in the Army? Will the trend toward the advancement of women soldiers that I witnessed in my career continue or will the talent that women bring to the military be marginalized? These are crucial questions, not just for the women who wear Army green, but also for the nation as a whole.

* * *

The future progress of military women will continue to reflect that of women in the broader society, just as it has in the past. Women soldiers have some reason for optimism.

In the 2000 election, women candidates from both parties made historic gains. Overall, women hold seventy-three seats in

cause she did not focus her full attention on giving me precise directions. Instead, she continued her duties, waving the line of cars ahead, checking the drivers' and passengers' proffered ID cards all the while rattling off a chain of directions for me. During all this, she even pulled over a driver who could not produce his ID. Her actions were a prototypical example of multitasking, a talent at which I believe women are especially adept.

Another time, a man MP came around to my car window, turned his back on his assigned lane of incoming traffic, and proceeded to give me a precise set of directions, including all turns and elapsed mileage to my destination building. He was completely zeroed in, focusing on the sole requirement of guiding me. Saddam Hussein could have walked through the gate with a Stinger missile on his shoulder and that young soldier would not have noticed.

When I relate this story, I ask people, "Who would you rather have at the gate?" But before they answer, I always say, "You want them both."

The Army needs soldiers who can be focused and direct and go straight for closure. But we also need soldiers with a broader view who can juggle multiple tasks and make a quick decision about what is important and what is not. Of course, these skills do not always divide along gender lines; the anecdote illustrates the importance of appreciating our differences.

An Army comprised of men and women serving their country side by side with mutual respect provides that optimum balance. I am proud of this Army and that it gave me the chance to live just such a life of service.

the House and Senate, more than doubling the thirty-two
women held in 1990. Five of the nation's governors are
women, and women fill 22 percent of state legislative seats.

These are impressive gains. And the trend will no doubt
tinue as both Democrats and Republicans groom women ca
dates for the important 2002 election. Commenting on
significance of the 2000 election, political scientist Sherry Bel
Jeffe noted, "The more women who serve in the Senate, the m
women who serve as governors, the more women there are f
which to choose presidential and vice presidential nominees."

But I personally think it will be a few years before we s
woman at the top of either party's national slate. The resistance
women in high leadership positions is just too deeply seated
America for there to be a major shift in the next two decades.
results of a recent Gallup Poll conducted in five Latin American
tions and the United States is revealing. When asked, "Do you
lieve your country will elect a female president in the next twe
years?" well over two thirds of those polled in Mexico, Colomb
Brazil, and El Salvador responded yes. Only 46 percent of Ame
cans answered affirmatively (just behind 47 percent of Argentine
But 57 percent of Americans polled believed government would
better if more women held public office. Significantly, across all t
nations polled, only 20 percent felt that women would do a bett
job than men at "directing the military."

Despite such polls, I remain optimistic about the future
women in the U.S. Army. The transformation of the military cu
rently will require greater participation of women in the defen
of our country.

After years as an Army staff officer and commander, my ol
servation about the synergistic contribution men and women so
diers make to the Army that I love so much can be summarize
in an anecdote I tell about visiting an Army post in the lat
1990s. I stopped at the gate during the morning rush hour t
ask directions from the Military Police on duty. The youn
woman MP at the gate was courteous, her salute as crisp as th
crease in her BDUs. But her instructions were rather vague be

Epilogue

A week after the June 2000 ceremony in the Pentagon central courtyard to celebrate the end of my Army service, I attended a retirement retreat at Fort Huachuca, the guest of Major General John Thomas, commanding general of the Intelligence Center and School. I had been expecting a very austere event, at which a small group would gather at the parade ground flagpole to salute the colors as they were lowered at the end of the day.

Instead, when my cousin Valerie Haygood Thompson, who had accompanied me to Arizona, and I arrived at Grierson Field, we found the post Army band and several hundred soldiers standing in formation before the podium. Among them was B Troop, a small ceremonial cavalry unit wearing the Army uniform of the frontier days. Their dark, broad-brimmed hats, wide suspenders, and riding boots silently evoked the Old West. For the rest of us, the uniform of the day was BDUs.

I was surprised and touched to have the opportunity to attend this final Army ritual with soldiers who represented every Army MOS with which I had been closely associated during thirty-two years of service. Although the World War II–era wooden classrooms in which I had attended the Advance Course as a young captain had been torn down, I drove past the old stucco bungalow where I had lived that year. Looking northwest, the high desert dropped away toward Tucson and the coppery Huachuca Mountains. Isolated columns of cloud drifted overhead, trailing skirts of rain so thin it felt like mist. Thunder echoed from the mountains.

The band played. General Thomas spoke briefly. Then I spoke. But I was so overcome with emotion that I cannot remember to this day the nature of the music or the words. But I will never forget when the band lowered their instruments and sang a cappella the words of that quintessential Army ballad, "Old soldiers never die. They just fade away."

* * *

And I never forget the words of one of our most revered leaders, General George C. Marshall. In 1951, as the former Secretary of State, he spoke to the graduating class of the U.S. Military Academy at West Point, several hundred young cadets, most of whom would be locked in bitter combat in the frozen mountains of Korea before the year was out:

> I think it is too early to talk to you regarding some of the trials and tribulations that are bound to be yours during your service to come. You will often be misunderstood. You will frequently find the democratic processes of this country difficult to assimilate in a military pattern. But never forget that this is a democracy and you are the servants of the people, and whatever complications may arise, you have a duty to your country which involves not only the final sacrifice if necessary, but a generous understanding of the role of an officer in a great democracy.

General Marshall's words speak to all of us who have chosen the military calling.

U.S. Army Grades and Insignia

GRADE	INSIGNIA	IF IN COMMAND, WHICH ECHELON
General	Four silver stars	Regional CINC
Lieutenant General	Three silver stars	Corps Commander
Major General	Two silver stars	Division Commander
Brigadier General	One silver star	Assistant Division Commander
Colonel	Silver eagle	Brigade Commander
Lieutenant Colonel	Silver oak leaf	Battalion Commander
Major	Gold oak leaf	
Captain	Two silver bars	Company Commander
First Lieutenant	One silver bar	
Second Lieutenant	One gold bar	Platoon Leader

WARRANT OFFICERS

Grade Five	Silver bar with five enamel white squares
Grade Four	Silver bar with four enamel black squares
Grade Three	Silver bar with three enamel black squares
Grade Two	Silver bar with two enamel black squares
Grade One	Silver bar with one enamel black square

NONCOMMISSIONED OFFICERS

Sergeant Major of the Army (E-9).	Same as Command Sergeant Major (below) but with two stars. Also wears distinctive red and white shield on lapel.
Command Sergeant Major (E-9).	Three chevrons above three arcs with a five-pointed star with a wreath around the star between the chevrons and arcs.
Sergeant Major (E-9).	Three chevrons above three arcs with a five-pointed star between the chevrons and arcs.
First Sergeant (E-8).	Three chevrons above three arcs with a diamond between the chevrons and arcs.
Master Sergeant (E-8).	Three chevrons above three arcs.
Sergeant First Class (E-7).	Three chevrons above two arcs.
Staff Sergeant (E-6).	Three chevrons above one arc.
Sergeant (E-5).	Three chevrons.
Corporal (E-4).	Two chevrons.

SPECIALISTS

Specialist (E-4).	Eagle device only.

OTHER ENLISTED

Private First Class (E-3).	One chevron above one arc.
Private (E-2).	One chevron.
Private (E-1).	None.

Glossary

CIA	Central Intelligence Agency
CID	Criminal Investigation Division
CINC	Commander-in-Chief
COO	Consideration of Others
DCSINT	Deputy Chief of Staff for Intelligence
DCSOPS	Deputy Chief of Staff for Operations and Plans
DCSPER	Deputy Chief of Staff for Personnel
DEFCON	Defense Condition
DIA	Defense Intelligence Agency
DMZ	Demilitarized Zone
DoD	Department of Defense
DPCA	Director of Personnel and Community Affairs
EO	Equal Opportunity
EW	Electronic Warfare
FGOD	Field-Grade Officer of the Day
FLNO	Foreign Liaison Officer
FORSCOM	Forces Command
FS	Field Station
GPS	Global Positioning System
GSC	General Staff College
HUMINT	Human Intelligence
IAV	Interim Armored Vehicle
ID	Infantry Division
IET	Initial Entry Training

IG	Inspector General
IMINT	Imagery Intelligence
INSCOM	Intelligence and Security Command
IO	Information Operations
JAG	Judge Advocate General
JOCCP	Junior Officer Cryptologic Career Program
JSA	Joint Security Area
MASINT	Measurement and Signature Intelligence
MI	Military Intelligence
MILPERCEN	Military Personnel Center
MIOAC	Military Intelligence Officer Advance Course
MOS	Military Occupational Specialty
MOU	Memorandum of Understanding
MP	Military Police
MWR	Morale, Welfare, and Recreation
NATO	North Atlantic Treaty Organization
NCO	Noncommissioned Officer
ODCSOPS	Office of the Deputy Chief of Staff for Operations and Plans
OER	Officer Efficiency Report
OPTEMPO	Operations Tempo
OSD	Office of the Secretary of Defense
OSUT	One Station Unit Training
POAC	Pentagon Officers Athletic Club
PT	Physical Training

RIF	Reduction in Force
ROK	Republic of Korea
ROTC	Reserve Officer Training Corps
RPM	Real Property Maintenance
SACO	Staff Action Control Office
SCIF	Special Compartmented Intelligence Facility
SIGINT	Signals Intelligence
SOF	Special Operations Forces
SOP	Standard Operating Procedure
TRADOC	Training and Doctrine Command
UCMJ	Uniform Code of Military Justice
UNC	United Nations Command
USAREUR	United States Army Europe
WAAC	Women's Army Auxiliary Corps
WAC	Women's Army Corps
WAREX	War Exercise
WMD	Weapons of Mass Destruction
XO	Executive Officer

Chronology, United States Army Service
Lieutenant General Claudia J. Kennedy

SOURCE OF COMMISSIONED SERVICE

Direct Appointment

MILITARY SCHOOLS ATTENDED

Women's Army Corps Officer Basic Course

Military Intelligence Officer Advance Course

United States Army Command and General Staff College

United States Army War College

EDUCATIONAL DEGREES

Southwestern at Memphis, BA Degree, Philosophy

FOREIGN LANGUAGE(S)

French, German

PROMOTIONS	DATES OF APPOINTMENT *(Note:* Selection to grade often occurred in year prior to appointment.)
Second Lieutenant	2 Jun 69
First Lieutenant	2 Jun 70
Captain	2 Jun 71
Major	10 Jul 79
Lieutenant Colonel	1 Jul 85
Colonel	1 Mar 91
Brigadier General	1 Oct 93
Major General	1 Nov 96
Lieutenant General	21 May 97

MAJOR DUTY ASSIGNMENTS

FROM	TO	ASSIGNMENT
Jan 70	May 71	Administrative Officer, G-1 (Personnel), United States Army Garrison, Fort Devens, Massachusetts
Jun 71	Jul 73	Women's Army Corps Recruiting Officer, United States Army Recruiting Main Station, Concord, New Hampshire
Aug 73	Aug 75	Commander, Staff and Faculty Company, United States Women's Army Corps Center and School, Fort McClellan, Alabama
Aug 75	Mar 76	Student, Military Intelligence Officer Advance Course, United States Army Intelligence Center and School, Fort Huachuca, Arizona
Mar 76	Jun 76	Student, Basic Electronic Warfare/Cryptologic Officer Course, United States Army Security Agency Training Center and School, Fort Devens, Massachusetts
Jul 76	Feb 77	Electronic Warfare Staff Officer, United States Army Security Agency Field Station, Camp Humphrey, United States Army, Korea
Feb 77	Jul 77	Strategic Intelligence Officer, 501st Military Intelligence Group (Provisional), United States Army, Korea
Jul 77	Jul 80	Cryptologic Staff Officer, United States Army Intelligence and Security Command, Military Intelligence Group (SIGINT/EW), with duty at National Security Agency, Fort George G. Meade, Maryland

Aug 80	Jun 81	Student, United States Army Command and General Staff College, Fort Leavenworth, Kansas
Jul 81	Mar 84	Assistant Operations Officer, later Operations Officer, United States Army Field Station Augsburg, United States Army Intelligence and Security Command, Germany
Mar 84	Jun 86	Staff Officer, Director of Training, Office of the Deputy Chief of Staff for Operations and Plans, Washington, D.C.
Jul 86	Jul 88	Commander, 3rd Operations Battalion, United States Army Field Station Augsburg, later Commander, 714th Military Intelligence Battalion, 701st Military Intelligence Brigade, United States Army Intelligence and Security Command, Germany
Jul 88	Jul 90	Commander, San Antonio Recruiting Battalion, 5th Recruiting Brigade, Fort Sam Houston, Texas
Aug 90	Jun 91	Student, United States Army War College, Carlisle, Pennsylvania
Jul 91	Mar 93	Commander, 703rd Military Intelligence Brigade, Kunia, Hawaii
Apr 93	Jul 94	Director, Intelligence, G-2, Forces Command, Fort McPherson, Georgia
Jul 94	Jul 95	Deputy Commander, United States Army Intelligence Center and Fort Huachuca/Assistant Commandant, United States Army Intelligence School, Fort Huachuca, Arizona
Jul 95	May 97	Assistant Deputy Chief of Staff for Intelligence, Office of the Deputy Chief of Staff for Intelligence, United States Army, Washington, D.C.
May 97	Jun 00	Deputy Chief of Staff for Intelligence, United States Army, Washington, D.C.
Retired	31 July 2000	

U.S. DECORATIONS AND BADGES

National Intelligence Distinguished Service Medal
Distinguished Service Medal
Legion of Merit (with 3 Oak Leaf Clusters)
Defense Meritorious Service Medal
Meritorious Service Medal (with 3 Oak Leaf Clusters)
Army Commendation Medal (with 3 Oak Leaf Clusters)
Army Staff Identification Badge

Index